How to Plan and Finance a Growing Business

How to Plan and Finance a Growing Business

Donald M. Dible
Editor

This publication is designed to provide accurate and authoritative information in regard to the subject matter covered. It is sold with the understanding that the publisher is not engaged in rendering legal, accounting or other professional service. If legal advice or other expert assistance is required, the services of a competent professional person should be sought.

—From a Declaration of Principles jointly adopted by a Committee of the American Bar Association and a Committee of Publishers

Printed in the United States of America

Originally published in modified form as *Winning the Money Game*

Chapter Fifteen first appeared in *The Pure Joy of Making More Money* © 1976 by Donald M. Dible

3422 Astoria Circle
Fairfield, California 94533

Distributed to the retail trade by Elsevier-Dutton Publishing Company, Inc.

Library of Congress Catalog Card Number: 79-57045

Introduction

Small business is the wellspring of our economy. But in these days of ever-spreading pollution, even the business wellspring is being fouled by increasing government regulations, the monopolistic practices of large corporations, and the encroachments of Big Labor.

What to do? Should you resign yourself to a Civil Service job; a gray flannel, organization man (or woman) job; or a "rank and file" position in a big labor organization? If pension plans, cost-of-living escalators, and paid vacations are your main concerns in life, then a mere job is all you deserve—you too are poisoning the economic well.

If, however, the prospect of shouldering the responsibility for launching a new enterprise appeals to you. If you don't mind working 60 to 80 hours a week in order to get a business going. If your attitude toward challenge is "Charge!", then you may have what it takes to make our economic well deeper and its waters sweeter.

Take the initiative! Join the hardy band of 14 million Americans who have their own businesses. But before you do—a word of caution. Don't do it until you've done your homework. Otherwise, you may join with millions of others who have failed in their attempts to establish a viable business.

How can you do your homework? Well, you can start by reading this book and following the advice of our experts.

The chapters in this book are based on a series of two-day seminars conducted in major cities across the country. Many of the attendees at these programs have subsequently prepared business plans, raised capital, and launched successful businesses. With perseverence and a little luck, you too may do so.

Welcome to the Free Enterprise System.

Donald M. Dible
Fairfield, California

Table of Contents

One

The American Small Business Owner

John L. Komives

SCOPE

When I begin a discussion of small business, I want my readers to comprehend the scope of the subject—just how many currently operating small businesses are we talking about? Unfortunately, there is no specific census of small businesses, no conclusive, reliable data available. We can't even be sure if the total number of small businesses is increasing or decreasing. Instead of quoting statisticians, we must generalize, basing our generalities on whatever information applies.

For example, about the best we can do with regard to business births and deaths is to check with the people at Dun and Bradstreet—an independent service organization that provides credit information on various businesses on request, for a fee. But Dun and Bradstreet usually does not gather information unless asked to do so by one of its clients who may be evaluating the credit-worthiness of a potential customer. Thus, unless a business is at

John L. Komines, Ph.D.; formerly served as the Director of the Center for Venture Management, a Milwaukee-based, not-for-profit, educational and research institute dedicated to the study of the entrepreneur and new enterprise formation. In 1975, Dr. Komives established the Lakeshore Group, Ltd., a management consulting firm. The firm specializes in working with smaller new and growing companies throughout the U.S. He also serves on the board of directors of twelve growth companies. He is a lecturer at Northwestern University Graduate School of Management.

least of modest size and requires trade credit in its operations, it probably won't be listed in the D & B data bank.

So we turn to the greatest of data banks, the federal government. A few years ago, the Small Business Administration indicated in an annual report that there were 5.3 million businesses in the U.S. In preparing its most recent annual report, the SBA did some research—mainly by getting data from the Internal Revenue Service on the number of taxpayers filing Schedule D with their returns–and subsequently announced that there are now 14 million businesses in the U.S.

More recently, it has been reported that there are more than 10 million proprietorships, partnerships, corporations, and Subchapter S corporations in the U.S. This figure does not include the 2 to 3 million farms, so we conclude that there are somewhere between 5.3 and 19 million business units in the U.S.

If we work, as I like to do, with the ball-park figure of 14 million businesses, we can determine that 7 to 8 million of these represent forms of self-employment. Thus, over 6 million businesses have at least one additional full-time employee.

SIZE OF THE SMALL BUSINESS COMMUNITY

The above figures lead us to consider another question—just how small is a "small business"? Most efforts to define the term wind up with too many exceptions. One way to tackle the problem is to talk about the largest business in the U.S.—General Motors. In fact, General Motors is the largest business in the world and has something like 800,000 employees worldwide. It's enormous. Last year, General Motors' sales were $63 billion. To me, $63 is a respectable sum of money, and I suspect it is to you, too. $6,300 or $63,000 are handsome sums, while $63 million is an awful lot. But $63 billion is very nearly beyond comprehension. It boggles the mind. Let's try to put it into perspective.

According to the *World Almanac*, there are on the order of 160 political entities that we call countries. (Not all of them belong to the United Nations.) Let's take all of these countries and rank them by gross national product (GNP, a measure of the goods and services produced by a country) from the largest to the smallest. You start off with the United States with a GNP in excess of $1.8 trillion. If you treat General Motors as a *country*, valuing its annual sales as a GNP, you will find that it ranks as the seventeenth largest *country* in the world. It comes in just behind the Netherlands, Spain, Mexico, and Brazil, all of whom are slightly larger than General Motors. Now you should have some feeling for the magnitude of the sales volume of the largest business in the United States.

Every year, *Fortune Magazine* publishes a list of the top 500 industrial companies in the U.S. Of course, General Motors is the largest. The 500th company of 1979 was Data General in Westboro, Massachusetts, with annual sales of $380 million. A few years ago, *Fortune* also started publishing a list of the second 500 largest industrial companies in the U.S. According to the *Fortune* roster for 1979, the 1,000th largest company in the U.S. was Virginia Chemical in Portsmouth, Virginia, with annual sales of $110 million.

Now we have accounted for the top 1,000 industrial companies in the U.S. (Banks, insurance companies, and department stores are not included here.) In going from Number 1 to Number 1,000, annual sales volume goes from $63 billion to $110 million. The sales volume of the 1,000th company is slightly less than .2% of the sales of the largest company. And we still have 13,999,000 companies unaccounted for in our list. I tend to consider these 13,999,000 businesses as being "medium" to "small" businesses. Furthermore, since our numbers *are* imprecise, I'll continue to use the figure 14 million when talking about the number of small businesses in the U.S.

BUSINESS CLASSIFICATIONS

In trying to classify small businesses, I like to refer to the chart on the next page that we have developed at the Center for Venture Management. The chart is designed to give you some insight into the nature of individual small businesses.

You will note that the left-hand side of the chart is broken down into three categories: Manufacturing, Wholesale/Retail, and Service. The distinction among these categories is based upon the management style, the personality, the instincts, and the motivations of the people who operate these different types of businesses. The boundaries of each classification are far from precise. I break them down this way because the art form of one business type is not readily transferable to the art form of another without a learning period or apprenticeship.

For example, if I am a banker and you come to me for a loan to use in starting a business, I'm going to ask you some questions about your work experience. Let's say that you want to open up a men's clothing store or some other sort of retail operation. However, all of your working experience has been in manufacturing. I wouldn't give you the loan. Most bankers wouldn't. You lack experience in that kind of business—that art form, if you will—and you don't know the traditions or the patterns that are part-and-parcel of doing business in that industry.

Let me tell you a little story I personally enjoy that illustrates some of the philosophical differences between a manufacturing business and a service business. I was sitting in the office of an advertising executive on whose board of directors I sat. (This business is a small, six-man operation.) The ad man was entertaining a client who owned and operated his own manufacturing company. It was after 5:00 p.m. The advertising guy whipped out the martinis from the refrigerator in his office, and we sat around enjoying the camaraderie. Meanwhile, the door to his office was

DECISION PROCESS— STYLE OF ENTREPRENEURSHIP / MANNER IN WHICH VALUE IS ADDED	MA and PA and SELF EMPLOYMENT: Ma and/or Pa make all decisions	CRAFTSMAN: Division of labor is evident	ORGANIZATION or VENTURE BUSINESS: Management responsibilities are shared by founders
MANUFACTURING: Converts raw materials or assembles components into finished goods.			
WHOLESALE/RETAIL: Transforms the location and modifies the size of the unit that is offered for sale.			
SERVICE: Packages and dispenses human capabilities at convenient locations and times.			
BUSINESS POPULATION DISTRIBUTION—BASE: 14,000,000 business entities	75%	20–22%	3–5%

BUSINESS CLASSIFICATIONS

open, and the manufacturing guy could look out into the area where the ad man's staff worked. By 5:30, the five people out there had folded up the stuff on their desks, straightened up whatever they were doing, put on their coats, and walked out. Finally, the manufacturing guy looked over to the advertising guy and said, "I couldn't stand to be in your business; I really couldn't. The thought that my inventory would get up every evening at quitting time and walk out is more than I can stand."

The top of the chart is also broken down into three categories: Ma-and-Pa (I also use the term self-employment), craftsman, and organization.

Ma and Pa

The Ma-and-Pa, or self-employment, business comprises between 70% and 75% of all businesses in the U.S. Typically, this category employs less than five people, has annual sales of less than $500,000, and has all its decisions made either by Ma or by Pa. The bookkeeping is handled on a simplified basis. Pa takes all the income and keeps it in his Money Pocket. When bills must be paid, disbursements are made from the Money Pocket. At the end of the accounting period, whatever is left over is what business-school students call "return on investment." Pa calls what's left "wages." Any way you look at it, what's left is profit. The system is quite primitive, but it works reasonably well at this level.

Craftsman

The craftsman type of business represents about 20% of the business community. Usually, this type of business has 10 to 30 employees, although I have seen craftsman businesses that had as many as 150 employees—but that's rare. What I'm discussing here is the *style* of business. With that in mind, consider that Henry Ford—the *original* Henry Ford—even when he had several hundred thousand employees and several billion dollars in sales, was still basically a craftsman entrepreneur. In fact, that was his downfall—he never graduated out of the craftsman category.

However, I don't want to confuse your perception of this category. Think of it in terms of 10 to 30 employees with $.5 million to $5 million in sales, clustering somewhere around $1.2 million. (It's always a major event in the life of that business when it breaks through the million-dollar annual sales mark.)

The craftsman business category includes such operations as tool and die shops, machine shops, printing plants, and building contractors. You also see craftsman category businesses in retailing. For example, the local retailer who may have 3, 4, 5—maybe even 10—stores around town is classified as a craftsman entrepreneur (as opposed to the single large outlet in town that may be owned by a national organization).

Now let's contrast that local chain-store retailer with the Ma-and-Pa shop where the owners do everything. In the craftsman business, you can begin to see evidence of a hierarchy in the organization. You will find managers besides the owners—a shop supervisor in the printing plant or a store manager in the local retail chain. Additionally, you will find rank-and-file employees.

In the craftsman business, you also begin to see something else—specialization of labor. You find people who are production specialists, bookkeepers, or office managers. This is the business category in which you find a great many self-made management and engineering types as owner-founders.

In our society, if you want to be successful in a large organization, you almost invariably have to have academic credentials. If you want to be an engineer, you have to have an engineering degree. In all of the "organization" types of business, you'll wind up as a technician if you don't have a B.S. degree in engineering. But you'll never be classified as an engineer. In the craftsman firm, you will find a lot of self-made engineers who didn't finish, or possibly never even started, the academic side of their engineering education but whose contributions to our society have been enormous. A great amount of the ingenuity of our economic and technical system really goes back to these craftsmen—the self-made, technical people.

The transition point between the craftsman and organization categories, in terms of annual sales volume, is around $6 million in manufacturing and $10 million in wholesale. Past that, the business is simply beyond the managerial capabilities of the craftsman-entrepreneur.

Organization or Venture Business

In discussing the "organization" category with a group in Japan, I found that they refer to this type of business structure as a "venture business." I think this term is a good one because an "organization" or "venture business" is a business that is characterized not so much by its size as by its *potential for growth* in its chosen market. That's the thing that makes it unique. Size is not necessarily a requirement for classification in this category since a new venture business may not yet have had the time to achieve substantial sales volume. This is the kind of business in which there is a rather sophisticated entrepreneurial operation. It isn't so much based upon a manual operations skill as it is upon a concept or an idea which is then brought into reality. It is also characterized by fairly early evidence of what I call "bureaucracy." I'm using the term bureaucracy in the sense that John Hall, the sociologist, would use it: Bureaucracy is the orderly planning and flow of work and events so that the amount of personal involvement is reduced and the amount of reliability, repeatability, and incidence of routine kinds of activity is increased.

I visited one venture business a number of years ago. At the time, it was less than a year old and had only five employees. While I was standing at the desk waiting to get through to the inner sanctum, a call came for the girl who was the receptionist, office manager, purchasing agent, personnel manager, and a number of other things. At that moment, she was also the credit manager. The caller was someone who wanted to place an order with the company. She told the caller that, before she could accept the order, she had to check the customer's credit standing, whereupon she hauled out the customer's file and a blue notebook above her desk. She checked the file, looked up in the notebook the company policy on extension of credit, got back on the phone, and said, "I'm sorry, Sir, but until you send us a check for at least 20% of your back bills, I can only ship you this order C.O.D."

In any other kind of business—in the Ma-and-Pa or the craftsman business—one of several other things would have happened. The call would have come in and the girl would have accepted the order and forgotten about it. Or she might have recalled that the customer was slow in paying his bills and said to her boss, "Hey Joe! Do we send this stuff or don't we?" Joe would have replied, "Hell, I don't know, let me think about it." The acceptance of the order would have involved the personal decision of the boss. But in the venture business, there would be no sense bothering some other person about a routine thing like credit when you have a company policy that covers it. These are the little behavior cues that you begin to notice in the operation of a venture business because the founders are thinking about growth and expansion. They can't be bothered with making personal decisions about something that should be routine. They start by infusing systems and procedures into the daily operations of the business.

PUBLICLY OWNED COMPANIES

Earlier, I pointed out that around 700,000, or 5%, of all U.S. businesses fell into the category of organization (or venture) businesses. Let's now look at this category from another point of view. There are about 1,500 companies listed on the New York Stock Exchange, about 1,000 on the American Stock Exchange, and roughly 50,000 that are traded over-the-counter. In the latter category, only about 8,000 companies have stock that is traded on the average of once a week. This suggests that there are only around 10,500 companies whose stocks are regularly traded in the public market. (There is simply a lack of public interest in, or demand for, the stock of the other 40,000 companies traded over-the-counter. However, they are still considered to be publicly traded companies.)

Now consider for a moment the objectives of the investment and venture-capital community. They hope to put their money into promising venture businesses that will, within four to seven years, become one of the 10,500 companies whose stock is regularly traded. In other words, when you launch a business using money from the venture-capital community, you are expected, within four to seven years, to build your business to a point where it joins the ranks of the top .1% of all U.S. businesses. Or, at the very least, you are expected to build a company that will be large enough to make an attractive candidate for a merger or acquisition. That's a pretty tall order and a mighty ambitious objective.

An article in *Forbes* reported an interview with the late Stanley Rubel, former editor of the annual *Guide to Venture Capital Sources*. Rubel was asked to comment on whether he thought it likely that the venture-capital subsidiary of a major corporation would be likely to find, and invest in, a budding Xerox or Polaroid. "Almost certainly not," said Rubel. The entrepreneur who takes backing from the likes of General Electric or the Sun

Oil Company knows that he is limiting his personal horizons. "He is," said Rubel, "the guy who won't mind being bought out at $4 million instead of building his company up to $25 million. He's not the truly independent type." I'd like to add that he's not the true organization or venture-business type of entrepreneur, either.

Now I'm not denying that you'll find some very successful people who have built companies that got up to $4 million in sales. The point I'm trying to make is that the venture-business entrepreneur is a guy who's not going to be satisfied with a company that's only reached $4 million in sales. He's going to be satisfied only after he has exhausted all the opportunities, challenges, and thrills of growing beyond the point where he can manage the business himself. (I'd like to suggest that some entrepreneurs go beyond their own endurance. For example, Jimmy Ling, the Texas tycoon, was constantly testing his ability to finance the next merger until he encountered Jones and Laughlin Steel, which proved to be his undoing in terms of marking the upper limit of his growth capability.)

CHARACTERISTICS OF ENTREPRENEURS

At this point, I'd like to move into a discussion of the characteristics of entrepreneurs. The information I'm relating to you is not limited to the bits and pieces of research that the Center for Venture Management had been directly involved in. We begged, borrowed, and stole additional information from all kinds of other people who were doing research in this field. We identified about 150 people who had done some sort of research in this field and had published their results. We did our best to establish and maintain contact with them and thereby arrived at an overview of the entire entrepreneurial phenomenon.

Entrepreneurship—Inborn or Learned?

First of all, we find that the family background of entrepreneurs is most interesting. On the order of 60% of all entrepreneurs come from families that provide a visible heritage of independent business. Now let me open up the boundaries of what constitutes a small business to include doctors, dentists, lawyers, and preachers, who often practice by themselves, particularly in small towns. The law practice in a small town might be the major business in the community. The preacher often has to make his congregation pay his way, and that constitutes his business. Of course, farmers who own and operate their own farms also fit into this expanded category. Using this expanded definition, the data suggest that as many as 80% of all entrepreneurs come from families where there is that heritage. Now when I refer to family heritage, I'm not saying that the *father* had to own and operate his own business. The relationship could have been with somebody else in the extended family system. But the kid that's going to become an entrepreneur at some future date has had *some* intimate contact with a relative's business, usually in the form of having worked part-time in the summer or after school and on week-ends.

Let me illustrate what I mean. I was helping a guy out a short time ago. He told me that he couldn't get an SBA loan. If you had met the guy, you would know why he didn't get the SBA loan. I've never before encountered such a personality. I even understand why the government bureaucrat threw him out of the shop. Anyway, I sat down with him because he asked me to walk through the business concept with him. Before I did, though, I yielded to my instinct to ask people about their background. How did they get to this spot, here? He proceeded to tell me how he learned to be a tool-and-die maker. "Well, my Dad was a tool-and-die maker." "Did he have his own shop?" "Oh, no. He worked all his life for Allis Chalmers." "Did he ever have his own business?"

"Well, yeah, he was a carpenter before he became a tool-and-die maker; and during the depression, he tried to start his own construction business, but it went broke after a couple of months." I sat there feeling frustrated because I knew, I just knew, that *somewhere* in this guy's background he had to have some contact with independent business. We started talking a little more, and it turned out that his two uncles had owned and operated a small chemical business that they had finally sold off. And during the years when he was in high school and college, this guy worked in that business part-time. But it took me the longest time during that interview to find this out. It *was* there; and I'll bet you that, in four out of five cases of attempted or successful entrepreneurship, you will find that heritage.

Now I'm often asked whether entrepreneurship can be taught or whether the urge is inherent. My answer is, "I don't know," which is a good academic response. But it is my feeling that entrepreneurs are heavily influenced by having been closely exposed to a model. If I'm unemployed or if I'm destitute or if I haven't got a job, then what can I do? One of the things that enters the mind of the potential entrepreneur: I can always start a business (although only 10% actually do try to become entrepreneurs—the other 90% proceed to look for another job).

I think it is possible that students taking a course in small business could be heavily influenced by the kind of material I'm presenting here. Schooling has an effect. It certainly has an effect on 20% of the population. But it also has another effect: through courses in entrepreneurship, your perception of a large business and your ability to visualize yourself as its founder are markedly increased. Most people think of a business as a small, independent Ma-and-Pa kind of thing. What I am trying to do here is to get you to open up your horizons and recognize that there are lots of other kinds of opportunities. The whole world is your oyster, not some little neighborhood or some little product. I think education can profoundly influence and increase your entrepreneurial expectations and goals. Ten years from now, when today's business students are in their early thirties and have just been fired, they might say to themselves, "This is sheer nonsense. I'm always going to get fired. The best thing for me to do for my own security is to start my own business." I like to say to these people, "If you can't hack it as an employ*ee,* why not become an employ*er?*"

Ethnic Background

In relating the entrepreneur to his family, we also find that immigrants have a much higher rate of entrepreneurship than do native Americans, particularly WASP's (White, Anglo-Saxon Protestants). It's fascinating to read about the Cubans in Southern Florida. Over one-third of the 300,000 Cubans that have come to this country now have their own independent businesses. One-third! Since immigrating, some of them have left Southern Florida. There is a little pocket of them not far from my office in Milwaukee who have braved a couple of winters and have become "natives." They've got their own little firms. One guy is importing cigars and has opened up a little shop; he's off and running. Back in Cuba, many of these immigrants were locked into their own, independent businesses. When they came to this country, they found that they were unable to practice law, banking, or medicine or to engage in any of the other nice WASP, establishment-type activities. Therefore, they had to begin a new social structure.

Consider also the case of the Bank of America: its beginnings provide a classic example of what can happen to a disgruntled immigrant. Amadeo P. Giannini was a fruit peddler who got turned down for a loan some 75 years ago. Although he had no professional background, he decided to start his own bank, the Bank of Italy. In ony 75 years, it has become the Bank of America, the largest bank in the world. Stories like this make me believe that the incidence of entrepreneurship among immigrants is primarily a reaction to alienation and not the result of some predisposition to starting a business traceable back to their native land.

There is an insightful book about immigrant businessmen called *Ethnic Enterprise in America,* by Ivan Light. In particular, Light talks about the Oriental entrepreneur—the Chinese and Japanese who settled in California, their family histories, and how they ended up forming businesses. He also discusses why they formed the kinds of businesses they did; and most importantly, he talks about the concentration of immigrants in certain neighborhoods—not only because they could communicate in their native language and feel comfortable in their own ethnic setting, but because within these neighborhoods they were able to set up self-help banking relationships. These became the source of start-up venture capital for ethnic minorities.

Childhood Work History

The childhood work history of entrepreneurs is also most interesting. We find that manifestations of entrepreneurship occur quite early in life. We have story after story after story. The typical one is that the kid, growing up, decides that he needs some money. He goes to his father and says, "I'd like to have some money." The father, because of this independent business heritage, says, "Well, if you want money, you go out and work for it. Earn it." So the bright kid grabs the lawnmower and goes down the street to start cutting lawns. The fascinating part of this story is that by the end of the summer, the aspiring entrepreneur is not cutting lawns anymore. He's got the neighbor's kids cutting the lawns, and this guy is rounding up customers, paying bills, sharpening the mower, and hustling new labor to man the machine.

You find the same thing with the paperboy. By the end of three months, he's got the biggest route in the district, and he hasn't thrown a paper in the last two weeks. He's got his father doing it on Sunday, and he's got other kids doing it on other days of the week while he collects the bills and sees to it that the operation is organized and running. The kids move out of the labor classification quite early.

I have a story about a kid who owned and sold houses at the age of twelve. I didn't believe the story, so I checked it out personally. It's true. The kid backed into the proposition. His father had failed in his own business in the middle of the depression. The kid went out and rasied enough money to buy a house. He got his father to sign for it. Eventually, the father was employed by his son in a very large business. My point is that, if you go back into the history of entrepreneurs, you will find many, many childhood manifestations of this characteristic.

Educational Background

There are two things that I want to say about the educational background of entrepreneurs. One, we have evidence that roughly 60% of them get thrown out of school or leave somewhere in their academic career. Not because of vandalism, or something really serious—they just get bored silly. They can't stand the constant yammering of their teachers, and they say, "To hell with it" and walk out. Many of them are drop-outs. Entrepreneurs in many ways are marginal individuals when viewed from the WASP standard of finished education.

The second point about education was indicated by Ed Roberts of MIT, who analyzed Boston's Route 128 high-technology companies. We at the Center found similar results in a study of 254 technical companies in the Palo Alto, California, area. (This study was conducted by Arnold Cooper of Purdue University.) The fellow with the bachelor's degree can expect to be reasonably successful in a given period of time. A person with a master's degree will be more successful in a shorter period of time. But if a person has a Ph.D. degree, he drops back down to the level of the bachelor's-degree holder in terms of the rate of success. It is fascinating to speculate about why this is true. I think that it is probably because the Ph.D. is like an inventor. The problem with the inventor is that he falls in love with his invention. A Ph.D. falls in love with his research and the product of his research. It's very difficult for an inventor to share his product or to permit it to be exploited.

In contrast, an entrepreneur builds a business without developing great emotional involvement with his product. He considers the product as simply a means to an end. But an inventor lies awake nights dreaming about how his product will give him a virtual monopoly. He thinks that he can charge any price for it that he wants, that everyone will come to him. That's sheer nonsense. The worst, worst, advice ever given to inventors are the words of Ralph Waldo Emerson: "Build a better mouse trap, and the world will beat a path to your door." Utter drivel. In one out of a million cases that may happen. In all the other 999,999 cases, you have to put together an organization to merchandise and market that better mouse trap in order to make any money.

Employment History

Now let's look briefly at the employment history of the entrepreneur. Based on our research in Palo Alto, close to one-third of the new businesses studied were started by people who had been fired by their former employers. When you analyze the circumstances surrounding their being fired, you find that entrepreneurs make terrible employees. They are constantly aggravating the boss to do other things, to get on with the job, to expand the product line. They are revolutionaries, constantly inciting other people. "This damn company; if we could just get a few more bucks in here, we could run with it this way."

If you look at the business cycle, you find that both ends play against this guy. If the employer's business is on the upswing, the potential entrepreneur will go to his boss and say, "I've got the greatest idea! I know how we can double our sales and our profits. If you'll just give me two assistants and let me get this thing launched, we'll be off and running." But this company is hell bent for leather trying desperately to meet the demands of their customers. So the boss says, "Look, for crying out loud, we're working our tails off just trying to fill the orders we've already got; and you come along and want to take time and money away from our main goal. Go away." On the other side of the business cycle, the guy goes into his boss and says, "I've got the greatest idea. I know, etc. etc." And the boss says, "Look, we're fighting for survival. We don't even know if we're going to make payroll next week, and you come in here with this harebrained scheme. Get lost!" Either way, the guy is going to be frustrated. So if you find a guy with a low tolerance for frustration, watch for this potential entrepreneurial thing.

Age

Very often, in discussing our research at the Center, I am asked to comment on the influence of a person's age on the likelihood that he will start a business. We find a real surge of entrepreneurship starting in people around 30 years of age and peaking somewhere between 32 and 35. From there, it decreases gradually until the age of 40. Between 40 on into the early 50's, we don't see much entrepreneurial interest. However, around the age of 55, we see a moderately increased level. Let's take a moment to analyze the various age groups.

1. Under 30. My instinct says that people under 30 generally don't make good entrepreneurs. This is my way of getting revenge on students who years ago used to say, "Don't trust anybody over 30." Now I say, "Don't invest in anybody under 30." Of course, I realize that this is a blind statement. What I am saying to you, though, is that it takes a certain amount of on-the-job experience after you get out of school before you become mature enough to cut your own way through the small business thicket. Your chances of success are much better if you learn the techniques of business while you are someone else's employee and then go out and start your own business.

2. The Magic of Being 32. The age of 32 (plus or minus a few months) seems to be the magic age for the Caucasian American male. Typically, he's married, has one child and a reasonably good career. He wakes up one morning at 5:00 a.m. and stares at the ceiling. Suddenly, it dawns on him that he is not immortal. It's really a terrifying discovery.

Reflecting on his future while evaluating his past, he decides, "What am I doing with my life? I've finished college; I've had a pretty successful working career of ten years, but I'm not progressing as fast as I'd like to be; and I'm not so committed to my job that I can't leave it at this time." One of the things that occurs to him is the possibility of starting his own business. At least he begins seriously to reflect on the idea for the first time in his life.

There are several reasons why anyone in his thirties is at an ideal age for starting a business. He's achieved a moderate level of maturity. He is old enough to have had a good bit of working experience, including some management responsibility; yet he's still young enough to have the enthusiasm, energy, and stamina necessary to sustain him while he puts in the grueling sixteen-hour days, seven-day weeks often required to launch a new business successfully.

Recent research on women entrepreneurs reveals that large numbers of women start their own business when they are between 35 and 45 years of age. In many cases this entrepreneurship follows a divorce. Often, new women entrepreneurs have arrived at an age when their children are old enough to survive her occasional absence from the home without ill effect.

These women prefer the flexibility of owning their own business to the rigid structures of an 8 to 5 wage job. In their own business, they can adjust their hours to meet the demands of their families as well as the demands of the enterprise. In non-divorce cases, the husband often proves to be most helpful and supportive.

3. The 40's and Early 50's. During this period, the American male is fairly well locked into rearing his family and making his way up the corporate employee ladder. He is an unlikely candidate for starting his own business.

4. The 55 Decision Point. Around the age of 55, interest in entrepreneurship picks up again. By this time, the children have grown up and left home; the individual has saved up a modest nest egg; and he is restless. Often, he feels that he has "topped-out" in his job. He considers a modest, one-man or Ma-and-Pa business as a realistic possibility. It's unlikely that he will try to start a major corporation—a venture business. He'll be content to earn a decent living and enjoy the independence of being his own boss.

TEAM ENTREPRENEURSHIP

We find that when a business is started by two, three, or four people, the potential for long-term success is much greater than it is for the lone founder. The problem that the lone founder has is his reluctance to let any of his employees share the responsibilities of managing the business. When every decision of any importance has to be made by one person, there are bound to be instances where progress actually stops while a decision awaits consideration. As a result, the growth of the business is limited by the physical and mental resources and endurance of the founder.

We have evidence at the Center (which corroborates the research of Professor Ed Roberts at MIT) that having two founders is much better than having one founder. We also find that three is better than two, and four is better than three. (The data base in the latter case is not substantial, but what data we do have support this assertion.)

Generally speaking, entrepreneurs and managers are two different kinds of people. The entrepreneur is a guy who, to a large extent, behaves intuitively. He sees something to do, and he goes and does it. His perceptual process is such that, when things finally get through his mental buffer-zone and he realizes that he has a problem demanding attention, he takes care of it immediately. For example, if the business is just struggling along and Friday is payday, an entrepreneur will not reflect until Thursday evening on the fact that he doesn't have enough money to meet the payroll. A manager would worry about this problem for the two weeks preceding payday.

Or the lone entrepreneur might decide, "What we really need is a special machine." He picks up the phone and says, "Hey, Joe, you got a special machine? You know, I heard that Warner & Swasey has a special machine that will allow me to make all kinds of cuts and hold really tight tolerances. Yeah. Okay, how much is it? Is that as sharp as your pencil is going to get? Where can I buy one used? Okay, I need it today." "You can't have it today." "Okay, then I'll have it yesterday. But I've got to have it because I'm late on this job and I've got to get this stuff out." This entrepreneur behaves in this fashion because it's his company. He started the company in order to have the freedom to operate in this way, a way that would be unthinkable to a manager—the manager plans ahead; the entrepreneur acts to solve. But as a team member in the multiple-entrepreneur category, the instinctive, intuitive entrepreneur cannot always behave as he wishes.

Now imagine this same set of circumstances with either two or three co-partners. They need not necessarily be *equal* partners. When I say that there are four founders, that doesn't necessarily mean that all four founders own equal shares of stock or have invested equal amounts of money. However, they are co-founders, and they have a feeling of equality with their fellow entrepreneur, even if he is the largest investor. It's a different form of equality from that of executive vice presidents without ownership or that of minority stockholders. But recognize that there is always a *lead* founder; there is always one strong guy who may have put the most money into it, or the most technology. He has the strength around which the team is built. But even in those cases where you have four founders who are not equal in power, strength, or capability, the lead entrepreneur cannot get on the phone and order that machine or make that decision or spend that money by himself. The first time he tries it, his co-founders will come to him and say, "Listen, we're in this business just as much as you are. When you commit us to a loan of $20,000—money which none of us has—the least you can do is discuss it with us beforehand. Our money and time is invested in this business too."

So the entrepreneur now has to think more carefully about his decisions, how his co-founders will react to them, and how he will defend himself. He is beginning to get involved in communications, something that a manager, but not an entrepreneur, does instinctively. A manager thinks about future events and tries to predict them and prepare for them with an orderly plan. He communicates with his key people and discusses the future plans. In the case of multiple entrepreneurship, the lead entrepreneur is forced to do some of these managerial tasks. Where there are three or four people who are involved and committed to the plan, the business begins to look like a managed company rather than an entrepreneur company.

Now there is a problem with becoming too managerial too soon, just as there are problems with not becoming managerial soon enough. I've seen firms, for example, that became managerial too soon. After the first sale is made, the founders go out and buy an expensive plant or expensive office space and furnish it with carpets and nice big rosewood desks. But beware: Any company that buys a Lear jet before it is seven years old or before it has gone through its second stock offering is doomed, doomed, doomed. The investors had better get their money out of that business as fast as they can because it does not have enough seasoning to ride out the business cycle. There are a lot of used Lear jets on the market.

BUSINESS TERMINATIONS

No discourse on small business would be complete without a discussion of failure rates. As you may have deduced, I am very much interested in studying organization or venture business types of companies. A few years ago, during the Center's Palo Alto study, we discovered an incredible turnover rate. You would pick up this year's phone book, compare it with one two years old, and find that an amazing number of technical companies were no longer listed. What happened? We found that, typically, the company was a small shop with anywhere from two to ten guys. At some point, they would either run out of money, lose interest, or experience some other small catastrophe. However, another guy with a two-to-ten-man outfit would suggest that they pool their talent and they would merge. Did the first business fail? I don't think so. However, it depends on the researcher doing the reporting as to what the statistics will show. The first business didn't fail in the sense that it went belly-up—bankrupt. The creditors may have had to wait longer to get paid than they would have liked; but financially, nobody got badly stung.

While there is an element of good luck that often characterizes businesses that survive and grow, it is clear to me that clever management and unflagging enthusiasm are essential. When these traits are present in the entrepreneur, the failure rates are much lower than the norm. It is consistently the smarter (and better educated) entrepreneur who makes a business succeed and reaps the rewards.

THE VALUE OF SMALL BUSINESS TO AMERICA

The contribution of small business to America is all but impossible to measure, but there is much evidence of its value. Clearly, the rate of invention and innovation is *much* higher in smaller enterprises. U.S. Department of Commerce studies show that 26 out of every 30 major inventions come from smaller enterprises. The contribution of small business also is seen in the fact that large corporation continuously require the many services and products of thousands of smaller enterprises. General Motors could not sell its cars without the support of 70,000 suppliers and distributors and the more than 1 million service enterprises such as gas stations, highway pavers, parts stores, body shops and numerous aftermarket suppliers.

Small business is the place where half the working population can find employment and dignity and a scale of work suited to their temperament. It is also the place where people can stretch their imaginations and find achievement and status without too many artificial restrictions such as academic degrees, manner of dress, etc. Small and growth businesses are truly the place where skilled and eager people can get ahead in this world. Entrepreneurs feel both a freedom from the restrictiveness of the large organization and a sense of responsibility and self reliance that comes from dealing directly in the marketplace.

SUMMARY

In spite of the grim figures on business deaths reported by some researchers, starting your own business continues to be the essence of The American Dream. As long as men (and women) have the gumption to go into business for themselves, the capitalistic system which has sustained this country for more than 200 years will continue to flourish.

Two

Farallon Industries: A Case History

Norman H. Moore

Farallon Industries is a venture still in mid-launch—not yet a clear success or failure. [Ed. Note: See Sequel and Epilogue at end of chapter.] I got into it in typical fashion. One day in February, 1970, I was sitting at my desk in an ailing airline operation quietly minding the ups and downs of that business when a former employee of mine (from the days when I was running the Electron Tube Division of Litton Industries) called to say that he was now operating a small company making a flashlight for the scuba industry; and in a small shop next door, two young fellows were working on a product that he thought had some potential for the same market. But they needed both money and management, and I was the only person he knew crazy enough even to look at it.

I asked what the product was, and he said, "A two-man submarine for scuba divers." I agreed that the product might ward off a few bankers and ultraconservative venture capitalists but that any reasonable man should certainly look at the opportunities in two-man submarines.

Would I come on over? I would. Following up such calls is an addiction. Some years ago a close associate exclaimed in utter

At the time this chapter was written, Norman H. Moore, Ph.D., was the Chairman of the Board of Farallon Industries, a scuba equipment manufacturer in Belmont, California.

frustration, "Moore, your long-range plan is the next telephone call." Well, this article tells how one such long-range plan is working out.

THE BEAST

That afternoon I drove over—it was only a couple of miles away—and saw, for the first time, The Beast. It was beautiful—international orange, nine feet long, three feet wide, about a foot high; it was sexy—pure James Bond; and it worked . . . well, sort of. (More of that later.) The two young fellows who had been working on it for the previous six months were both eminently qualified to develop a device to descend and maneuver 100 feet under the ocean—they both had B.A. degrees in psychology from San Jose State University, both were 24 years old, and neither had taken any courses in science or engineering. But they had already built two of them and were working on this one, their third model.

An hour later I called an associate of mine to come look—we had been examining a variety of possible new ventures over the previous six months. We spent most of the next couple of weeks looking at the product, the field, the individuals.

We became fascinated by the whole venture, particularly by the audacity and enthusiasm of the two young fellows, whose only real qualifications were a tremendous love of scuba diving, vivid imagination, boundless enthusiasm, and considerable natural mechanical ability. They had decided that a two-man wet submersible could be made small enough and light enough to fit in the back of a station wagon, be driven to a beach, unloaded by hand, launched in shallow water, and then flown. I use "flown" appropriately, for the unit, as it was finally developed, really operated under water like a plane in the sky. It came to have a single lever joy-stick that permitted all the maneuvers of an acrobatic plane. The two young men had designed and fabricated the fiberglas molds, had them shot with fiberglas, had assembled two units, and had actually descended 35 feet with one of them. That there was no management experience between the two fellows, no real marketing plan, was unimportant. It was like falling in love with a beautiful girl—nothing else mattered. And besides, you only live once.

IN THE BEGINNING . . .

By April 1, 1970, we had a corporation formed. The young fellows' Submersible Systems became Farallon Industries—named for the islands off San Francisco. Also, the Spanish word *farallones* meant "guiding light," which we thought appropriate. Our goal was to sell 50 units in the first year. Our forecast showed break-even by the end of the year.

One of the young men became president; the other, vice president; my associate became chairman of the board; and I, a board member. My associate had decided that the project was more in his realm than mine—the problem was more in mechanical design and fabrication, and he was a mechanical engineer by original training. I was a physicist—rather, my businessmen friends think I must be a physicist; my physicist friends think I must be a businessman. Anyhow, my associate took over as chairman.

He and I each agreed to put in $40,000 in a complex arrangement that would have resulted (had $80,000 been all that was required) in stock ownership of about 35% of the company for each of us. The remaining 30% was to be split between the two young men; they also had options that would enable them eventually to reach 48% ownership.

By May we realized that some of the performance figures the young men had been quoting on the machine they had already built and flown had included, shall we say, "expected" as well as "achieved" speed and maneuverability. To be specific, the *three* knots mentioned were more like *one,* the maneuverability was marginal—the machines floundered along. The range with two 100-ampere-hour 12-volt truck batteries was about one-fifth that listed on their product sheet. By June, 1970, we all realized we had a tiger by the tail, that a low-speed, high-efficiency underwater propulsion system was something we needed but didn't yet have, that submersible ballast and control systems were pretty subtle, and that we had a lot of engineering ahead of us. By July, as complexity and cost rose, we all began to question the size of the market, particularly as price had to rise. By August, we realized that we needed a lower-cost, simpler device and began modeling a new product that looked more like a small torpedo to tow a diver.

It was not a unique idea. At least 50 varieties of diver propulsion vehicles have been carried at least through the model stage, but up until the Farallon unit, no one had put good solid engineering and tooling into them, nor sold them in any quantity. By September, my associate had brought aboard as chief engineer a top mechanical designer who had been our chief engineer in an earlier very successful venture—the Litton Microwave Oven. We had started that division from scratch in 1963. It now does $50,000,000 a year, *very* profitably. By October, we had the first torpedo-like DPV (Diver Propulsion Vehicle) in the water; by November, we were in production; and in December, we delivered $10,000 worth to customers—the Farallon DPV MK-I was launched.

Also by November, my associate was wanting out—or at least no more in—so we made up a prospectus to try to interest some outside investors. A short effort at raising $150,000 for one-third of the company convinced us that this was not a very salable commodity. But I'm always the optimist, so I said I would keep putting enough money in to see us through the National Sporting Goods Show at the McCormick Place in Chicago in February, 1971, one of the biggest trade shows in the world. In addition, one of the two young fellows wanted to drop out to go to law school.

So Ralph Shamlian, the remaining young man, who was president, and I went to the NSGA show, took a 10 x 10 foot booth and filled it with our big, beautiful two-man submarine at $2,495, up from $1,495 list price in the original brochure, and a bunch of our DPV MK–I at $395 list. As I've always done in any business I've been associated with, I did booth duty every hour, every day except for coffee breaks. No food until dinner.

About the middle of the third day, I saw a good-looking gray-haired man standing about 20 feet away observing us for about the fourth time in three days. I walked over and in my shy way said, "Who are you? You've been casing us every day." He chuckled and replied, "I'm the show manager. You have the best-looking small booth in the whole show, and I don't have to tell you that you have more foot-traffic per square foot of booth than anyone else here."

It was pretty heady stuff—no IBM, you understand, but we took orders for 41 DPV's at about $300 dealer cost and one DTV (Diver Transport Vehicle) at $1,495 dealer cost which, with accessories, added up to about $15,000 in orders. In January through June, 1971, the little company shipped $130,000 worth of DPV's and one DTV to some of the worst credit risks you ever saw!

THE SCUBA MARKET

Scuba equipment is marketed in the U.S. through about 1,100 outlets. Gross sales of all forms of scuba equipment sold through these outlets are between $60 million and $70 million per year, including masks, fins, snorkels, tanks, wet suits, and instruments. The market is growing upwards at a rate of 15% per year. It is served by eight so-called full-line manufacturers and another half dozen or so smaller specialty houses like ourselves. Altogether, sales at manufacturer level total about between $40 and $45 million a year.

The biggest is U.S. Divers	$14,000,000
next is Voit	8,000,000
then Scubapro	7,000,000
Dacor	4,000,000
Healthway	2,100,000
Imperial	1,300,000
Sportsways	1,200,000
Seamless Rubber (Nemrod)	1,000,000
White Stag	1,000,000

They don't really hand me their books for inspection, so these are educated guesses, but the first three (U.S. Divers, Voit, and Scubapro) do two-thirds of the total sales in the market.

The sport first began to climb out of the hairy-chested hero status in the late 1950's. Along with its commercial and military counterparts, it was bathed in—or perhaps drowned in—propaganda about the coming world of "inner space." There was a resultant early rapid growth followed by a disillusioning cutback as it was discovered that a sustaining market just wasn't yet there.

Then in the mid-60's a slower, steadier growth set in—this is the source of the 15% growth figure. At this point, there are four or five organizations which train divers and issue certificates saying that the diver has passed certain tests. Most scuba shops will not put compressed air in a diver's tank unless he has one of these certificates in his possession; it is a dangerous world into which the scuba diver descends, and he must be trained for it. A diver at 60 feet without air is in at least as dangerous an environment as a private pilot at 6,000 feet without fuel.

Today there are approximately 900,000 people who carry scuba diver certificates; another 150,000 receive training each year. Unfortunately, only approximately 15% to 20% of the latter are female, and scuba diving isn't really going to become popular until that percentage increases significantly. But there is hope. Brightly colored, well-tailored wet suits and "apres-scuba" clothes are now being marketed by White Stag and others, and light-weight, high-pressure aluminum tanks are on their way. Also, new and better instrumentation and other safety items are becoming generally available.

INITIAL CUSTOMERS

Now, back to Farallon's entry into the market. The direct customers of the scuba manufacturer were the nearly 1,100 retail outlets—half of these were departments of full-line sporting goods stores; the other half were one-man or man-and-wife shops catering to the scuba market or perhaps scuba and one other market, such as skiing or public safety (the latter goes with scuba because both markets need high-pressure air-filling facilities).

Not all of the 1,100 scuba equipment outlets carried a full-enough line to be fair targets for the Farallon DPV. In fact, there were a lot of people in the industry who gratuitously offered us the advice that there were *no* valid targets for a product that sold for $395 in a market where a complete outfit—mask, fins, snorkel, tank, regulator, pressure gauge, depth gauge, inflatable vest, and wet suit could be purchased for $300. And as for the two-man submarine—forget it! Well, in the latter case they were certainly right. The $1,495 unit my associate and I first looked at had been raised to $2,495 by show time; if somebody today *insists* we build one for him, we'll do it for $4,995.

But back in early 1971, we still had high hopes for the submarine. We sold one at the show—I did it myself—to a dealer located . . I guarantee you will *never* guess where. For use off the Southern California coast? In the Bahamas? In the Mediterranean? No! In something called Table Rock Lake, a 40-mile-long lake on the border between Missouri and Arkansas. That still amazes me—a submarine in Missouri! However, by the time we had a unit we were proud enough of to sell, the dealer had cancelled the order. He put it succinctly: "I get to have a submarine or a wife." And if you had met his wife—believe me, he made the right decision. Our submarine is sexy, but his wife is a real doll.

We really did sell one—to the U.S. Navy. I vividly recall the way we got that order. Again I was sitting at my desk, which was now at Farallon (the airline had been mercifully buried), when I received a call from a man who identified himself as an employee of the Naval Undersea Research and Development Center in San Diego. He said he had in front of him a one-page sheet. One side was headed *Farallon DTV MK-II* and had a photograph of the machine; the other side listed detailed specifications, including by now:

Speed:	3 mph
Depth:	300 feet
Range:	5 miles

He asked if it was for real. I told him it was. He asked if it did what the specifications said. I said, "Yes, and then some." By that time, we had a very sophisticated unit with a single joy-stick control that permitted the machine to maneuver like an acrobatic plane. Solid state speed control produced a smoothly variable thrust of from 10 to 100 pounds—and that is a lot of thrust—in a very efficient way. He asked about delivery. I said "30 days." And if he wanted it in black? "Still 30 days." He said, "You mean you really can build one from scratch in 30 days?" I said, "Yes." He asked who I was and if I was authorized to speak for the company. I said I owned it—or most of it. (I could have added, "More than I intended," but more of that later.) He said, "You had better not be kidding, for a Navy Contracting Officer will be calling you within 30 minutes." Then he added: "Just one thing. When you're talking to him, please don't call it a submarine. Call it an 'Underwater Power Unit, with electrical and motive power.' Only the Pentagon is authorized to buy submarines."

Within 30 minutes, a man from the Navy Purchasing Office in Pasadena called. We went through the same set of questions. Apparently he found my answers incredible, because when it came to the 30-day delivery, he said, "And if I put in a clause that says, 'contract may be cancelled at no cost to the government if not delivered in 30 days,' *then* what is the delivery?" I replied, "30 days." Then he gave me the navy contract number and added, "My watch says 2:30 p.m., June 12, 1971, and the contract delivery date is going to be set for July 12, 1971, with cancellation permitted at no cost to the government if not delivered by then. Now how do you feel?" I said, "Great—I have a contract I didn't have yesterday." He repeated his concern about the delivery date and asked if I was worried. I wasn't. There was a pause. Then he said quietly: "Maybe *I* had better start worrying. I'm not sure I can process all the paperwork in time to *take* delivery in 30 days."

On the 30th day, the "Underwater Power Unit" was ready for delivery, but the Navy couldn't get use of the pier at Scripps Marine Biological Station in La Jolla until the 33rd day. That day, we delivered the sexiest looking jet black UPU the Navy ever bought.

We demonstrated that within ten minutes of opening the doors of our mini-van we could have it in the water and operational. And that day we trained two Navy and four Scripps divers to operate it. They all were absolutely blown out of their minds by it. And we did get paid. But that is almost the only government money we have yet received for anything—and I like it that way!

That was the one and only DTV we ever sold. We did loan two to be used in the TV series *Primus,* which had the most cornball scripts and acting yet seen on TV—but it sure gave us great publicity. And by the way, in over five months of use. the completely untrained actors using them had no problems at all.

The producers of *Primus* also used six of our DPV's. The recognition from TV was so great that one day, while walking two blocks from my car to Abercrombie & Fitch in downtown New York carrying a DPV, I got stopped by a number of absolute strangers who wanted to know "Didn't I see that on TV?" As a result of that exposure, a variety of new James Bond stuff we designed was used in the filming of *The Day of the Dolphin,* with George C. Scott.

So the submarine was an artistic and engineering triumph, but a financial disaster!

The DPV, however, began to catch on.

TRAVELING SALESMEN

After the 1971 National Sporting Goods Show, Ralph headed back to California to get production going—after all, it was only a ten-man company—and I headed south and west with my oldest son, the marketing manager for a water ski company, that had also been exhibiting at Chicago. We drove out to visit the commercial diving concerns in the New Orleans area—Taylor Diving, Dick Evans Diving, Sub-Sea International. Taylor is one of the largest in the industry, and I wanted to see the chief engineer.

I obeyed a rule I try never to violate: *Never* call ahead for an appointment if you are trying to sell something to a customer whose first reaction is likely to be, "I don't need it" or "I can't afford it." He will ask why you want to see him, and you will get turned off by phone. It's much tougher to refuse to listen to the story of the anvil salesman if he has lugged his demo ten miles to your doorstep and is sitting there with it, obviously tired, hot, and thirsty.

The receptionist's desk was located on the center of the first floor of a two-story well, with offices leading off the reception area and the second-floor balcony. She said, "I'm sorry, the chief engineer is very busy today, but I'll call and ask if he can see you. What shall I say you want to see him about?"

I said I would like to show him our DPV for possible use in his operations. She called him and then said, "He regrets he just can't see you today, but he has no use for any scuba equipment since all his divers use only hardhat gear."

So I was just standing there, temporizing, hoping lightning would strike, showing the DPV to the secretary, other people waiting in the lobby, the janitor—anything to stall—when a second-floor office door opened, a man came out, glanced down, retreated into his office and, through the receptionist, said, "Oh well, if he's here, send him up; I didn't realize he'd come all the way out here."

And so four hours later, after he had not only looked at the DPV himself but called in five other men to study it, he said, "That's the first piece of professional gear I've ever seen come out of the scuba industry—too bad we don't have any use for it." Then he smiled—"But we'll find some." (He also asked how we made them for that price.)

Since then, they and many other commercial diving concerns have bought quite a number of our DPV's for inspecting oil lines, water lines, and sewer lines. Marine biology stations, university laboratories, and government laboratories are also making increasing use of them.

By the time we arrived back in California four weeks and 4,000 miles later, we had called on over 50 sport scuba and commercial diving firms in places like Alamo Heights, Austin, Barstow, Baton Rouge, Crowley, Del Rio—through Langtry, Morgan City, New Braunfels, Opelousas—clear through to Yucca and Zachary. I had taken orders from one in every three of the potential customers for DPV's—in fact, for four of them at a time from a dealer in Galveston who asked if he could pay in advance by personal check. I said "yes" with alacrity and had steak for dinner that night.

TAKING STOCK

By now I had decided that Farallon was, in fact, a business, but a business that was going to take a lot more time and money than we had originally estimated—though there's nothing new about that in the venture capital business.

Upon my return, I offered to continue funding the operation on the basis of loans to the company, convertible to stock at $1.00 per share, taking over as chairman and chief executive officer. The offer was immediately accepted, and Farallon kept going. By December 31, 1970, $140,000 had been put in; by June of 1971, $200,000 more was required. By June, we had successfully sold over 400 DPV MK-I's to dealers, though collecting from a few of them was a real hassle. Also in June, we began delivery of a DPV MK-II, which included all the improvements building 400 MK-I's suggested, raising the price to $450 list. In July, we brought out a DPV MK-III, with solid-state variable speed control, for $595 list; and by late fall, a DPV MK-IV, with three instead of two batteries and additional thrust, at $795 list.

We had discovered that, for a fair percent of our customers, price was not the prime determinant—performance was. I am sure that motorcycle and snowmobile manufacturers before us had discovered the same thing. The MK–I had delivered 15 pounds of thrust; the new MK–II, 30 pounds; the variable speed MK–III, 40 pounds maximum; the MK–IV, 50 pounds maximum.

NEAR DISASTER

Getting all that performance was at least 50% accident. We had begun shipping the DPV MK–I in December, 1970. Performance in terms of pounds of thrust and pounds of thrust per horsepower were about on a par with what might be expected—we had even paid a marine engineering firm $1,500 to go over our design in mid-1970, and they reported it was giving within 10% of theoretically possible performance.

One day in mid-April, 1971, while casually operating a DPV in our test-tank—one of those 12-foot-diameter-three-foot-high pools you can buy at Sears—someone noticed that the DPV acted very dead in the water. When we put a spring scale to it and measured thrust, it was only about 10 pounds instead of the expected 15.

We took another and another and another unit off the production line; the thrusts all measured from about 9 to 15 pounds, with most around 10. Consternation reigned. We started to look for binding bearings, bad brushes, demagnetized motors, bad seals, bad gears, misshapen propellers. Nothing jibed; nothing correlated.

For ten days and nights, and I do mean nights, no one went home until he was too tired to stand up. And about the third or fourth day, we began to get calls from the field saying things like, "My unit doesn't seem to perform like the one you demonstrated." We knew, we knew . . . we just didn't know why.

Around 8 p.m. on the tenth evening, just staring in dismay and fatigue at two units, one good, one bad, I asked the chief engineer, "Do you see a difference in the gap between the body and the kort nozzle on those two units? And do you suppose that could have anything to do with it?"

It had everything to do with it. The subcontractor who spun our kort nozzles had casually moved a pivot point in his spinning operations, which had made what seemed to him a negligible change in nozzle shape. In the blending of curves, we had never noticed it, and now in the field we had nearly 300 DPV's, some of which were good, some bad. And we had no way of telling which were which.

All this we realized between 8 and 10 p.m. that night. But between then and 6 a.m. the next morning, using *Bondo,* that wonderful material used to fill bumps on cars before repainting, we had fashioned a new contour onto the old kort nozzle that not only took 9-pound performance to 15 pounds, our original number, but on up to 20—far beyond the marine engineer's reported possible limit.

By noon that day, we were in session with a rubber molder; and within five more days, we began shipping the "Farallon Thrust Augmenter" free to all 300 owners in the field and along with the 100 units going along our production line. Our customers were delighted.

If 20 pounds was possible, what was the limit? Lots of work had been done on *high*-power, *high*-speed, *high*-thrust design—for submarines, torpedos, ships, and even for high-power, low-speed tugs. Now we really got to work, realizing that no one had ever tried to maximize efficiency in *low*-speed, *low*-power, *low*-thrust underwater devices. Although the power in trolling motors was still well above ours, even it had never been optimized. Data for our problem were nonexistent, so we set up a tow tank—remember, I was once a physicist a long time ago—and got to work. Understand that, when using battery power, efficiency is *tremendously* important.

We not only varied kort nozzle shape but propeller shape and speed as well. For our original 324-watt input, thrust crept up and up from the original 15 to 20, to 25, and finally, to 30 pounds. We used a little theory and a lot of cut and try. It was the results of this work we incorporated in our MK–II, which came to market in June, 1971.

Three months later, as we were visiting the G.E. marine systems plant in Philadelphia, their Technical Director casually asked the performance figure of our MK–II which, as a good peddler, I just happened to have under my arm. (You may note my right arm is now 3" longer than my left.) When I told him, he asked me to repeat it. Then he got out his slide rule and said, "We consider 40 to 50 pounds of thrust per horsepower good underwater propulsion design, 60 pounds to be asymptote of the curve, and you are delivering 70. How in hell do you do it? So I told him about the pains of progress. And I spent the rest of the day with his propulsion experts, who viewed our device with amazement.

NEED FOR MORE PRODUCTS

Back at the ranch! Even with the MK–II, III, and IV and a high-power underwater movie light, we still didn't have a viable business. We needed more products to make it—under-$50 products, we felt.

At the Marine Technology Show in Washington in August, 1971, we saw a device designed by engineers at the same Naval Undersea Center that had bought our submarine—a hypodermic-type device that would kill sharks by exploding a CO_2 cartridge inside their bodies. We saw it on a Wednesday. Ralph flew back to California that night and got together with Ash Hollingsworth, our chief engineer. By the following Wednesday, they had designed and built a repeater version of it called the "Shark Dart," and

Ralph had flown to San Diego and obtained a license to manufacture the device for the non-military market.

That was mid-August. Within 90 days we began shipping five variations of the Shark Dart, all tooled for injection-molded parts. We quickly increased the variations to seven and, within the following three months, delivered over 2,000 of them. Steady orders now continue at several hundred a month. The Apollo Fifteen recovery team carried them, and soon so will Air Force air-sea rescue teams, but still over 99% of our orders have been to sport divers. We already have a number of letters from divers thanking us for producing a device which saved their lives.

ON THE ROAD AGAIN

While Ralph flew back to California to get the Shark Dart going, I called my wife in California and said, "Come on east. This fall is going to be slow and a good time to visit a lot of dealers. Let's buy a car and drive it west, calling on as many dealers as possible." In the 80-day period between August 18 and November 6, 1971, when we arrived in San Francisco, we traveled 12,060 miles, called on 157 dealers, and sold DPV's to just over half of them. The DPV was the most expensive inventory item, by a factor of three, any of them had ever bought for their shop. The most unlikely sale was made at a Howard Johnson's motel in Ithaca, New York, to a dealer who tried both the DPV and the 350-watt movie light in the motel pool at 1:00 a.m., then tried to buy my demo out of my hands at 2:00 a.m. Instead, I had a new one on its way by 9 the next morning, air freight from San Francisco.

DESIGN STANDARDS

All the engineering and tooling didn't come cheap, but we try to design and fabricate everything we make so that no one else will be tempted to try to do it better or cheaper. By December 31, 1971, over $400,000 had been put into the company. Sales for the year, the company's first, were $256,000. The Shark Dart sales had overcome the expected plunge in third and fourth quarter sales in DPV's.

Early 1972 started out with a bang, between DPV's and Shark Darts. In the spring, we came up with a MK-V at $995, with a maximum of 60 pounds of thrust, and a MK-VI at $1,295, with 90 pounds maximum thrust for the burgeoning commercial and nascent military market. By the way, holding on to a MK-VI is exactly like trying to hold onto a 90-pound sack of cement—you don't do it for long—so for the MK-V and MK-VI, named respectively the "UDT Special Mission" and "High-Speed Special Mission," we sell something I call a pogo stick that fastens to the unit and catches you in the fanny. The MK-VI will tow a fully equipped 200-pound diver at 3.7 mph—which is really moving under water. And we have a way to rig two of them in parallel. And it is this MK-VI which has really obsoleted our original wet submarine. The MK-VI is less costly than the sub ever was, lighter, and more maneuverable. (But it just isn't as glamorous.)

SEEING THE LIGHT

However, we still needed more under-$50 products. Ralph then came up with the idea of illuminated underwater instruments; and through the spring, summer, and fall, we all worked on them. Joining us in mid-summer was Norm MacLeod, an ex-aerospace engineer who had come by one day to try to get us to back him in bringing to market an underwater detection system for the military, a goal that he had worked on in a small two-man company that had foundered for lack of financial backing. We told him that we didn't have the money or the inclination to tackle that market, but we liked what we saw of him and some of his other ideas for non-military markets. We asked him to join us as vice president of operations.

By August, we brought the first illuminated instrument, a pressure gauge, to market; by October, a depth gauge; by November, a compass and a combination pressure/depth gauge.

By December, our problem was the kind that most companies wish *they* had—more orders than ability to deliver. We went into January, 1973 with over 1,000 unfilled orders.

Now, it should no more have been possible for a new, upstart company to come out with the first illuminated underwater gauges in late 1972 than for me to fly to the moon on a broomstick. This should have been done long ago. The devices represent nothing that is either revolutionary or technologically difficult. It is just a matter of taking good engineering and innovation to a consumer field that hasn't had much. And to go night diving or cave diving or even daylight diving in murky water and be unable to read your instruments except by using a hand flashlight is like going private flying at night and having to read your instrument panel by flashlight. Both are dangerous.

In two weeks, the 1973 National Sporting Goods Show opens, this time in Houston, and we will have a couple of more new products to show—also under $50 each. And our backlog will all be caught up even if every supervisor's wife works at the assembly bench—and they all have! I should add here that Norm MacLeod's wife and three sons assemble so much at home that we refer to them as the Cottage Industry Division.

SUMMARY

Well, that's how one company got started. Every forecast of time, money, performance, and market was wrong. Only one of the original products was ever sold. And the company isn't completely out of the woods yet. At the end of the first three years, total investment equalled total sales.

Would we sell the company for the investment in it? No way! Remember, I'm an optimist . . . . But in 1973, the company should do between $750,000 and $1,000,000 and be in the black—of course, that's what I thought about 1972 in January of that year.

But we now have 550 dealers in the U.S. and others in England, Switzerland, Japan, Australia, South Africa, Venezuela, Israel—over 20 countries in all. We'll soon be out with a wrist-mount size digital depth gauge, using a light-emitting diode readout, accurate to 1 or 2 feet in 300. But we don't have the last of the bugs out of it yet. And we have another model that is equally accurate to 2,000 feet.

Today, that young psychology-major-president is now close to his engineering degree . . . well, sort of. Each time he comes up with a good new idea, we award him credit toward his B.S. at Farallon Engineering School. But occasionally we also have to let him know that his psychology background would indicate the B.S. should stand for something else.

SEQUEL — July, 1974

The above paper was delivered in February, 1973. It took another year to get all the bugs out of the digital depth gauge, but it is now in production. The company has continued to add new products—moldable mouthpiece snorkels and digital thermometers—and soon we will begin shipment of the Farallon "Decomputer," a cigarette-pack-sized wrist-mounted device that simulates the action of body tissues and accurately indicates to the diver his decompression status.

The company didn't climb into the black until January, 1974, three years and ten months after incorporation; but by June, 1974, sales and profits have risen so fast that possibly all operating losses of the first three years and nine months will be earned back by the five-year mark: March 31, 1975.

Sales were $830,000 in 1973, will be about $2,000,000 in 1974, and will reach $3,500,000 to $4,000,000 in 1975. So the company, now headed by a much more experienced but still only 28-year-old psychology graduate, is off and running.

EPILOGUE – October, 1979

In July, 1977, a small privately held corporation purchased Farallon in a bulk stock transfer. The major Farallon stockholders were removed, and a new management team was brought in. Farallon became a wholly owned subsidiary of American Underwater Products (A.U.P.), which does its marketing under the name of Oceanic. Farallon and Oceanic were competing firms when Farallon was purchased and still operate with separate financial and commercial identities. Both companies enjoy similar growth paths and operate at the upper ends of their market's price range.

Purposes

In 1977, both companies marketed masks, fins, snorkels, DPV's, underwater lights, and instruments in retail "dive shops." In addition, Oceanic was successfully marketing underwater camera equipment and movie lighting. In Farallon, Oceanic saw an innovator in the field—an innovator that needed some guidance in marketing and in research and development but that could help A.U.P. to shorten its long-range product-development goals by about three years. Since the acquisition, A.U.P. has continued to redesign its reliable original products, as well as adding new members to the product line. Three or four new products are introduced each year.

A Changing Market

The typical Farallon/Oceanic customer is an experienced diver who may be in underwater photography. He or she probably enjoys an upper-middle-class income (the equipment is fairly costly) and likes to travel.

The number of women entering the sport has increased in recent years, and women now make up a viable part of the diving industry's consumer market. Trying to appeal to female tastes, the industry has experimented with the cosmetic use of color in underwater equipment, especially wetsuits. Also, advertising is now aimed at both male and female divers. The industry has not tapped a possible lucrative market—teenagers—primarily because of the financial demands of the sport and the legal liability problems inherent in matching minors with a potentially very dangerous pursuit.

Despite the participation of women, the sport's popularity—and market—has grown more slowly than, say, the popularity of tennis and the market for tennis equipment, largely because diving is a nonspectator sport. The participant is active but not on display. Hence, diving appeals to people who enjoy performing the sport more than performing for the appreciation of others.

In addition to the changes in the market brought on by the growth of the sport, the retail dive shop owner has changed since the start-up of Farallon Industries. Dive shops were originally run by hobbyists whose hobby had grown into a store. Today, because the market has grown, common business people have scented profits in diving equipment and have brought better managerial skills to its retailing. Likewise, the older hobbyist owners have become more sophisticated in their business dealings, becoming more aware of inventory levels, controls, and mature approaches to finance. Since more profits are to be made, the owners are bringing in professional helpers, such as bookkeepers and accountants, to help develop financial strength and professional methods.

A.U.P. is interested in continued growth, but not to the point of sacrificing quality in products. A.U.P. products and market impact, the company feels, are based on innovative technology. Technological development itself has affected the market. During the last 10 years, lighter-weight, more compact underwater equipment has become available, appealing to many men and to the growing number of women divers, as well as to youths who dive. Publicity generated by loaning equipment to television and movie companies has helped to make the underwater environment less alien, has stimulated consumer awareness, and therefore has also expanded the market.

The industry as a whole has enjoyed a steady growth rate of 15–20% for the past three or four years. Domestic sales through approximately 1,800 retail dive shops are in the millions of dollars, and both Oceanic and Farallon sell internationally at the retail level to foreign dive shops. The domestic and international consumer markets keep them busy enough so that they do not pursue government sales.

Keys to Success

The company's vice president of finance feels that there are several concepts key to the success and the profits of Farallon/Oceanic and other companies as well.

1. Be aware of your company's "fit" in its industry. Look at the total picture. Be aware of your strengths but recognize and cover your weaknesses—*every* company has weakness.

2. Make every employee accountable and responsible for his or her share of the job. Make sure employees *know* that they are accountable and responsible.

3. Employees will *be* accountable and responsible if the company maintains and interesting climate which functions by teamwork. Farallon/Oceanic employees are interested in their jobs since many of them are practicing underwater photographers and scuba divers.

4. Identify and understand the complexion of your company sufficiently well so that you are aware of its changes. You must be flexible and ready to adapt.

5. Management must be capable of maintaining the company and growing itself as the company expands. Here is where flexibility is needed—management must be able to adjust the company to meet day-to-day changes as well as longer term growth requirements.

To apply these five principles well, management needs a system of reporting that enables them to understand and trace, on a day-to-day basis, any and all changes that are taking place in each department, what those changes are in response to, and what further changes are needed.

Farallon Industries, the little company that started out in 1970 trying to manufacture and sell a two-man submarine, has gone through many phases of a maturing process that has now brought it success. Almost nothing about the company has remained the same, except its guiding precept of bringing quality, technologically innovative products to the scuba diving marketplace. Farallon's survival and growth attests to the importance of flexibility, adaptability, and change to long-term profits.

Three

Employment Contracts and Liability of the Entrepreneur

Thomas A. Skornia

Say you are working as an engineer for some high-technology firm, and you decide to leave their employ to start your own company. What is your liability to this former employer in regard to ideas you may take with you? This paper will first consider such liability and then discuss the obviously related topic: How do you, as a successful entrepreneur, protect your *own* plans and operations from budding entrepreneurs in *your* employ?

LIABILITY OF THE ENTREPRENEUR

Depending on the nature of the business, the entrepreneur leaving one company to start another may have a rough exit if his former employer thinks he has taken with him some key ideas. Can this difficulty be avoided? Probably not entirely, but I can suggest a couple of guidelines.

Cardinal Rule One, I think, is that you take with you nothing that is tangible—certainly nothing by way of actual prototypes or

At the time this chapter was written, Thomas A. Skornia was a Senior Partner with the San Francisco firm of Skornia, Rosenblum & Gyemant, attorneys-at-law.

parts, blueprints or drawings, or laboratory notebooks. That is, take nothing tangible that you could be accused of using to your benefit or the benefit of your subsequent employer in the same field.

Now there are intangibles—certain things in your head that you automatically and necessarily take with you. These include standard know-how and possibly the ability to duplicate or replicate certain processes or parts. There is nothing much you can do about such knowledge other than to avoid operating in that area or to erase it from your mind as best you can. However, the courts will be very reluctant to prevent you from using standard know-how in a particular business or field because it is part of your ability to make a living. To prohibit you from using it would be against the public policy which is set forth in statutes such as California's Business and Professions Code prohibiting noncompetition agreements. To avoid other areas of unfair competition, make no misuse or close use of a trade name or a trademark, and make no infringement of patent positions or what-have-you. Now again, these are general guidelines; the only way that you can be certain is to discuss the specific facts of your case with a lawyer who has some experience in this field. Discuss with him what you've been doing with your former employer and what you are likely to be doing for your new company. Your lawyer should be able to spell out some guidelines for you as to what your course of conduct should be over the early months of the formation of the new business.

Now there is one other aspect in the law which is still fairly ill defined—the question of recruitment of additional employees from the former employer, otherwise known as raiding. Frequently, two or three people who want to found a new company just leave a particular employer in a group and begin to set up their own operation. About three or four months later, they find that they need some other competent people to operate in specific divisions or sections of their firm. Naturally, the best place to go is to the well where you know the quality of the water. So you go back to your former employer and you start hiring. You take one in March, two in April, four in May; you skip June and July; and then you take six in August. This gets very aggravating to your former employer. The way I usually put it—amputation should not be done in sections. There's a lot of blood lost every time you take another segment of the leg. What you should do, I think—if you know there are certain minimum numbers of key employees that you want, and if your former employer is the only place you can get them—is take them all at once. As long as you're going to take the risk of getting them, get it over with and let the pain subside; anesthetize it in the best way you can at the time, but then don't go back for more. A year or two later, when you want to get lower-level people? That's another matter.

EMPLOYMENT CONTRACTS

You've gotten away from your former employer; you've started your own company; it's going well. Now you want to protect your ideas—perhaps better than your former employer protected his. What you must consider at this juncture is the topic of employment contracts.

There are basically two kinds of employment contracts: oral and written. In the oral agreement, you agree to hire a guy and pay him X dollars per year once or twice a month. That contract is acceptable as an employment agreement so long as neither one of you decides to terminate it. The State Labor Code is likely to add a lot of provisions to that oral agreement which you aren't even aware of with respect to termination periods and other rights and liabilities of the parties. By and large, for lower-level employees, it's probably satisfactory to have oral agreements because the likelihood of a dispute which will be of material importance to the company is fairly small. But when you are talking about founders and key employees, I think it's of great importance that the agreement—whatever it is—be written down as clearly as possible so that the company on one side and the founder or key employee on the other know what their respective rights and liabilities are. (In some cases—at the outset, for instance—the founder may be the company's only employee. But I want to postulate that we now have a company that is operating and has perhaps three or four key founders and as many as half a dozen key employees.) Thus, you must ask yourself the following questions: When your company is successful in securing a large amount of investment capital, what sort of arrangements will you want to have with your other founders and key employees? What will the venture capitalists and finance people look for in regard to your arrangements with the other founders and key employees? You as founder and the capitalists as investors must be extremely concerned with protecting the new company—you want to keep the good people and get rid of the bad ones without letting them get away with the bacon at a key time in the development of your company. How do you do this? There are two main subheadings under the topic of Employment Contracts that apply to the problem. They are "incentives and lock-ins" (keeping everyone happy) and "disciplines and lockouts" (protecting yourself from someone who is unhappy).

Incentives and Lock-ins

Consider that there are two important moments in a company's dealings with a founder or key employee—when you hire him and when you find it necessary, if you do, to fire him. Once you have determined that an individual is competent and likely to do a good job for you, you make sure that he stays in. If it turns out that your judgment was wrong, it's important that you have the means expeditiously and finally to get him out because it can be a very serious point of dispute and aggravation to have a disgruntled key employee or founder around with whom you cannot make an adequate or satisfactory termination settlement. Therefore, the termination provisions should be set down in advance along with the provision for compensation and benefits during the time he was working for you.

At this point, let me define compensation and fringe benefits as I use the terms. This may seem to be fairly obvious, but I want to make it clear that compensation has to do with the amount of equity, or stock, that a founder or key employee will receive or purchase at the time he comes to work for the company. That, I suggest, is the area in which the greatest incentive, the greatest carrot followed also by the largest stick, can be applied to the people who have to make this company go and succeed. When we talk about equity compensation and equity incentives, the numbers sometimes get staggering. I have in mind a specific example. We assisted a company in incorporating in 1969, and it went public in the fall of 1972. The eight founders paid an aggregate of $60,000 for what turned out to be about 42.5% of the company. When the company went public, that 42.5% was valued at $9 million based on the offering price of the stock. Now in anybody's book, that is a nice capital appreciation in a four-year period.

If you have a company and if the founders and key people expect growth such as that in the example (which is not an unreasonable expectation) and see themselves meeting the performance milestones month by month and year by year, they're going to be working very hard for themselves, for you, and for the shareholders. Money is, after all, the objective in a profit-making corporation. So I suggest to you that equity compensation really is the key provision. You can pay a guy a lot of ordinary income; you can pay him a lot of fringe benefits; you can look after his retirement (hopefully this is 30 or 40 years away because you probably want a bunch of young guys who can stand the pace at the time that you are setting up your company). But the equity incentive of supermoney in "Adam Smith" and George Goodman's terms is the *real* incentive.

Now how do you assure that there is a fair balance between input or effort and compensation or repayment in the form of an equity position? Let me suggest a typical situation which obviously will vary depending upon the management position of the employee and his experience. Some employees you can buy cheaply; others you have to pay a lot of money for; hopefully, you can recognize the difference. When you are negotiating with your founders and key employees, you don't leave any money on the table. Presumably they don't either. But negotiating, like other human processes, is not a perfect art.

For example: Let's say we have a company with four founders who together are going to put in the $100,000 seed capital which is necessary to build a pre-production prototype of whatever it is they are going into business with. They are ultimately going to ask for $1 million and more from the venture capital community and other finance sources in order to get into production with this prototype and make the company a success. When they form the firm, let's say that they all decide to be equal participants in the equity. One of them will be president; the other three will perform perhaps the finance function, the manufacturing function, and the marketing function. Assume they each put in $25,000 and each take down a quarter of the original equity. Then, about four or five months later, they are in a position to sell half of the company, if you will, for $1 million, a ratio of 10:1. In effect, they have bought 50% of the company for themselves for $100,000; they sell the other 50% to outside investors for $1 million. Clearly, there is a lot of gain right there, and presumptively there is going to be some more if the company is successful and enjoys good earnings. In three to four years, assuming the company continues to be profitable and the stock is publicly traded, the financial community might value that stock at a high price-to-earnings multiple. That's a powerful incentive.

Going further with our example, the original $100,000 would buy a million shares at 10¢ per share. Let's say that's at par value, and it's sold at exactly the par value to the founders. The outsiders will pay for their million shares $1 per share. So the gain at the time of the initial outside financing is already 90¢ per share. Hopefully, the company will go public at $7 or $8 a share, and everybody has made a lot of money. However, making money is dependent upon the presence of the four key individuals.

These four people are expected to function as the chief people in their specific areas. It's very important that they stay with you during the founding period. If they don't, you must be in a position to recruit a substitute—somebody of equal standing who will be equally motivated. The only way I can suggest to do that is to be able to offer the substitute the same equity position which the departing individual had initially. This means forfeiture on the part of the departing employee or, as I like to put it, a scale of vesting the equity related to the period that a person stays there.

Say an individual leaves the company during the first year, and the company has a right to buy back his equity at the price he originally paid. Here the theory is that he hasn't stayed long enough really to have earned any of it. But if he leaves in the thirteenth month after start-up, he gets to keep a quarter of it; and if he leaves in the twenty-fifth month, having completed two years but not three, he would keep half of it—the other half would be bought back by the company.

A vesting period of four years is recommended based on the assumption that this should be enough time to establish the company firmly in the marketplace. By this time, the founder being considered here would have made the contribution expected of him by his co-founders and investors. Having done so, he would be entitled to keep all of his equity position.

It's important that such an understanding be written down and that the provisions be carefully drafted, either in the employment agreement or in a separate agreement which may be tied to the employment agreement. In this way, everyone understands what will happen to his stock position in the event he leaves—either voluntarily or by being terminated for cause.

Let's assume that, at this point, we have compensation and fringe benefits defined. We have established a vesting or forfeiture schedule for the equity incentive. We are now concerned about the continued availability of the key individual if he leaves voluntarily, if you discharge him for cause, or if the other founders collectively decide to discharge him without cause, allowing him to keep his equity incentive. That individual may still be valuable, not necessarily as an employee but because of what he knows about the company, what he knows about the market, and what current information he has picked up during his tenure with the company. You may want to retain him as a consultant. I would then suggest that, in drafting the employment agreement, you consider the possibility of including a consulting option. In this way, you have the right to retain him as an independent contractor or consultant for some reasonable period of time at a reasonable level of compensation should he terminate his employment. You may decide to pay him his original salary or some reasonable percentage of that salary for a period of time during which he will hold himself available to do consulting. You may then call upon him at reasonable times and places to consult for the company and assist it in its continuing development program.

It is very important that the provisions for termination in the contract be *very clearly* drafted. This is especially true in the case of someone who has a large equity position because the courts generally look upon forfeitures with disfavor. Let's say that a key employee is terminated. Subsequently, in accordance with the provisions of the employment agreement, the company decides to exercise its right to buy back the equity position at the price originally paid. At this time, the equity may have a much greater value, or at least a *potentially* greater value, than it did when it was originally purchased. If litigation develops over this matter (and it probably will if the stock has significantly increased in value), the court will scrutinize the agreement very carefully to find out whether you have the right to terminate the individual under the circumstances involved. If the agreement is not clearly worded, the result may be lengthy litigation. It may involve a lot of discovery on behalf of the departing employee against the company and a lot of general harassment and expense. You can avoid this very simply if you have a reasonably well-drafted and generally self-enforcing termination provision.

When I say well-drafted and self-enforcing, I am particularly concerned with the equity position. An ideal method would be to place the initial stock in escrow with some neutral third party—the company counsel, the company accountant, or perhaps even a bank escrow department. The neutral party would hold the stock certificates for that initial equity position under instructions that, if a notice of termination specifying facts A, B, and C is delivered to the employee with a copy to the escrow holder, the stock held in the escrow on his behalf would automatically come back to the company upon payment to the escrow holder of the initial purchase price. That then puts the burden of initiating litigation on the shoulders of the employee who is departing.

Consider the problems if you do not have that kind of a provision. Let's say that you fire an employee, you make a demand that he return his stock certificates, and you tender him a check. If he does not return the stock, there is only one way that you are going to be able to get it back—that is to file a lawsuit. From the company's point of view, I think it is much better to put the burden of a lawsuit on the other side. Very frequently the question of who has to sue determines whether or not suit is brought at all because of the costs, time, effort, and energy involved in bringing litigation.

To sum up: The one thing you inherently want to avoid is litigation. It is the least productive kind of business you can possibly engage in, even if you are a lawyer (and I say that as a lawyer who has a firm that does litigation). In our operation, commercial litigation is generally looked upon as kind of a Thursday loss leader at the supermarket. Because of the agony of going through the process, there is no way that you can make either money or friends with litigation even if you ultimately win. Again, clearly drafted and relatively certain agreements in the area of employment is one way to avoid the possible disaster of litigation.

So far, then, we have talked a little bit about the clearness of the provisions in the employment contract; we have discussed provision for a self-enforcing escrow to be able to bring back this equity position upon notification to the employee and the escrow holder; and thirdly, we discussed a consulting option in the event that an employee is discharged or leaves.

Disciplines and Lockouts

In California, one has to be fairly imaginative about covering down-side risk in the event of the departure of a key employee who may be in the possession of various proprietary information and company trade secrets. The Business and Professions Code in California is very restrictive about the circumstances and time during which you can impose a noncompetition agreement or covenant upon a departing employee. Generally, the rule is that you *cannot* impose a noncompetition covenant. One of the few exceptions is in the case of a sale of substantially all the stock or all the assets of a going business whether it be a corporation or a partnership. Then you may only impose a noncompetition covenant to the extent necessary to vindicate the ongoing goodwill of the continuing business. Therefore, the noncompetition covenant has to be restricted in time and in geography. If an individual leaves from a plant that operates principally in San Francisco, with its markets restricted to northern California, and if his ability to compete effectively may be restricted to a two- or three-year period, then the noncompetition covenant should be restricted to three years and to perhaps the ten counties of the San Francisco Bay Area. If he wants to move to southern California and compete in that market where you do not operate, he can probably do so. As you can see, even when you buy a business, you may be very limited in the way that you can restrict the previous owner's ability to compete with you.

With respect to a departing employee who does not own a substantial equity position, say 25% or more of the company, you probably *cannot* restrict, in any significant way, his ability to compete. That is, you cannot enforce a provision which says that, during the two years after the employee leaves, he shall not work for any company which is in the same industry, line of business, or competition with the former employer. That is against public policy on the grounds that no company should be in the position of depriving a man of his right to make a living. Otherwise, he would have to retrain himself and start out in some other field, which may take a long period of time and which may be very difficult to do depending upon his age and circumstances.

So what do you do? Well, what you do is write a very carefully defined provision that deals with unfair competition. Of course, you cannot prohibit competition generally, but you can—and the law will permit you to do so—prevent what is known as *unfair* competition. That involves such things as the misuse of a trademark or a trade name, the misappropriation or application of trade secrets or patented positions, or the misuse of a list of customers (which may be partially secret or inside information in the eyes of the company from which employment the individual is leaving). When it comes to matters of proprietary data and trade secrets, high-technology companies are particularly sensitive. In that area, a strongly worded, carefully drafted provision preventing use of what is defined as proprietary data and trade secrets will prevent the employee from using that information in other employment. In practice, you debrief your departing employee; you send his new employer (presumably a competitor) a letter quoting from the employment agreement and indicating perhaps the field, particular product line, or research and development project in which the individual has been working; and you indicate that it is your counsel's opinion that the agreement prohibits the individual from working in that specific area of the business—prohibits *as a matter of law.* Furthermore, if it comes to your attention that he *is* working in that field, litigation will be inevitable.

Finally, in connection with trade secrets and proprietary data, a provision should be included in the agreement in which the employee specifically consents, in advance, to the application to himself of certain injunctive relief, which a court is authorized to give, in the event he violates or breaches that provision of the agreement. Injunctive relief refers to an injunction—an order by the court that an individual will not and shall not continue to misuse the proprietary data and trade secrets of the former employer for his own benefit or the benefit of some competing employer. Now that is the law anyway; and a court of equity can and will give you, as the plaintiff employer, a temporary restraining order and ultimately a preliminary injunction against this kind of unfair competition. But you have to make a very strong showing. You have to prepare your moving papers and affidavits quickly, and you have to prove to the court that there is a very substantial danger of irreparable injury if the court does not order the individual to refrain from engaging in specific conduct. In obtaining such an order, it is a great help to have a provision in the employment agreement by which the employee has agreed to the nature of any trade secrets, at least by way of general category, and has consented in advance to the entry and application against him of injunctive relief.

For example, consider this fairly standard case with which we dealt. The departing individual happened to be the Director of Research and Development of the company in question. Now obviously, that's the clearest possible case. When we received notice that he was leaving (about a half a day in advance), we took the precaution of having an investigator monitor his whereabouts over the subsequent weekend. He left the plant on Thursday afternoon, carrying with him a large briefcase containing what we believed to be some of the plans for the major research and development project of our client company. He was monitored over the weekend; and by the following Tuesday at 9:00 a.m., we had a temporary restraining order which, a week later, was turned into a preliminary injunction. The injunction then lasted for a period of 18 months.

The above series of events took place four years ago. To my knowledge, that individual, because of the grossly unethical character of his conduct, has not worked regularly for a competitor in the industry since then. Based on the speed and ease with which we were able to get a preliminary injunction, it was fairly obvious to other people in the industry that his was very bad conduct; and they were not interested in being associated with him. We were able to get that injunction primarily because there were a couple of clear paragraphs in the employment agreement that we were able to show to the judge and say, "Look, we've already defined this and here are the affidavits showing that he is violating the agreement. He has agreed in the contract to the entry of a temporary restraining order." We got one on an hour's notice. So I suggest to you again to make your employment agreements clear and thorough.

OTHER LIABILITIES OF THE ENTREPRENEUR

In closing this discussion, I wish to state that I believe the most important liabilities of the entrepreneur to be to himself and his family. When you start your own business, you hope that someday it will be a public company listed on the New York Stock Exchange. Certainly that is what your investors want to hear. They want to be able to see the market out there and the profit margins that will permit you to reach those goals. If you are going to build that kind of a company where none exists today, you're going to have to do as the founding fathers of the United States did: pledge your lives, your fortunes, and your sacred honor to that undertaking. That means 16 hours a day six or seven days a week for a long period of time. That means sacrifice to yourself and to your family and children in a very meaningful and real way. That liability, once you embark upon it, is not reversible unless you get out. And probably you will be locked in by your investors and your co-founders and by the kinds of contract provisions I have suggested. Once you make that decision, you have got to be prepared to stay and be prepared for total dedication—to invest everything that you have by way of money, energy, and devotion. I suggest to you that, as Harry Truman put it, if you feel you're not up to standing that kind of heat, then perhaps the kitchen is not the place for you.

Four

The Founding Team and the Board of Directors

Leonard Mautner

When a group of young, would-be entrepreneurs think about starting a new business, one of the first items to be considered might be "The Founding Team and the Board of Directors" because in many ways the experience and quality of the founding team is perhaps the single most important ingredient in the building of a successful business. If a program presented to venture capitalists and backers of young businesses is properly organized by an experienced management team, the venture capitalists will look further into the deal; if the founding group appears to be inexperienced and perhaps naive, it is quite probable that the deal will "pass."

BACKGROUND OF OUR FIRM

Perhaps I should start out my discussion with a few introductory remarks about Goodman & Mautner, Ltd. We are a private, limited partnership and have been engaged in the venture capital business for the last five years. My partner, David M. Goodman, and I are

Leonard Mautner is a General Partner in the Los Angeles venture capital firm of Goodman & Mautner, Ltd.

the general partners of the firm. Each of us has been involved in venture capital activities for more than fifteen years. Among our limited partners are several investment banking firms and some of their partners as well as a number of business executives with whom we have been associated over the years. Currently, our portfolio includes some eighteen companies, the greatest number of which are located on the west coast. Several start-ups are included in the group as well as several rather more mature companies; roughly half of our portfolio companies are now publicly held. The businesses are generally high-technology ventures, and a number of them are oriented around the information-processing and computer industry—although we have a lively venture going in the egg carton field, and one of our newest investments is in a young distributor of foreign auto car parts. Within this group of companies, I think we have had the full range of problems that can beset a venture capital portfolio. We have had one bankruptcy, a merger, and several "sickies"; six presidents have been replaced; and we have had some interesting quarrels among members of the founding team. We have also had a chance to observe the interaction between the founding team and the board of directors in a number of difficult situations.

I think it might be appropriate to share with you several of our experiences and also those of some of our associates in the venture capital business. At the outset, let me emphasize the importance we attach to the quality of the founding team and how the team gets along with its board of directors, who generally represent the investors backing the enterprise.

When we consider going into a new deal, we figuratively try to thread the program through a series of "wickets." A proposed venture that can successfully navigate through the following four wickets receives our very serious attention.

- *First and foremost:* the quality of the management team. By this I mean the previous business experience of the founding members and their relative strengths in the various disciplines that constitute the necessary management tasks: general management, finance, marketing, engineering, production.

- *Second:* the market and everything we need to know about it—for example, how big it is, how much of it is penetrable by our company, with whom we must share it, what the methods and costs in distribution are. Of these elements, we feel we must develop an exquisite understanding.

- *Third:* the product. We ask: What need does it fill? What does it replace? How is it used? What is new and novel about it? What patent protection (if any) is available? Above all, How does it fit into the marketplace? Giving the product third priority seems to emphasize that, while it may be considered necessary in starting a new business, the product is by no means all that is required. This approach tends to offset the enthusiasm of the group who comes to show us a new product and says, "We developed it after-hours in our garage. It was a team effort. There is nothing like it available now. It works twice as fast, costs only half as much to make, and is edible in case of emergency. We can't wait to get started because we should be able to sell lots of them."

  When we press the team—How will they go about marketing the product? How, in fact, do they propose to organize a business to manufacture and distribute the product? Who has had the experience in doing this?—we often get some pretty naive answers. Those of us with engineering experience tend to think of the product first. We perceive the need for some item or device and feel that, after a solution to that problem is found, the rest of the program is pretty straightforward. Unfortunately this is not the case.

- *Fourth:* the business plan. If we have a good team that knows the marketplace, and if they have a good product or series of products with which to enter that market, then they ought to be able to put together a plan which shows over the next three to five years what amount of capital will be required, what the several phases of development might be, and how the thing all fits together. In a university course entitled "Entrepreneural Skills I," this would be considered the final exam. In Don Dible's book, *Up Your Own Organization,* this subject is discussed at some length. Suffice it to say that, if the whole project makes sense, the business plan will be a good distillation of it and the entrepreneurs as well as potential backers will be able to see one version of how the entire venture could get started.

OBJECTIVES AND BUSINESS CONCEPTS

Before we talk about specifics for a founding team and a board of directors, I think it is important to examine the kind of business being planned and to inquire into the objectives of the entrepreneurs. We can then look at the objectives of the financial backers and finally at the objectives of proposed members of the board of directors.

What kind of a business will it be? Will it be a small consulting and design firm with sales of perhaps $1 million a year or a small manufacturing company with sales of about $3 million per year? Perhaps we are planning to develop a medium-size manufacturing company making computer peripherals (or something related to that industry) with a sales rate of $10–$20 million a year. By examining carefully the goals that you hope to achieve in the business, you can then look around and see whether you have the management talent on the team to build an organization of the kind you have in mind. Further, when you look for investment support, you will be able to describe to them the kind of business you plan to build as well as what the subsequent capital requirements will be.

I recognize at the outset that it is often quite difficult for a new group of entrepreneurs to predict what kind and size of business will develop in five years; it may seem like a futile exercise to predict so far ahead when one may be uncertain of the immediate future. But consider the words of one of my former associates, who was extremely talented, very successful, and possibly slightly arrogant: "Always be prepared for success." Certainly you, as a founding entrepreneur, should be bullish about the program. You undoubtedly recognize some of the possible pitfalls. But you must have a clear view of what it is that you want the business to become before you can examine whether you have a powerful enough founding team and decide who you wish to have as investors and as members of your board. It may be that you have planned to run the business in several phases and not try and bring in the heavier financial guns until you are ready for phase 2; phase 1 might be carried on by the investment of the founding team and some members of their families. If it is your objective, for example, to build a small consulting firm whose revenues will consist primarily of consulting fees, royalties, and the like, you ought to be able to do it with a relatively small capitalization and participation primarily by friends and associates. On the other hand, if you are going to force your way into a marketplace which is dominated by three well-entrenched manufacturers, then you ought to take a close look at what sort of resources, both financial and managerial, you will have to bring to bear to make the venture that you have in mind into a viable enterprise.

To summarize: Very much like an experimenter in a chemistry or physics laboratory, you must go about the design of the "experiment" in great detail. It is only by carefully describing what you hope to accomplish and how you expect to go about it that you can gain support from the kinds of talented associates and backers you will need to help you get there.

THE FOUNDING TEAM

As a way of illustrating to you the method by which we evaluate the quality of the founding team, let's suppose that we are reviewing a prospectus for a deal that has just arrived on my desk. First of all, we usually "qualify it" by examining the way in which the deal came to us. If one of our associates in the venture capital field had called us and said "we are sending over a deal to you which we think is quite interesting and which we would like you to examine carefully," you'll tend to take a close look at it. If it is a "Bluebird" that comes in the door by virtue of the fact that we are listed in a directory of venture capital firms, it will probably have to have exceptional merit to get the same attention. That's all part of salesmanship. It reminds me of the clever cartoon that appeared in the *New Yorker* not so long ago. It depicts a scene very much like the Gates of Heaven: the applicant is applying for admission and is at the top step looking forward expectantly. The archangel in charge of the gate mechanism is looking down sternly and questioningly at the new arrival. He summarizes it all by his question: "You realize, of course, that it doesn't depend on who you are but who you know. Who do you know?"

After we have looked over the prospectus and understand the nature of the business, we turn to the resumes of the founding team. We scrutinize the business record of the leader of the group, the proposed president. Ideally, we would like to see that the former division manager of the XYZ Co. (age 35–40), who has had a few years of responsibility behind him successfully managing a division, has taken off and started a new company. Possibly he has on his team several of the executives who worked with him in the division or in prior business associations. The men are familiar with one another and know how to work together as a team. They have a first-rate marketing man on the team who is thoroughly familiar with the proposed market for the company; they have good support for finance, engineering, and production.

As we look over the career pattern of each member of the founding team, we like to think that a phone call to any of their previous bosses (and we frequently make such calls) would get us a first-rate reading on any of them. We expect to find shortcomings, but we like to see enough talent so the team as a whole is strong enough to carry out its objectives.

The typical team for a specific high-technology venture may have substantial engineering strength and may also be reasonably strong in, say, project management or manufacturing. The biggest weaknesses seem to be in marketing and finance. What will frequently put us on guard is a team of men coming out of the aerospace industry and going into, say, sailboats. Their team may know how to deal with plastics and materials, marine design, and possibly even production management, but they may have a very sketchy knowledge of the sailboat marketplace. They have only an intuitive feel that the market is ready for something new and that they are the people to bring it out. They have a new technology, never before used in making boats. . . .

Not so long ago we had a chance to invest in a company making high-protein food additives out of dehydrated whole fish. One founder had a Ph.D. in nutrition; he really knew all about amino acids and the efficacy of the product. The company owned an operating pilot plant which manufactured a product that was awfully good (my wife baked it into a loaf of bread and it was quite tasty)—but the team had no real ability or understanding for marketing the product, nor did they have a strong management team with financial expertise, nor an understanding of sources of supply and FDA food-regulation requirements. We labored mightily to help the team get organized, but we had to give it up as a bad job.

Another sad case that comes to mind is that of the young entrepreneur with a small mechanical job-shop looking for diversification out of the aerospace business. He chose to go into a new type of professional audio-recording technique without a real, in-depth understanding of the marketplace. We gave him moral support but no money and told him to pick a better market opportunity. With his enthusiasm, he was able to raise other funds and give it a go; it sputtered for a while and then burned out.

Because the results in these cases are often disastrous, we can't help but repeat the admonition which comes from one of the memorable musical comedies, "You gotta know the territory." From this detailed knowledge of the marketplace comes the requirement for a really first-class marketing man on the management team. He will clearly recognize the importance of doing the necessary homework to prepare the plan, and he will understand the business you want to build. (Don Dible has certainly emphasized this in *Up Your Own Organization.*) In addition, when doing the market research to justify what you are going to do in the marketplace, don't do the armchair type of "top-down" market research, such as: Of the umpteen million left-handed babies born last year in the United States, 30% buy an average of 1.2 teething rings per year, which adds up to a market of 26 million. We only aim to penetrate 5%, so we expect sales of about 1.3 million units. This is all too vague. What venture capitalists expect to see are the results of *detailed field work*—the specifics of the first customers he will sell to, in what quantities, at what price, yielding what gross profit margins; the specific competitors he will displace, what kind of sales and profits they enjoy, what kind of a response he has had from his sampling of the marketplace with the first run of prototypes. Most importantly, how many orders or tentative orders does he actually have in hand?

To summarize: the recent operating experience and the success in management roles of the various members of the founding team—specifically oriented to the kind of business that you plan to conduct—constitute the measures by which venture capitalists evaluate the quality of the founding team.

DEDICATION

In the course of the previous discussion, I hope we have properly stressed the dedication the members of the founding team must have in starting a new business. Being an entrepreneur in a new business is very much like being in politics. According to Harry Truman, "If you can't stand the heat, stay out of the kitchen." The tremendous dedication required by all members of the founding team of a new small business is so consuming that, unless you are prepared to put everything else aside in order to make the business succeed, you ought to give serious thought as to whether or not you really want to do it. Certainly in the early formative years of a new business, the demands upon the founders are so heavy that the prospect shouldn't be considered lightly. Heel-dragging by the aerospace business shouldn't by itself be considered a clear signal to start your own business. There may be other alternatives. If, after a sober reflection on all the factors involved, some of you elect not to go into business for yourselves, I have made a useful contribution—as useful as encouraging others who are really prepared to go ahead and do it.

In a case study on new business and entrepreneurs carried out several years ago by the staff of the Sloan School at MIT, this matter of dedication was considered. It was reported by E. B. Roberts in *Technology Review* (December 1970). In particular, the study showed a high correlation between the career patterns of young entrepreneurs and those of their fathers. In about 50% of the cases, the fathers were self-employed. (Apparently it runs in families.) Perhaps sadly, there was a high incidence of divorce in the life pattern of the young entrepreneurs. The message is straightforward: the commitment required to start a new business is nearly total. One must be sure his family circumstances and relationships are strong enough to co-exist with the needs of the emerging business. Recognize that you may have to spend a lot less time with your wife (or husband) and kids for the three to five years it takes to get the business off the ground.

In a similar way, it is often requisite to the founding team, especially the president, to make a substantial personal investment in the financing of the new business. Venture capitalists and backers usually take it as a mark of dedication, commitment, and sincerity if the founding team has contributed perhaps 10% of their net worth to the capital pool to get the business started.

To the members of the founding team, then, let me leave you with this admonition—after you put the business plan together in rough draft, take a good long look at the requirements that the business will impose upon the founders. Make sure that you are all prepared to enter into it with the degree of commitment required to make it work. Recognize your own abilities; some people are better at starting businesses than they are at running them. The president should personally evaluate the members of his team in the same way he anticipates some of his potential backers will do to assure himself that he has the right combination.

A SPECIAL ISSUE

A special problem sometimes encountered in forming a founding team is the relative equity ownership among the members of the team. Our experience has been that a five-man "democratic team" is a hard way to go about organizing the business; democracy may be a sensible way to organize a political program, but it doesn't seem to be feasible for a young high-technology business. It is far better to have one person in the group as a clear leader. It is also a good idea when organizing the founding team to consider the appropriate participation of the various members and set up a "management stock pool" in which stock is purchased by the founding members, vesting ownership with them over a period of three or four years. Suppose it turns out after a short period of time that one of the founders finds the degree of commitment more than he can support; he wants to back out. Then there is a prearranged plan for him to sell back at least a portion of his stock to the management pool, from which it can be resold to his replacement, who will also have to be a key member of the management team. It may even turn out after six months that the president, for one reason or another, wants to leave and take his stock with him. Obviously a new president must be found, and he must be given proper incentives. My suggestion is that this matter should be considered at the outset so that you avoid a built-in problem which careful planning might have overcome. The "Buy-Out Provisions" which are sometimes established between the principals of a partnership are a similar method of avoiding conflicts and difficulties among close associates. In contemplating the details of such a separation, one is reminded of the parable of the two kids disagreeing over how to divide up the 50% ownership each has in a layer cake: "*You* cut it in half, and *I* get to pick which half."

THE BOARD OF DIRECTORS

If your business plan roughly fits the pattern of the majority of businesses we have examined recently, the chances are that your board will consist of between five and seven people. There are differing theories among venture capitalists as to what constitutes the optimum composition of the board. One view holds that it is useful to have only one member of the management team on the board (say the president), with perhaps four outside people. This is in support of the concept that the board can then review the performance of any of the management team with the president in complete candor. Others hold that this separation need not be so rigid and that, on a seven-man board, perhaps two or even three of the management team should be represented. This representation of management will suffice in those cases where the predominant investment position and/or the controlling stockholder position lies outside the management team. Obviously that can be modified by the election of management nominees with a greater or lesser degree of independence, where control rests with the management group.

This brings up the question of control, and perhaps a few words ought to be said about that. Frequently we encounter management groups who are very much concerned about control. They feel that, unless they have absolute control of the Board of Directors, the control and direction of the business will fall to the representatives of the major stockholder groups to the detriment of the long-term future of the business. For my part, being as objective as I can, I believe this represents an immature attitude on the part of the potential management group. However, in order to really answer the question, one must carefully examine the objectives of the management team as well as the objectives of the investors who may be represented by their nominees on the board of directors. Sometimes, when we query the president of the new company with respect to his personal objectives, he says "I am starting this business to make a lot of money. My goal is to build a personal equity which is worth $1 million after taxes. And I am prepared to sell out whenever the business will let me support that position." Another president may say, "I want to build a good viable business in my field. If it goes along as we have planned, I could see us doing $10 million in sales volume—possibly more—

within five years. If I can maintain a 10% equity interest, then I think I'll come out all right. Mainly I want the feeling that I can build a good, profitable, successful business because I think I can do it." What wasn't said is that he has the ego and believes he has the ability to carry it off; he wants a shot at doing it and is willing to share the rewards with his team and his backers. There's obviously a lot of variation in these objectives; the drives for power take many forms.

The long-range objectives of a venture capitalist may not be too different from those of the entrepreneurs. Over a five-year period, we may look for a 10:1 return on our investment. However, there may be a substantial point of difference; we would like to look forward to having a liquid investment position somewhere in the latter part of a three- to five-year period, whereas the entrepreneur may be quite satisfied to remain "in" as a founder-manager indefinitely. We then go back to the overall objectives and business concept. If you are going to build a business big enough and successful enough to become public, then the liquidity and growth in value that we have established as our targets can be met. Alternatively, the goal of the business may be to build up to a certain volume of sales and earnings and then to merge it into a larger company with complementary product lines. In any case, there is a unanimity of objectives in the sense that *if* the entrepreneur and his team can build a successful and profitable business, there will be substantial capital appreciation in the process. If they're really fortunate enough to build one of those "winners," then they will make a lot of money even though their individual ownership may be small.

Suppose, on the other hand, the management group has a fairly flexible notion of where they want to go and does not have a very good plan for getting there. In fact, they aren't even looking for advice on how to do it. In this case, the entrepreneurs may view the whole undertaking much more from the standpoint of an antagonist/protagonist relationship; their fundamental desire is to have the fun of running the ship without too much interference. Consequently, they might want to divide the equity ownership and the proportions of the board of directors in a way that will make their control unquestionable.

The discussion of investment objectives of the participants as well as the relative proportions of the board of directors is perhaps too involved to go into at length here. I might add the observation that, in our experience, the most successful ventures have been those in which the outside investors have had a "majority ownership" position with effective control of the board during growth periods, even though the management group may have had a very substantial ownership—and in fact "ran the company." It is our feeling that the entrepreneurs learning how to run the business deserve all the help they can get. When the system functions properly, the entrepreneurs are not only pleased with the support their directors and investors can give but find there is a good deal of problem-solving in which both groups can participate.

In our view, the relationships between the management team and the board of directors should be fairly straightforward. The management team runs the company; the board does not. The board has a responsibility to the shareholders to see that the management carries out their responsibilities properly. The management team looks to the board much as they might to an in-house management-consultant group. If the board of directors has been carefully selected, their members have "been there before." Examples of questions with which an experienced board can help a management team: How do I arrange for a licensing deal in Japan? My controller says I should lease the equipment from the XYZ Company rather than the ABC Company—has he analyzed the tradeoffs properly? We want to sell a big order to Xerox, but they say we have no financial backing. Can you help us to convince them otherwise? How much business can we swing on the present capitalization? Are the operating ratios that we are encountering with respect to receivables, payables, and inventory feasible for our kind of business in our stage of growth? Are we getting a reasonable deal from our banks on receivables compared to other situations with which you are aware?

The essence of the argument is that management may be "too close to the trees to see the forest," and it takes the objective viewpoint of a competent observer away from the pressures of the business to see the problems in proper perspective. If the directors have been picked properly, several of them will be familiar with businesses of comparable size in this field of activity and should be able to make useful comments on these matters. An important point to remember: The most useful members of the board of directors are often those who have had detailed operating experience with problems similar to those at hand. For a business with potential production or manufacturing problems, a board member with production experience might be preferred to the dentist who happens to be an investor and a friend of the president. The well-organized president will work out the essential issues with his management team and then propose alternatives to the board for their consideration. On key issues, management proposes and the board disposes. In the ultimate, if the management team performs badly, it is up to the board to recognize that a change in management is required and to act accordingly.

SELECTION OF BOARD MEMBERS

If you are uncertain as to where to find quality members for your board of directors, talk to your proposed venture capital sources or to your friends in business. Consider the problem as entirely analogous to finding a good dentist or a good physician; seek out the opinion of those whose judgment you have reason to respect and those who are knowledgeable about the qualifications of possible board members, potential management team members, or even venture capital sources. Put all the opinions you collect together before you make your specific selections.

Not all venture capitalists willing to serve on the board are able to devote enough time to a specific venture; hence, they may not be sufficiently familiar with the operating problems in the detail necessary to make useful suggestions. For example, it is unreasonable to expect that a director who only meets with management on a quarterly basis and is only generally familiar with the industry can be counted on to help on a detailed issue of marketing strategy.

TYPICAL MANAGEMENT PROBLEMS

This discussion might be closed by considering some typical problems that have been solved through interaction between the board and the management team.

Subject: The Option Plan

The company is a "new start" and has been going perhaps six to twelve months. Management feels that it would like to introduce an option plan to reward some of the new key employees they are bringing in. Do any of the directors have any ideas as to how this should be done? Director A says, "We just introduced a new option plan in the XYZ Company about three months ago. I am also a director of XYZ, and I think I can get you a copy to look over. I think it would be applicable to the size business we are planning to build here. Alternatively, the PQR Company is initiating a program of direct stock purchase by the employees. This would also be interesting to consider. Suppose I get a copy of that one also. You men can review it and circulate copies to the other directors with your comments; then at our next meeting we can consider how we might go about it."

Subject: Bank Financing

The president points out that the company has been financing its receivables through Bank X. He thinks that they should be able to build up added sales volume over the next six months, giving the business a continuing record of profitability. Will this performance support a combination receivable and inventory line of credit? Do any of the directors have any suggestions as to an alternative bank that could give us the desired kind of financing arrangement? Director B offers to take the president to meet a senior executive at the desired bank in order to initiate the necessary discussions.

Subject: Replacement of Key Management

The board has been reviewing operating results for the company and finds that sales are consistently below the established targets. The president has been diligently trying to shore up the vice president of marketing, hoping to improve the situation, but it has persisted for four months. Some of the field personnel support the position that their boss is not equal to his job. The president has reluctantly concluded that he is ready for a new vice president of marketing. He has two good candidates lined up. Can any of the board help either by interviewing the men or by obtaining additional information about them? The connections of the members of the board with industry and their ability to obtain information about potential employees can often be very useful to the president of the company.

Subject: We're Out of Cash

The company has been operating with only marginal profitability for the last nine months. Although there have been two infusions of capital since the company was organized and the product is getting satisfactory acceptance, there is a general realization that another twelve months of marginal profitability and a substantially greater marketing effort are required to obtain the kind of performance and profitability that the board feels makes for viability. There is a general consensus among the board, after much discussion, that it might make sense to consider having the company acquired by a larger organization, one with more marketing clout, to make the venture move forward with more vigor. Several of the directors, by virtue of their connections with executives in several candidate companies, agree to work with the president on a committee carrying out the delicate overtures prior to a possible merger.

Subject: How to Cut Up the Pie

One final example is the interesting debate—to which there is no "correct" solution—that took place between the management and board members of a successful young company that went public about a year ago. They are now operating at an $8 million sales level, with a net of about 10% after tax. What level of earnings should they set as their target for the end of their current fiscal year? In the past, when they were a privately held company, they had established a bonus plan for the key executives; should they now continue that at the same level? At first, this position seems reasonable. However, the manager of one newly acquired division has made a case for spending more for research and development to support the expanded product line he needs to meet next year's sales forecast. Finally, one of the founders, a principal stockholder, raised the question of the potential effect on their stock price in the marketplace with respect to the reported earnings. He pointed out that, at a 30-times multiple, 5¢ more a share in earnings would boost the price of their stock about $1.50. Wouldn't this be a good thing to do? The problem is really the allocation of resources: Reward the management and employees, invest in the future via research and development, or boost the price of the stock via improved earnings? What's the best trade-off?

I hope those of you who are planning to start a business get to the point where you will be able to debate such interesting alternatives at a meeting of your board of directors. It's the kind of operating management problem that comes as the reward for running a successful enterprise. There is a great deal of challenge and satisfaction in reaching this point, and perhaps these are the best motivators of all.

Five

How to Prepare a Business Plan

Donald M. Dible

According to statistics assembled by Dun & Bradstreet, Inc., almost half of all business failures are caused by poor management, including lack of experience in the industry, lack of managerial experience, unbalanced experience, and simple incompetence. One very important way to reduce the likelihood of business failure is to prepare a good business plan (also referred to as a proposal, prospectus, brochure, or offering circular).

DEFINING THE BUSINESS PLAN

Let's start by explaining just what a business plan is. Fundamentally, a business plan is a *written* document prepared by the individual or individuals responsible for starting and operating a company. Properly executed, a business plan is a realistic statement of company goals and objectives along with a detailed description of the steps necessary to achieve those goals. Some people might call it a "Game Plan."

Donald M. Dible is the founder of The Entrepreneur Press and author of Up Your OWN Organization! A Handbook of How to Start and Finance a New Business.

PRIMARY FUNCTION OF THE BUSINESS PLAN

Probably the most important function of a business plan is that it forces the preparers to organize their thinking about the future of their business concept. It tends to eliminate "seat of the pants" management and replace it with the penetrating insight of reasoned logic. Like doing a "take-home" exam, the preparation of a business plan is quite likely to reveal to us just as much of what we *don't* know about our business as it will of what we *do* know. Not surprisingly, in business as in school, it's what you *don't* know that hurts you. It's one thing to think you know all there is to know about a given subject; it's quite another to *prove* that you know it by putting your thoughts into writing. Not only that, but once you have put the ideas and plans on paper, you can proceed to implement your plan confident in the knowledge that you have done your very best to insure success.

In addition to setting forth goals and objectives and the steps necessary to achieve them, a business plan should also provide information about the conditions prevailing in the industry. Are there problems such as shortages of raw materials? Excessive price cutting due to heavy competition? Restrictive government regulation under consideration? Labor disputes?

The business plan should provide for milestones against which company progress can be measured. Examples might include renting a building and readying it for your business needs, the completion of product development, the assembly of a working model, landing the first order, shipping the first order, *getting paid* for the first order, and so forth.

The amount of detail incorporated into a business plan depends to a great extent on what you hope to accomplish by preparing it. If you hope to raise substantial capital from sophisticated investors, you'd be well advised to leave no stone unturned in your search for background information. On the other hand, if your plan is to be used for internal purposes only, you may get by with a good deal less effort. REMEMBER: You are the primary beneficiary of a well-prepared plan!

SPECIAL INTEREST GROUPS

There are many people whose information needs you should consider when preparing your business plan:

Bankers

Virtually every business needs the services of a commercial banker. Since banks are an important source of loan money for any business, it's a good idea to develop a friendly and candid relationship with your banker at the earliest possible opportunity. The best way to start is by presenting him with a copy of your business plan as soon as it is completed. Your ability to meet sales and profit objectives specified in the plan will go a long way toward establishing your credit-worthiness. (Since most businesses do not have business plans, the fact that your company does have one will give your banker a very favorable impression of you in relation to his other customers.)

Suppliers

The survival and growth of almost any business depends on its ability to secure and maintain trade credit from its suppliers. Usually, suppliers will provide 30-day credit to their customers on an open account basis *provided* the customer can demonstrate his credit-worthiness. Even without substantial cash reserves, a small business may succeed in establishing a line of credit by persuading the supplier that its chances of survival are good. In such a case, a business plan does the trick. The plan gives substance and form to what may only be an idea at the time the credit is established.

Customers

When a small company tries to land a big contract, there are often doubts in the customer's mind as to the ability of the small company to produce on schedule. Often, small company bids are rejected out-of-hand on the grounds that their ability to produce is questionable. A well-executed business plan can show the steps and the time required to double or triple plant capacity and may prove to be just what the doctor ordered to win your customer's favor *and* get his order.

Investors

It is not only wise, it's a moral obligation to do any and everything within reason to protect the money invested by backers. The conscientious preparation of a business plan goes a long way toward satisfying this obligation.

Most often, the primary function of the business plan is to serve as a fund-raising document. No professional investor would consider putting money into a deal that was not documented with a business plan. Verbal presentations by the principals are considered important. However, the business plan is *the* information source on which the final investment decision is based.

Employees

Many small companies, operating in low-overhead facilities, have difficulty recruiting capable employees. In some instances, the goals and objectives of the company as set forth in the business plan can be an important factor in influencing a decision to join the firm.

WHO SHOULD PREPARE THE PLAN?

A point that occasionally comes up at my seminars on "How to Build a Million-Dollar Business" has to do with just who should prepare the business plan. Assuming that the business is operated by more than one principal, each individual should contribute his efforts to the project. This team effort tends to produce a set of projections and expectations that everyone can live with. It also serves to make clear to everyone the importance and interdependent nature of their combined talents. Often, the willingness of each team member to contribute his time and effort to this joint undertaking serves to test the individual level of commitment to the venture. When the business is first conceived, a number of people may want to get on the bandwagon—for a free ride. The joint preparation of the business plan may provide the first opportunity to identify and get rid of weak sisters and lazy opportunists.

WHERE TO GET HELP

The preceding notwithstanding, those contributing to the preparation of a business plan need not be limited to the principals of the business. A small army of outsiders stand ready to lend their expert help and guidance.

Business Consultants

Business consultants can be an important source of help in preparing your business plan and in assisting you in securing financing for your company. Unfortunately, business consultants are not generally regulated or licensed, and almost anyone can hang out a "Business Consultant" shingle. Therefore, be certain to check references carefully before engaging a business consultant's services.

Normally, a consultant will require a monthly retainer, a small percentage of any monies raised through his efforts, and the opportunity to secure a modest stock interest in the company at the same price paid by the investors. In return, the company can expect the following analysis:

1. Are the company's prospects viable at all?
2. How much money is required by the company?
3. Should the financing be debt or equity?
4. What weaknesses exist in the company's management team, and can these weaknesses be remedied?

The consultant will then provide guidance in the preparation or revision of the business plan, rehearse the management team for their presentation to the investors, and direct or introduce the team to likely sources of capital.

Lawyers

Lawyers who regularly serve the needs of small business clients (*many* do not!) can provide a great deal of assistance in such matters as choosing the legal form the business should take (proprietorship, partnership, or corporation), selecting the most suitable financial instruments (different classes of stock, debentures, warrants, options, notes, etc.), preparing employment agreements, and avoiding litigation with former employers, competitors, and employees. Some lawyers may even be able to let you review (in strict confidence) the business plan of one of their other clients (with that client's permission, of course).

Certified Public Accountants

Unless members of the management team have had accounting experience, the assistance of a qualified accountant can be extremely important in the preparation of past, present, and future (projected or *pro forma*) financial statements. Also, the accountant is generally qualified to provide assistance in tax planning—something not to be overlooked in preparing the business plan.

Bankers

On almost every working day of his life, your banker is involved in analyzing financial statements and evaluating a great variety of different businesses. With this perspective, your banker can be an important source of advice and counsel in preparing and evaluating your business plan. Also, if your business does not qualify for a bank loan, your banker may be able to suggest a number of other sources of financing—loan or equity—as appropriate to your situation.

Stockbrokers

Depending on the condition of the stock market, your broker may be selling a great many "new issues" of recently registered stock.

When stocks are initially offered to the market, a prospectus, or offering circular, is distributed describing the securities to be issued and the company issuing them. These prospectuses of other companies (available from your broker) should give you a great many ideas on how to prepare your own business plan.

Your stockbroker can also be of help in evaluating your business plan. He should have considerable insight into the types of businesses currently favored by investors and can pass this information on to you.

Customers

From a customer's point of view, the more suppliers he has, the more competitive will be the bidding for his business. Therefore, it is often the case that a customer or potential customer will give you whatever assistance he can in gathering information for your business plan. This may include access to industry forecasts and surveys, letters of intent to buy from you at some future date, and detailed specifications on current and projected product requirements.

Suppliers

Except in times of severe shortages, suppliers are always delighted to see new customers come along. Doesn't it seem logical, therefore, that your suppliers should be glad to help you in any way they can? Of course it does. Just ask them.

Government Agencies

The Small Business Administration and the Department of Commerce provide an enormous number of services for the small businessman. Personal assistance and guidance in preparing or packaging a business plan is just one of these services. These government agencies also publish mountains of literature, some of which should be helpful in the preparation of your business plan, regardless of the type of business you plan to start.

THE MINI-PROPOSAL

If your business plan is to be used to raise risk or equity capital, there are a few more things that you should know at this point. Most investors are very, very busy people who place a high dollar value on their time. If you think a lawyer's hourly fees are high, consider the value of time to a man who manages millions of dollars in investment money.

Picture this: Mr. Moneybags, a harried investor, has just returned from a three-day business trip. The president of one of his portfolio companies is in the hospital with an ulcer, and Mr. Moneybags is trying his best to keep the investment from going down the tubes in the meantime. As Moneybags enters his office, he groans quietly upon seeing the huge pile of new requests for money overflowing from his "In" basket and onto his desk. (Many investors see 100 to 200 proposals a month.) He knows he won't get a chance to look at any of these new deals until he finishes studying the latest reports from the companies in which he has already invested money. (Some investors have *daily* telephone conversations with the principals of *each* of their portfolio companies.)

As the day draws to a close, Moneybags eyes the stack of new proposals on his desk and decides to go through a quick first-pass to weed out the obvious "whizzers." (A whizzer is a plan with no apparent merit that "whizzes" from the "In" basket to the trash can.) Finally, he ends up with two stacks. One contains big, fat proposals. The other contains mini-proposals—brief, three- or four-page summaries of business plans sent in to determine whether there is any interest at all. If there is interest, Moneybags will then request a full-blown formal business plan. If he is normal, Moneybags is going to review the mini-proposals before he gets around to looking at the unsolicited, big fat business plans. Here is what Moneybags looks for when scanning the mini-proposal:

Amount of Capital Required

Depending on the total amount of money an investor has to work with, he tends to develop a dollar range of investments which he prefers. He may like $100,000 to $200,000 deals. On the other hand, he may not be interested if the capital required is less than $1 million. Many investors maintain that it takes just as much work to manage a small investment as it does a larger one, and therefore they invest as large a sum of money in a deal as they feel is prudent.

Type of Industry

Most professional investors are not willing to invest in any deal in an industry with which they are not familiar. Investors tend to develop lists of industries in which they are interested in investing and lists of industries in which they are definitely *not* interested in investing. One investor came up with the following lists:

Areas Preferred for Investment	Areas Avoided for Investment
Cable Television (CATV)	Computer Hardware
Chemicals & Plastics	Computer Software
Communications	Construction
Consumer Products	Electronic Data Processing
Education	Food (Processing)
Environmental Control	Food (Franchising)
Finance & Financial Services	Hotels, Motels & Restaurants
Health Services	Leasing
Manufacturing	Leisure Time
Marketing	Metal Fabrication & Processing
Medical Equipment & Instrumentation	Motion Pictures
Optics & Lasers	Natural Resources
Pharmaceuticals	Oil & Gas
Proprietary Technology	Real Estate
Service	Retailing & Wholesaling

In some cases, the decision to avoid a given area for investment may be based on a recent unfavorable experience in that industry. An investor who has just lost a substantial percentage of his capital in a bankrupt computer company would be unlikely to invest again in that industry in the near future.

Maturity of the Enterprise

The younger a company is in terms of years and in sales figures relative to its ultimate potential size, the more time an investor must devote to monitoring it. Company maturities are generally related to the type of financing sought. The following is a list of the five most common types of financing arranged through investors:

Seed In this case, all that exists is an idea for a product, possibly a plan, and possibly a proposed company team. This represents the highest possible risk investment opportunity.

Start-up Here there is usually a prototype product (or a well-defined service); a plan and a team exist; but no operating history has been established. Since visualization of the business concept is easier here than it is in the case of seed financing, this situation is more attractive to investors. However, risk is still considered quite high; and the cost of equity financing is also usually substantial in terms of what the founders must surrender to obtain backing.

Mezzanine In this stage, a company has withstood the rigors of start-up, usually has a record of service billings or product shipments (including an adequate manufacturing capacity and capability), a customer list (albeit a small one), and a financial record (whether profitable or not) that will permit an analysis of progress to date versus dollars spent.

Growth At this stage, a business has usually established its viability as a commercial operation; but it is unable to generate sufficient cash flow or to attract adequate debt financing at manageable interest rates to permit the rapid growth possible with its proven products (or services) and available staffing. Characteristically, this problem is typified by an inability to handle the cash differential between accounts receivable (on orders shipped) and accounts payable (on raw materials and parts in inventory) while trying to increase sales volume.

Bridge This type of funding frequently takes the form of debt instruments with warrants or options attached (called "kickers" or "sweeteners") for the later purchase of company stock at a price established at the time the debt is incurred. The term "bridge" derives from the fact that this form of financing is generally used to provide funds to sustain operations while the company is in the process of securities registration for a public offering of stock.

Sales and Profit Projections

The next item to be covered in the mini-proposal should be an estimate of sales and profits three to five years out. Unless your firm anticipates a sales volume of at least $10 million within the first three to five years, the chances are that you will not be interesting to a sophisticated investor. Million dollar sales figures represent a very respectable small business and should provide the founder with a handsome personal income. However, such a company is referred to as "the living dead" by members of the investment community since it does not provide potential for substantial long-term growth.

Management Team

The final item that should be covered in the mini-proposal is the management team. Every major investor I know continually maintains that he would rather invest in a top-notch management team with a mediocre product than in a top-notch product with a mediocre management team. Detailed resumes are not appropriate in the mini-proposal. However, a brief summary of the highlights of the careers of each of the founders should be included in the body of the mini-proposal.

THE FORMAL BUSINESS PLAN

When the founders have managed sufficiently to interest the investors in their mini-proposal, the investors will request that the founders provide them with a formal business proposal. This is the document that in most cases will determine whether or not the investors and founders will reach a point of serious negotiation in the financing of the new enterprise.

Every key aspect of the proposed business should be covered in detail in this document. The founders should try to communicate a sense of thoroughness and a feeling that "We're ready for anything!" The following is devoted to a brief discussion of the many items that should receive consideration. A more detailed discussion of the contents of the business plan is beyond the scope of this chapter. In fact, fully one third of my book *Up Your OWN Organization! A Handbook on How to Start and Finance a New Business* deals with this topic. Let me summarize, however, those items which should be included in any formal business plan:

Introduction

A one- or two-page summary of the concept is intended to encourage the reader to study the huge amount of detailed information contained in the business plan.

Table of Contents

Different investors have their own favorite areas of interest in a business plan, such as financial statements, market data, autobiographical information on the founders, etc. Make it easy for Moneybags to find what he's looking for; remember the value of his time.

Operating History of the Business

Here you should cover the highlights of the company's history, including all dates of major significance such as time of incorporation, relocation, etc. If the company previously served markets it no longer serves, that point should be covered here.

Directors or Limited Partners

If the company is incorporated, the names and corporate affiliation of the directors should be indicated here. If the business is a limited partnership, the names and corporate affiliations of the limited partners should be indicated.

The Management Team

A brief resume of each principal in the business should be furnished here. Detailed autobiographies should be reserved for the Appendix. The brief resumes should make clear the recent experience of each principal and his qualifications for accomplishing the stated objectives of the company.

Compensation and Incentives

The level of compensation of each principal should be indicated. (Bear in mind that the willingness of every principal to draw a modest salary and commit a significant percentage of his own net worth to the business is a strong measure of his level of commitment to the enterprise.) Employment contracts, non-competition agreements, buy-out arrangements, trade secret and proprietary information agreements, and patent assignment agreements should be indicated here. Stock option, warrants, bonus, profit sharing or other incentive plans should also be listed.

Outside Professionals Rendering Service to the Company

This section of the plan should list the attorneys (corporation and patent), accountants, insurance agents and carriers, investment bankers, commercial bankers, management consultants, advertising agency, and public relations firm that serve the business. Any fee arrangements with these professionals should also be indicated.

Organization Chart

A one-page diagram showing the responsibilities and channels of communication, work, and authority in the company should be provided.

Capital Required and How It Will Be Used

Remember, Moneybags has his favorite range of investment capital. Indicate how much you need to achieve the stated company objectives and *exactly* what you intend to do with it. One of Moneybag's fellow venture capitalists once told a large audience of investors that the young, hot-shot president of one of his portfolio companies used a large percentage of new financing as a down-payment on a company jet. This disposition of the financing had not been provided for in the business plan. Not surprisingly, the young hot-shot was shot out of his presidential saddle and the jet plane contract of sale was voided. Be very specific when indicating the use to which the new capital will be put. "Working capital" just doesn't hack it.

Summary of Company's Present Financial Condition

How much money has previously been committed to the company, who were the investors and lenders, and how was the money used? A current balance sheet should also be included here. The nature of all financings including classes of stock, warrants, options, debentures, etc., should also be covered.

Major Products

Every major product in the company's existing or proposed product line should be described in terms of the following detail:

Photographs or Drawings Although your command of the English language may be excellent, you may still have some difficulty in communicating the nature of your product using words alone. If your product can be photographed or drawn, include pictures in the business plan.

Product Uses Describe in detail the primary uses to which your product can be put, the function it serves, the reasons why people buy products of this type at all, and any new uses to which your product might be put. For example, Johnson and Johnson baby shampoo is a product that was serving the baby market. But one day, someone at Johnson and Johnson decided to suggest to the consumer that it was just fine for adults who had to wash their hair frequently. As a result of discovering this new use for their product, Johnson and Johnson has enjoyed a very substantial increase in sales.

Unique Characteristics One of the major considerations applied in evaluating the product offerings of any company has to do with whether or not these products are unique. If a product falls into the category referred to as a "commodity," the product becomes subject to severe price competition, and its sale price winds up being almost exactly the same as that of any other product of its kind offered to the marketplace. Examples of commodities are things such as wheat, gold, cattle, and eggs. Some of the characteristics which give uniqueness to a product are suggested below:

1. *Size* In many product areas, a manufacturer can give himself a major advantage if he can maintain the function of an item while he makes it smaller. For example, stereophonic speaker systems used to be enormous. With advances in technology, it was possible to obtain very fine reproduction in systems that were small enough to fit on a bookshelf.
   In other instances, the ability to make the product bigger can provide an important competitive advantage. Certain fruits and vegetables make more profit for their producers if they can be grown in larger sizes. Similarly, it has been the tendency of wine producers in recent years to package their product in larger containers. This has proven to be a highly successful marketing innovation.

2. *Weight* When a product must be transported from one location to another, weight can be very important. A great deal of money is spent each year in trying to develop lighter yet still durable shipping containers. Most freight charges are based on weight; the lighter the shipping container, the less the transportation cost. This becomes particularly important when air freight shipments are involved. Lightweight ten-speed bicycles command a very important place in their market because of the efficiency possible in propelling them.

3. *Quality* In most marketing situations, all things being equal, the best quality product is desirable and almost invariably will produce customer loyalty.

4. *Prestige* Many expensive products are purchased because their ownership suggests prestige. The plush corporate aircraft, the expensive luxury automobile, the first-class section on transcontinental airplanes, all have an inherent element of prestige. Properly marketed, such prestige factors can produce significant profits.

5. *Durability* The willingness of customers to buy certain items depends on the durability of those items. Particularly when a worn-out product must be replaced by a highly paid repairman, durability can be of

paramount importance and will justify a very much higher price than a less durable competing product.

6. *Convenience* All it takes is one trip to the supermarket to appreciate the importance of convenience in improving the marketability of any product. Every year, sales of convenience foods continue to increase their percentage of all food sold. You find foods frozen, freeze-dried, canned, pickled, salted, and dehydrated all in the name of saving the housewife time in the kitchen. Often convenience is coupled with efficiency; in any business, efficiency means lower cost in the long run. Frequently convenience and improved efficiency can be important selling points when trying to win new customers for your product.

7. *Appearance* Not surprisingly, a good-looking product enjoys a significant advantage over a similar product that does not share the same design elegance. Even such simple things as color can be important in product marketing. Back in the old days when Henry Ford offered automobiles in "any color you want as long as it's black," he had a near monopoly and no marketing problems. As soon as his competitors started offering color options, Ford had to go along or lose his commanding position in that marketplace. In a great many industrial markets today, considerable money is spent for the services of industrial designers to insure that the appearance of the finished product does not suffer in comparison to the offerings of competitors.

8. *Price* Everything else being equal, a lower priced product should enjoy a higher volume of sales than its competitors. However, price cutting is not necessarily a wise competitive strategy. When pricing any product, decisions should be made on the basis of maximizing profits.

9. *Serviceability* If your product is complicated and subject to occasional breakdown, it is very important to have a network of service facilities available to insure customer satisfaction. One of the reasons some foreign automobiles do not enjoy a higher sales volume in this country is because of the shortage of authorized repair stations able to provide maintenance. Even a product seemingly as simple as an office typewriter is subject to occasional breakdown. It is comforting indeed

to call your local manufacturer's service agent and receive repair service within a few hours.

Delivery When products must be furnished on short notice, delivery performance can be a great competitive advantage. If your product is to be one small part of a very large system, you may be certain that the manufacturer of the major system will be vitally concerned with your ability to deliver the goods on time before he will consider giving you an order. In many cases, delivery can be even more important than price.

Warranty Obligations In many product areas, particularly where machinery is involved, product warranties are common. In describing your major products, you should provide a detailed description of your warranty obligations to customers and what this may cost the company in terms of service expenses during the warranty period.

Profit Margins and Cost Considerations The business plan should discuss the manufacturing cost for the product; the cost of servicing the product during the warranty period; what percentage of the selling price constitutes sales and promotion expenses; and finally, what profit margin is expected for each product.

Protection Available It is not enough for a product to be unique in the marketplace to make it an attractive part of the company's overall product line. Ideally this product uniqueness should be protectable.

- **Patents**

  If the product is patentable or already patented, a discussion of the patent claims, real or proposed, should be included in the business plan. If patent protection already exists, the expiration date of the patent should also be noted.

- **Trade Secrets**
  If a product represents the embodiment of a trade secret, this fact should be duly noted. Please recognize that a well-kept trade secret may constitute a more valuable form of protection than a patent. For example, had the formula for Coca-Cola been patented, that patent would have expired in 1917.

Know-How and Human Skill In some product areas, the ability to deliver the merchandise may depend heavily upon the services of a few talented individuals. If this is the case, it should certainly be brought out in the business plan.

Technological Advantage Many industries are involved in product areas where technological change is commonplace. Occasionally, an advance in technological capability will occur, giving the company originating this feature a significant competitive advantage. Unfortunately, it may only be a matter of time before competitors are able to reproduce this technological advance. However, such an advance does take *time* to duplicate, and during this period the originator may enjoy a virtual monopoly.

Research and Development Costs In order to remain competitive in a product area where technology evolves rapidly, it is important that the costs of a continuing research and development program be recognized and acknowledged. If this is relevant to your industry, be sure to mention it in your business plan.

Product Liability There is a growing tendency on the part of customers of all kinds to hold the supplier accountable for problems which may later result from the failure of the product. If an automobile fails to function properly due to the failure of one of its moving parts, the automobile manufacturer or his parts supplier may sustain product liability. If a child, playing with a toy, is accidentally injured because a part of the toy is sharp or can be swallowed or represents some other kind of hazard, the manufacturer may sustain product liability and be obliged to pay heavy penalties in the event of an unfavorable court judgment. Product liability is an area of growing concern for suppliers in all major markets.

The Market to Be Served

What overall market do you wish to serve? What trade associations and trade publications serve this market? What are the growth characteristics of this market? These are just a few of the many items that you should discuss in the marketing section of your business plan.

Market Studies Available? The New York Chapter of the American Marketing Association publishes an annual *International Directory of Marketing Research Houses and Services.* In this directory, you will find the names, addresses, and research specialties of hundreds of research firms eager to supply you with information about the markets you wish to serve. In many cases, these market research firms have mass-produced market surveys available to anyone who has the price of purchase. Other market research firms only provide their services on an individual client basis. Some examples of market research firms include:

Stanford Research Institute
333 Ravenswood Avenue
Menlo Park, California 94025

Arthur D. Little, Inc.
25 Acorn Park
Cambridge, Massachusetts 02140

Battelle Memorial Institute
505 King Avenue
Columbus, Ohio 43201

Frost and Sullivan, Inc.
106 Fulton Street
New York, New York 10038

Predicasts, Inc.
200 University Circle Research Center
11001 Cedar Avenue
Cleveland, Ohio 44106

In addition to market studies available from private research firms, you will find that trade associations typically provide their membership with annual industry surveys. Also, most trade publications dedicate at least one issue a year to a review of marketing trends in the industry served.

Ease of Entry This heading has to do with the difficulty a would-be competitor might experience in starting his company. If the initial amount of capital required is small and the skill level required is modest, you may be relatively certain that a large number of competitors will enter the field if the market itself is expanding rapidly. For this reason, most investors shy away from industries where the ease of entry is great.

Overall Growth Rate If the market you propose to serve is not growing at a rate significantly faster than our gross national product (the measure of goods and services produced in this country), it is unlikely that your company will have much chance for rapid growth. You should give serious consideration to analyzing the overall growth potential in your industry.

Identify Potential Customers by Name It is not enough in the business plan to indicate that there are large numbers of customers. Major customers or customer groups should be identified as precisely as possible so as to make more realistic your estimates of future sales.

Identify Competitors by Name It is rare indeed that a business serves a marketplace free of competition. This section of the business plan should include an in-depth evaluation of the strengths and weaknesses of your competition and how you hope to deal with them in the marketplace.

Indicate Percentage Market Share Expectations Total sales volume in a given industry is not generally an adequate measure of the viability of a business in that industry. An important indicator of marketing effectiveness is the figure for market share. This represents the percentage of the total market available that your company has captured. Your business plan should indicate the market share you now have, plans for securing a larger percentage of market share, and how you expect to achieve that improved level.

Market Strategy

Bringing any product to the marketplace successfully requires the formulation of a marketing strategy—a plan for gaining a foothold for your product and winning a significant share of the overall market.

Zero in on Market Segments Earlier in your business plan, you discussed the various segments of your market. Here you should indicate the particular segment or segments on which you plan to zero in. Since reaching each segment may require a different marketing strategy and substantial marketing expense, the number of segments selected for initial penetration should be limited.

For example, if you want to make laundry soap, here are some of the market segments available to you:

1. Institutional laundries such as hospitals and hotels
2. Home laundry markets—i.e., housewives
3. Laundry service agencies such as diaper services and commercial laundry and dry cleaning establishments
4. Janitorial agencies
5. Government agencies

Channels of Distribution Each market segment that you select may be reached by a number of different channels of distribution. The following is a very small sample of the channels available to you.

1. Your own salesmen
2. Manufacturer's representatives and agents
3. Wholesalers
4. Distributors
5. Jobbers
6. Direct mail
7. Retailers
8. Factory outlets
9. Direct salesmen
10. Vending machines

Now let's use our laundry soap example and see how two of the possible market segments might be reached through some of the above channels of distribution.

Institutional Laundries: You might use your own sales force or a manufacturer's representative organization to make calls on these customers. Alternatively, the institution may buy its soap from a distributor or wholesaler.

Home Laundries: Your sales force might call on all sorts of retail outlets that serve the housewife directly, such as supermarkets, variety stores, discount drug stores, etc. Possibly a manufacturer's representative organization could also call on these retailers. The stores might buy from the wholesalers that stock your merchandise.

An interesting way of approaching the housewife in need of laundry products is with a direct selling (door-to-door or party-plan) organization such as the giant Amway Corporation uses. Avon uses a similar "Shop without going shopping" approach in selling cosmetics.

Many housewives do their wash at coin-operated laundries. Generally, soap is available at these establishments in small packages dispensed by vending machines.

Having segmented your market, you may discover that your competitors are using a limited number of channels of distribution to serve this segment. With a little ingenuity, you may open up an entirely new channel of distribution and capture a large market share from your competitors. On the other hand, your efforts may significantly increase overall demand and in this way permit you the opportunity to build a profitable enterprise.

Advertising Plans If your marketing scheme calls for an advertising program of any size, it is recommended that you engage the services of a professional agency. They can assist you in planning the overall campaign, write your advertising copy, and select the best media mix from among television, radio, newspapers, magazines, direct mail, billboards, advertising specialties, etc.

Push versus Pull A basic marketing concept has to do with the notion of "push *versus* pull." By "push," we mean those actions necessary to get the product out in front of the consumer. It means filling channels of distribution with your product so that a potential buyer can't miss it when making a purchasing decision. It means getting your product into the store.

To develop "push," you may offer your salesmen special prizes as incentives plus large commissions, you may give prizes and bonuses ("spiffs") to your dealer's salesmen, you may offer your dealers extra-large discounts, you will certainly provide prompt delivery, and you may offer very attractive credit or payment terms to your dealers. All of this will be backed up by extensive advertising in trade publications and other trade media.

By "pull," we mean those activities designed to produce heavy buyer demand. This may be achieved through the use of contests, sweepstakes, premiums (give-aways), special offers, low price, quick service, refunds, discounts and discount coupons, special product features, and a large-scale advertising campaign aimed at your buyers.

Product producers may rely on either "push," "pull," or a combination of both to accomplish their marketing objectives. However, before a marketing program is launched, these promotional methods should be understood and the appropriate approach consciously selected.

Methods of Financing Sales While many sales are made on a cash basis, others require the use of some type of special financing arrangement. Your business plan should indicate whether goods will be offered on a thirty-day or extended credit basis, or on a rental or lease basis. The methods employed to finance sales not only affect sales volume, they also have a profound effect on the company's cash flow and capital requirements.

Pricing Strategy Pricing obviously has a major impact on sales and profits. In most cases, lower prices mean the sale of a greater number of individual items. While increased sales and resulting manufacturing volume may not appreciably lower the cost of manufacturing the goods, total profits may rise.

Whenever pricing is considered, the total of all costs must be analyzed carefully to determine a pricing "floor." Not only must labor and materials be calculated, but overhead expenses such as marketing outlays must also be included in evaluating costs.

Pricing should take into account wholesaler and retailer discounts, salesmen's or brokers' commissions, competitor's pricing policies with regard to "positioning" in the product spectrum (Do you want to be known as a producer of inexpensive, medium-priced, or expensive goods?), and an assessment of how much the customer is willing to pay.

Sales Organizations Most small businesses selling outside their immediate geographic region rely on commission salesmen or manufacturer's representatives as a sales force. Larger organizations establish their own salaried sales force. Indicate the approach you plan to take.

Manufacturing Economics

This is the area of the business plan in which the production side of the business is analyzed in some detail.

Assembly Characteristics The manufacturing nature of the product is an important consideration in determining the capital necessary to finance inventory. For example, if the product is to be available "off the shelf," then an inventory must continually be maintained. This represents a more or less fixed capital expense as well as the risk that the products may become obsolete while sitting on the shelf. A less risky mode of operation is a business where the product is custom made to order. This is sometimes referred to as a "job shop" business and generally does not lend itself to economies of large-scale manufacturing. One way around this problem is to modularize your product line in such a way that many of the products utilize standard parts.

Make or Buy—Vertical Integration? In most small businesses, it is necessary to buy component parts in a finished state for use in the production of your company's product. Unless the volume of these parts that you require is very large, it may be much cheaper to buy them from a major outside supplier than it would be to manufacture them in-house. As your sales volume grows, however, you may decide to make the small parts you need as building blocks for your larger and more complicated products. The characteristic of owning all the facilities required to produce raw materials and make parts on through ownership of retail outlets is referred to as "vertical integration."

Product Cost Breakdown At this point, it would be appropriate to furnish a discussion as to whether or not the end product represents a high level of material costs or labor costs. If it should turn out that the labor content is high (i.e., a labor-intensive product), it may be a good idea to give some consideration to the possibility of foreign assembly. Many underdeveloped countries have large labor pools that can perform manufacturing functions at a very low cost. If this is applicable to your business, you should certainly discuss it in your business plan.

Tooling Costs Most manufacturing organizations require the use of certain kinds of tools to effect the manufacturing process. These tools may be such things as lathes, end mills, polishing and grinding equipment, and power tools of all sorts. The cost of such equipment can be quite high, and methods of financing it should be discussed in the business plan.

Specialized Equipment In many industries, very specialized equipment is necessary to produce the finished product. Typically, this specialized equipment does not enjoy a ready resale market should it become necessary to liquidate the assets of the company. For this reason, the risk involved in furnishing a manufacturing facility with such equipment should be analyzed in the business plan.

Economies of Scale In most businesses, a certain level of operation is necessary to insure profitability. If substantial capital is tied up in plant and equipment (fixed costs), it may prove to be very expensive to manufacture your product in small quantities. However, as you are able to utilize your equipment on a more or less continual basis—say you employ two or three shifts—you may realize very substantial economies of scale. It's the old story of high volume means low unit overhead. Obviously, this axiom does not apply in all cases, but it occurs commonly enough to be a part of every businessman's vocabulary.

Supplier Relationships In any business that utilizes the goods and services of other suppliers, the relationships with those suppliers can be of critical importance to the ongoing success and growth of the business. A good working relationship between your company and its suppliers decreases the likelihood of production delays due to late shipments or late receipt of component parts and increases the availability of trade credit.

Availability of Raw Materials Some industries are habitually plagued with shortages of raw materials, while others are subject to seasonal or intermittant raw-material shortages which wreak havoc with manufacturing time tables. An analysis of the availability of raw materials may constitute an important part of your business plan.

APPENDIX TO THE FORMAL BUSINESS PLAN

The Appendix should contain the background data upon which much of the formal business plan is based as well as any miscellaneous, supporting information that will help to explain the business concept.

Pro Forma Projections

Conservatively prepared sales forecasts, cash flow and income statements, balance sheets, and projected staff and plant requirements should be presented here. Many investors like to see projections for the first five years as follows: monthly for the first six months, quarterly for the following eighteen months, and annually for the following three years.

Legal Structure of the Business

The full details of the legal structure (partnership, proprietorship, or corporation) of the business should be laid out here.

Founders' Resumes and Financial Statements

Complete details of the founders' backgrounds and accomplishments should be furnished here, along with personal financial statements.

Founders' Compensation

Salary requirements and equity positions of all of the founders should be revealed at this point.

Market Surveys

Any available market surveys relating to the proposed venture should be included in the Appendix to the business plan.

RECOMMENDED READING

Batten, J. D. *Beyond Management by Objectives.* New York: American Management Association, 1966.

Campbell, David. *If You Don't Know Where You're Going, You'll Probably End Up Somewhere Else.* Niles, Il.: Argus Communications, 1974.

Dible, Donald M. *Up Your OWN Organization! A Handbook on How to Start and Finance a New Business.* Santa Clara, Ca.: The Entrepreneur Press, 1974.

Kepner, Charles H., and Tregoe, Benjamin B. *The Rational Manager: A Systematic Approach to Problem Solving and Decision Making.* New York: McGraw-Hill Book Company, 1965.

Mali, Paul. *Managing by Objectives: An Operating Guide to Faster and More Profitable Results.* New York: Wiley-Interscience of John Wiley & Sons, Inc., 1972.

Markstein, David L. *Money Raising and Planning for the Small Business.* Chicago: Henry Regnery Company, 1974.

Mockler, Robert J. *Business Planning and Policy Formulation.* Englewood Cliffs, N.J.: Prentice-Hall, Inc., 1975.

Myer, John N. *Understanding Financial Statements: A Handbook for Executives, Investors and Students.* A Mentor Executive Library Book. New York: The New American Library, 1964.

Wall Street Journal Staff. *Here Comes Tomorrow! Living and Working in the Year 2000.* Princeton, N.J.: Dow Jones Books, 1967.

Six

How to Plan Marketing Strategy

Richard A. Drossler

WHAT IS MARKETING?

Marketing is often defined as "The creation of demand" or "The creation of customers." It is not just putting your product up for sale and hiring a few salesmen to call on customers. Looking at some of the functions of marketing may yield a better definition, since marketing encompasses everything up to and including making a successful sale and keeping the customer sold. Marketing includes:

- Selling
- Pricing
- Market research
- Advertising
- Developing a competitive strategy
- Product planning
- Market intelligence
- Projecting a corporate identity
- Public relations
- Financial public relations
- Promoting the products
- And a lot of planning, strategizing, and budgeting

Richard A. Drossler is Chairman of the Board of Drossler Research Corporation, a San Francisco-based marketing research firm.

Marketing is the nitty-gritty of your business. It must take place every minute of your corporate life, or the enterprise will be drowned by marketing-oriented competitors.

As I see it, there are four key concepts that form the foundation of a solid marketing function in the successful enterprise:

- Customer orientation
- Concern with market share
- Competitive focus
- Future consciousness

These concepts support the development of a winning marketing strategy.

Customer Orientation

The successful marketer has his primary orientation toward the customer. He is acutely aware of who the customers are and what their needs are in buying the product. And he knows how and why they buy the products they do. He makes it his point to know what really "turns them on."

Concern with Market Share

In preparing the business plan, an estimate of the size of the market is important. But often overlooked and even more important is a clear perception of market share—the percentage of the total market that your company can actually get.

A marketer has little control over the size of the total market, i.e., the customer demand. But he does have control over how much of that demand he will get by the strategy he selects and the skill with which he carries it out.

Marketing is not just going out and finding some customers. The marketer is trying to get his piece of the total pie. When Hertz says, "We're Number One," they are saying they have the largest share of the market. Every marketing man wants to be Number One in his market. And anyone who wants to raise money and start a successful business should be concerned with identifying the right market for him and getting as big a share of it as possible. In almost every industry, big or small, the highest profit margins are made by the companies with the largest market share.

Competitive Focus

It is surprising to me how many companies plan their marketing programs without considering what the competition is doing or likely to do. The essence of marketing strategy is to focus on competition. Think of it this way: They do not give a Nobel Prize in business. Your rewards in business are not earned on the basis of the elegance of your corporate offices or the artistic merits of your advertising or the academic credentials of your R & D man—although these may help. The rewards in business come from beating out the competition, and the best way to do that is to know who they are and how they operate.

Future Consciousness

It is important to know what the marketplace is like today. A knowledge of past trends is also important. But maintaining a consciousness and orientation to the future is vital to the successful enterprise—it is the fourth cornerstone of marketing strategy.

Let's say that the industry you plan to go into has been growing at the rate of 25% for the past several years. This might indicate a very attractive opportunity. However, a lot of other, much stronger companies might be attracted by this growth history and may be making plans to move in. The result could be heavy competition, price cutting, and severe profit pressure. If this is the case, you surely do not want to invest your time and your money in that market. On the other hand, the market might be maturing and levelling off to 3% or 4% growth per year. Worse, it might be declining. So before you jump in with your life savings, get a reading on future growth potential and on what new competitors there might be.

Consciousness of the future and its problems and opportunities must be maintained by the successful marketer and built into his marketing strategy.

These four key concepts underlying marketing strategy demand a planned, analytical approach to the marketing effort. This "heads up" marketing thinking is needed to match the "seat of the pants" skills of the salesman.

HOW TO PLAN STRATEGY

The essence of marketing strategy is how you meet the needs of the marketplace better than your competitor. It is the overall plan of action, the driving force behind your marketing efforts.

Having an explicitly stated marketing strategy defines the posture you will take and guides the development of the tactical marketing programs such as advertising, pricing, packaging, distribution, etc. (We use the terms "strategy" and "tactics" somewhat in the military sense. Strategy is the overall battle plan and tactics are the programs for carrying it out.)

In order to build a marketing strategy for your company, I believe you should take the following approach:

- Analyze the present and future market situation
- Shape your product to fit the market
- Understand yourself
- Understand your competition
- Select and clearly state your strategy

These are the five major points we will address in this discussion.

Analyze the Market Situation

The first step in developing marketing strategy is to analyze the present and future market situation and the opportunities that lie in this situation.

Market Size and Growth The *size of the market* is often the first thing the new entrepreneur looks at—and it is one of the first things looked at by the venture capitalist considering an investment. Knowing the size of the market is indeed important, but equally important is an accurate forecast of the *growth rate potential.*

What is an attractive market growth for investment? A new entrepreneur should be entering a market that is growing at the rate of 15%, 20%, or even 100% or more per year. (This is market growth, *not* company sales.) This may seem like a tough requirement, but if the market is growing at less than 15% a year, there just is not going to be enough "up-side" potential to increase the value of your equity in the venture by 10 times or 100 times, which is what you should be shooting for.

We live in a changing world. To analyze the growth-rate potential for a market, it is necessary to look not only at projections of past trends. It is also very important to understand the pressures that are coming to bear on the realization of that growth. These days, for example, the actions of the federal government may have an extremely important effect on creating or destroying market opportunity. The ban on cyclamates severely crippled the diet soft drink industry literally overnight and just about permanently wiped out Diet-Rite Cola, once the leading diet drink. (Now there is talk of lifting the cyclamate ban, as it may not be harmful.) On the other hand, a recent government safety regulation was issued requiring that trailer trucks be able to stop without skidding or jack-knifing. It is estimated that this action created a market of $100 to $150 million per year for electronic anti-skid devices. The entrepreneur must be sensitive to these kinds of pressures in his industry. The key is to think them all the way through to the implications on problems and opportunities that might arise.

Market Segments Next it is important to understand the market segments. Few products have universal appeal or appeal to every potential buyer for the same reasons. Almost all markets are made up of different segments who buy and use the product in different ways and for different reasons. Identifying the market segments is particularly important to the new and smaller entrepreneur in that it helps him to identify a niche in the marketplace that may not be adequately served by bigger competitors. It may not be necessary to fight head-on with the big guys if you can find a piece of the market where you can be strong. Thus, segmenting the market helps the marketer to focus his resources on a narrower target, increasing the competitive power he can bring to bear.

How do you segment the market? There are many ways. Geographic segmentation is one of the most obvious. In many industries, there are usually local or regional marketers who are not large nationally but who are Number One in their geographic area. Although small in total, within their geographic "segment" they have the marketing and profit clout of the largest company.

Geography is only one way to segment the marketplace. Other market segments may be more productive. The beer industry, for example, segments the market into heavy and light users. Something like 10% of the beer drinkers drink 80% of the beer. Obviously, their use patterns and favorite brands of beer would be much different from those of the light users who drink beer only occasionally. The classic Schaefer beer slogan, "The one beer to have when you're having more than one," and Budweiser's "Pick a pair of six-packs" are appealing to this heavy-user market segment. On the other hand, Miller's "The champagne of bottled beer" is not going to appeal to the guy who slugs down a case a day.

There are also more subtle market segments. In the trucking industry, the requirements of the owner-operator, who drives his own truck, are much different from those of the fleet operator, who may be operating hundreds of trucks. Not only do they have different product requirements, but they also buy differently. The fleet operator most likely specifies not only the make of truck he buys but also the makes of the major components. The owner-operator will most often buy whatever components are on the truck he sees at the dealership.

The hospital market has some segments that are not immediately obvious. There are great differences in products purchased and in the method of purchase among hospitals, depending on whether they are administered by a professional hospital administrator or by a doctor-administrator. This difference can strongly affect the market for hospital equipment or supplies because the professional administrator frequently has different values, decision-making processes, product acceptance criteria, and management style than the doctor-administrator.

The market for cameras and photographic products and services can be segmented into the amateur picture-taker and professional or serious photographer. These two segments have different needs, buy different products, and have a completely different attitude about price, which can sharply affect marketing strategy.

Who are the Customers Once the broad segments of the market have been identified, it is then crucial to understand who the customers are within your target segments. It is amazing how many companies do not have a detailed idea of who their customers or prospects are. Many firms are basically interested in selling their products to anybody who will buy them. This is fine as long as the world is beating a path to your door—but more often it is necessary to go out and find the customers. Knowing who they are likely to be and what they are looking for increases immensely your chances of finding them.

In the case of industrial products or services, it is often possible to list every individual customer or prospect. One venture capitalist has commented that one of the first things he looks for in evaluating a business plan/proposal is not only the overall size of the market but who the first five customers are likely to be. This is a strong indicator to him that the entrepreneur really understands his market.

There are many industries where individual customers are identifiable. If you are selling to the general aviation market, for example, it is possible to obtain registration data on the owners of all aircraft by make and model from the Federal Aviation Administration. The FAA data is on computer tapes. (Similarly, all automobile registrations are available on computer tapes.) There are services which will provide this information. If you have a new instrument that is to be sold to aircraft owners you can get a list of every single individual who would be a prospect.

For consumer products or services, it is equally important to identify who your best customers are likely to be, even if they cannot be identified individually. Are they young, middle-aged, or older? What is their income level? How well educated are they? What products are they using now that would compete with or substitute for your product? How do they live their lives? If you are selling a camping product, you need to know how many and what kind of people go camping.

What Are the Needs of the Customer In addition to knowing who the customers are, it is crucial to know what their needs are—what motivates them to buy or not to buy your product. To the customer, a product is not so much an object as the fulfillment of his needs. That is why the old advertising rule still holds good—"sell the sizzle, not the steak."

Take the case of Farallon Industries. Farallon is a very successful small company marketing products to scuba divers. In just a few years, it has achieved an enviable reputation in this market for supplying top-quality and highly desirable products such as diving gauges and small underwater vehicles. The fundamental product strategy of this company is to look at the needs of the diver and meet those needs better than the competition, with well-engineered products. The key is not in the engineering, which is fairly simple, but in identifying needs and supplying benefits that others do not.

One of Farallon's first products was an illuminated depth gauge. Accurate reading of the depth gauge in deep water is literally a life-or-death matter to divers. Until Farallon came along, it was necessary to carry a flashlight to read depth gauges, which was cumbersome and could lead to error. It is not hard to see that Farallon spotted a critical customer need and supplied it with the very simple product improvement of illuminating the gauges. This is not fancy engineering—just a good perception of the customer's needs. With this simple perception of the market, Farallon has become a leader in its industry. The company took the time to find about its customers and their needs and built its product strategy in line with those needs.

The physical characteristics of the product are only part of what supplies customer benefits. There are also the *psychic* needs that are supplied by the image of the product in the user's mind. These psychic benefits are just as important as the specific operating features of the product. The interweaving of the physical characteristics and the psychic benefits needed by the customer is the key to a successful product or line of products and can form the basis of a winning market strategy.

The field of consumer products provides many examples of products chosen for their psychic benefits rather than for physical differences from other brands. Morton Salt is just one example. It is by far the largest selling brand of salt, yet it is chemically the same as other brands. The psychic benefits of "When it rains it pours" and the familiar blue box are much more important to the consumer than its chemical properties.

Psychic benefits are important in industrial goods, too. Let me tell you about a successful start-up company in the electronics field. The company was created to make and sell small computer memory circuits. They had some minor product innovations, but basically the electronics of their circuits were the same as their competitors'. However, their real product difference was psychological. Memory circuit boards sold by competitors were pretty much of a commodity item, and they looked it. They were made out of dull gray plastic with printed circuitry on them. Since they just got stuck into the back of the computer, no one cared much about their appearance.

But this new firm of bold marketers took an important if seemingly insignificant step. They made the circuit boards out of bright blue plastic with red and yellow circuitry. And they encased sample boards in a clear lucite plastic case for the salesmen to use when demonstrating the product. People were impressed—they felt that somehow these circuit boards were outstanding. They wanted to hear more about them. And they bought. Within a year, this brand-new company was one of the leading sellers of circuit boards, although the only substantial product difference was psychological. They appealed to the need for excitement, the need to feel good about the product, which is a need that every customer has, whether it is a housewife shopping in the supermarket or an electronics engineer specifying computer components.

The Buying Process The final key to analyzing the market situation in order to spot opportunities is to understand the buying process—the stages that your customers go through from the time they have a need for the general benefits you can supply until they actually buy and use your product. It is extremely helpful to develop a "Buying Process Model" for your product. This is nothing more than an explicit and very simple statement of the buying process.

Such a model, regardless of how simple it is, can help you to understand how your product can relate to the customer's life and how your product can fit in better than your competitors' product. Not only can it help spot marketing opportunities, but it can help to monitor problem areas and forecast success.

Here is an example of a simple, but very effective buying process model that is often used in consumer products:

NEED
AWARENESS
TRIAL
REPURCHASE

Quite simply, it describes the process whereby consumers buy and use a product. First, they feel a need for the product. (This is a need for the product category, not for any particular brand.) They have a headache and need a remedy. This is called "primary demand." Next, they become aware of the specific products (aspirin, analgesics, etc.) and the various brands available to fill their need. Then, based on their perception of the benefits offered by each of the brands they know about, they try one. Perhaps they try Excedrin because it is twice as strong, or Bayer because it works twice as fast, or Bufferin because it does not cause stomach upset. Then, finally, if they are satisfied, they will repurchase the product.

The consumer products marketer must be aware of each stage of this buying/use process and, most importantly, be able to shape his tactics differently for each stage of the buying process, covering the customer's differing needs at each stage.

At the *need* stage, the marketer must create primary demand—not for his brand, but for the product category. Someone must convince a headache sufferer to use a remedy rather than just waiting for the pain to go away by itself. Some marketers concentrate mainly on building primary demand—especially if they are dominant in their product category. This is a particularly good strategy for someone with an innovative product that is opening a whole new category. If you are the only airline flying to Hawaii, your strategy might very productively be to sell the beauties and benefits of going to Hawaii. There is no need to sell the reasons to fly on your airline—people will have to if they go to Hawaii. This strategy of creating primary demand or increasing the total market size is a good strategy for the market leader, who will gain most from market expansion, but it could be a poor strategy for a company with a small market share because the greatest return from this effort will go to the larger competitors.

The next task is to create *awareness*. People cannot buy your product if they do not know it exists, regardless of how good it is. And in many consumer product categories, very little product differentiation exists. Often, the largest share of market goes to the brands which have the greatest awareness or name recognition. Building brand awareness involves completely different tactics than creating new demand or getting the customer to try your product. Advertising, for example, need not give reasons to buy—the key is to get your name across.

But stimulating *trial* of the product is another matter. It is at this stage that the customer considers the virtues of all brands he is aware of and selects the one that offers the most benefits. This is where the sale is closed. Tactics at the trial stage must be aimed at differentiating your product from its competition and giving better reasons to buy. Also extremely important and often forgotten is the fact that the product must be available when and where the customer wants to buy it. Sales of new products are often hurt because customers cannot find them in the store. Your advertising compaign might stimulate immense interest, but the product must be on the shelf to be bought, or the campaign is wasted.

Finally, in the case of most consumer products and many industrial products, *repurchase* is immensely important. The user must be satisfied enough to buy the product again and again, or the producer will be out of business. Repurchase can be aided by advertising, but the most important factor is the satisfied customer. The product must perform, or we have lost the future sale. It is here, at the repurchase part of the buying process, that the physical characteristics of the product and the use experience are important. If we want them to fly to Hawaii again, we must be sure they had a good time on their first visit.

Now why is it important to lay out the stages of the buying process as we have done? The formulation of your strategy must take into account which stages of the buying process you will address and how to address them. The customer's needs change at each stage, so your product must change at each stage—bearing in mind that the product is actually a bundle of benefits filling customer needs. As the needs change from one stage of the buying process to the next, you must meet those needs differently—by stimulating primary demand, by creating awareness, by selling against competition, by the set-up of your distribution system, and by the physical characterists of your product—depending on the stage of the buying process.

Having a buying process model is an excellent way of monitoring how well you are doing. By measuring awareness levels, trial rates, repeat-purchase rates, etc., one can see the degree of success being achieved at each stage of the buying process and therefore where more or less marketing emphasis is needed. We frequently see companies who have excellent products and advertising that emphasizes the product features vs. features of competitive products but whose sales are sluggish. They often have good trial and repeat-purchase rates among those aware of them. But because they have not attempted to create raw awareness, they are little known and their total sales are low. Clearly, their strategy would be to stimulate new awareness.

By monitoring your success at each step in the buying process, you can learn how your strategy is working and what adjustment is needed.

Shape Your Product to Fit the Market

Once you have analyzed the market for your product and you understand the customers and their needs, the next major step in planning your marketing strategy is to shape your product to fit the market.

There is a tendency for entrepreneurs to overemphasize the product itself. Often the entrepreneur has decided to start his own company because he has invented a new product or has a technical innovation in the design or production of the product. This focuses his attention on the product itself and may cause him to lose sight of the much more important concept—the positioning of the product in relation to the market. Selling refrigerators to

Eskimos is a poor business venture—not because refrigerators are a poor product, but because the product is aimed at the wrong market. The successful marketer must continually be concerned with shaping his product to fit the marketplace and with finding markets that fit the shape of his product.

Product Positioning—Finding Your Niche in the Market Finding the right niche in the market is often a wiser strategy for the small or new entrepreneur than attacking the market as a whole, despite the attractiveness of the total market projections. Usually larger competitors, through economies of scale, are better able to address the broad marketplace. The "low overhead" rationale given by the small firm to justify low prices is often a myth. Usually the small firm is just cutting its own profit. And it is a poor strategy for the growth-oriented small entrepreneur to be satisfied with low profitability, for he is likely to stay small.

However, large companies are often not willing to take on ventures that are less than very large. Most billion-dollar corporations will not look at a venture that produces less than $50 million annual revenue. Yet some of these "smaller" opportunities are just right for the smaller entrepreneur. In effect, then, by picking a niche in the marketplace too small for the big companies, the entrepreneur can eliminate the biggest, most powerful competitors. This can go a long way toward making a very profitable market for him.

As an example, consider the hypothetical case of a small manufacturer of leafsprings for trucks. Manufacturing truck springs is a very competitive business. The technology is not sophisticated. The manufacturing processes have been around for 50 years. It is a growing market, but the real profits are being made by the big companies because of economies of scale in both manufacturing and marketing. It was hard for this small manufacturer to make any real money or even to grow. If he tried a bigger advertising campaign, the big firms could always step up their budgets and overwhelm his efforts. He could not cut price because his margins were already thinner than those of his competititors. He finally just gave up selling truck springs. But he gave up creatively.

He stopped selling *truck* springs, but he started selling springs for *swimming pool diving boards.* He repositioned the same product and found a niche in a new market. In a short time, he became the major factor in diving boards and was able to increase his margins because there was no strong competition and because the market was willing to pay more. By becoming the largest factor in this new market, this manufacturer achieved the marketing power he was unable to achieve with the very same product in the original market.

Just as our spring manufacturer found a niche in the market by repositioning his product, it is important to find the right niche for a new product. The most profitable niche is the one with the least competition. The field of small, hand-held electronic calculators, for example, quickly became intensely competitive. Two years after the first one was introduced, prices for the simple, arithmetic models dropped to one-tenth their original price due to this intense competition. But one manufacturer, Hewlett-Packard, found a niche in the market without any competition at all until just recently. They produced a much more sophisticated calculator designed to meet the needs of the scientist or engineer. Their calculator is not only priced much higher than other calculators, but they have been able to maintain that price for a long period of time, with resulting increases in profitability. By choosing the right niche for your product and shaping the product to fit the needs of that market, you can enjoy a virtual monopoly in many cases.

Establish a Unique Selling Proposition Every product is bought for a reason—to fill some need of the customer. To the extent that competitive products address the same need, the customer will see no difference and competition is increased. The product that offers a unique reason to buy will be differentiated from its competition. The successful marketing strategy seeks to establish this "unique selling proposition" (USP) because it *adds value to the product in the buyer's mind* beyond that offered by competitive products.

Hewlett-Packard had a very obvious USP—the actual features of their calculator. The things it could do for the scientist were much more extensive than the simpler models on the market could do. No other calculators had these features, so the USP was established. Hewlett-Packard did a fine job in pointing out these product differences.

However, it is not always possible to have truly unique product features. Value may have to be added to the product with a less obvious USP. This is exactly what was done with the computer memory circuits we discussed earlier. The USP there was the bright, modern, high-quality appearance of the memory boards. This added value to the product in the buyer's mind, as the sales results demonstrated. In planning your strategy, it is strongly recommended that you establish a USP and write it down for everyone to see and understand. This will be the cornerstone to positioning your product in its niche in the market.

Pricing There are many ways to establish a Unique Selling Proposition. Pricing is one of the strongest, although there are many markets where the price of the product is relatively unimportant. The key is to *price according to the market, not according to costs.* Of course, the costs of your product must be kept in mind so that you know if you are in a viable business situation. But buyers basically do not care what your costs are; they only consider the price they are willing to pay. That is why pricing is and should be a marketing function, not just a financial or accounting function.

The best pricing strategy is to charge what the market will bear—but be very sensitive to changes in the market. If the market will no longer pay the price, drop it (or be satisfied with a declining share). If the price drops below costs, either cut costs or get out of the market—it is not viable for you. (This, of course, refers to long-term price levels, not short-term fluctuations. Sometimes it is desirable to lose money for awhile until competition shakes down. This is particularly true if you have the largest share of a fast-growing market.)

Cutting price to gain market share can be a good strategy. But price cuts are often quickly followed by competition. If this is the only USP, it is a shaky strategy unless there is some reason to believe competitors will not follow or unless you have a higher margin and can hold out at the low price longer than competition.

Being aware of the different needs of different market segments can often lead to a highly creative and profitable pricing strategy. Suppose you were the manufacturer of work gloves. You would probably find that there are three distinct market segments for your product:

- Businesses, such as manufacturing plants, who may purchase dozens of gloves every week as they are worn out by their workers.
- Laborers and construction workers, who buy their own gloves, say one or two pairs a month.
- Householders and "do-it-yourselfers" who may buy a pair of gloves only every year or so.

Clearly, attitudes toward the price would be different among these three market segments. The first two would be very price conscious and would probably also have considerable brand consciousness. On the other hand, the once-a-year buyer would probably not have any particular brand awareness and would probably not buy on the basis of price. He probably buys whatever they have in the store at whatever price they charge, just as long as the gloves do the job.

In setting the price for the gloves, it would be a poor strategy to set the same price for all three types of buyers. If it is low enough to appeal to the "professional" users, it is probably much lower than the householder would be willing to pay, so the extra profit available from that market segment would be thrown away. Conversely, if the price were set at the level the householder would pay, the large volume "professional" market would be lost because some competitor would be willing to give them a better price to get the business.

The dilemma can be solved in several ways through creative pricing and product positioning strategy. One way would be to sell two "lines" of gloves under two brand names—a lower-priced professional line and a higher-priced consumer line. They would be sold through different outlets so they would probably not compete with each other. The second strategy would be a pure pricing strategy. It would be to sell the same line of gloves but to set a high price for a single pair and then sell packages of these at a sharply reduced per-unit price (to appeal to the laborer buying his own gloves). There would also be a price per gross at a very low per-unit price to appeal to the business buyer. In this way, all three market segments are paying the "maximum" price they are willing to pay, and profits are optimized.

Pricing can be one of the most powerful tools for marketing strategy. It is important that it be a marketing function and that the marketer understands fully the cost and profit implications of pricing strategy.

Understand Yourself

Some elements of the strategy planning process are not as precise or as clear as pricing, yet may have as much or more influence on ultimate success. One of these is to have a realistic understanding of your own situation and the intent of your marketing efforts.

Understand Your Company Situation Entrepreneurs are notorious optimists. So are marketing people. They have the attraction of anticipated success to pull them forward over the hurdles of a competitive world. This optimism is necessary. But in planning marketing strategy, cold, realistic analysis is also needed—most importantly applied to understanding your company situation and your strategic motives.

First of all, you should have a clear appraisal of your company's resources. Especially in a start-up company, there is just not enough money to do everything. This is why a market segmentation strategy is important. It allows you to focus your limited resources on one part of the market to maximize the impact.

One of our clients, a small firm with a new product for smokers, had an initial advertising and marketing research budget of less than $5,000—virtually nothing for a consumer product. But they knew their limitations. Through some small-scale research, they identified their best prospects and developed an advertising message that would have maximum impact on these prospects. The firm concentrated all of its advertising in a full-page newspaper advertisement in just one city. They put all their direct selling efforts in that one city, pushing for maximum distribution and shelf display. In that one city, the impact was so strong that they achieved enough profit to move on to other cities. Within one year, that firm was in national distribution and could afford over $1 million a year just for advertising.

Appraise your skills as well as your limitations. Define in writing what your capabilities are. What is unique about your venture that competitors do not have? Are you strong in marketing? Do you have a technical innovation? How long will it last? Is your skill in management of opportunity rather than a specific technical advantage? How will your company be different from competition? What can you do better? What are your true costs? How will they be reduced by increased volume? These are the kinds of questions that can help to achieve some real leverage for you in your marketing strategy.

It is also important to be realistic about the pressures on your company, whether they be cost pressures, competitive pressures, pressures of timing, or financial pressures. At one time during the development of its new Citation jet aircraft, Cessna Aviation reportedly had 40% of its corporate assets tied up in the R & D for that plane. This was nearly two years before it was able to be put on the market. Cessna had never before made or sold a jet aircraft. Needless to say, that firm had to be absolutely realistic in understanding the pressures on it and in developing a flawless marketing strategy. Failure to gain a substantial position in this new market could have endangered the entire corporation. Fortunately for Cessna, they did develop and execute an excellent strategy, and in the last two years the Citation has been the largest selling corporate jet.

Having a buying process model, as we have seen earlier, is a good way to understand the market. It is also a good way to understand your company situation in the marketplace. When you have developed the buying process model for your market, you should then address each step in the buying process and delineate your strengths and weaknesses at each of those steps. Is there really a "primary demand" or basic need for the product you are selling? What is the awareness level of your brand? How do the customers regard your brand? Would they choose your brand or the competitor's? Why? How is your distribution—is your product available when and where people buy? What is your trial rate—are people who are aware of your product buying it? What is your repeat purchase rate—will customers buy your product again? Why not? Knowing your strengths and weaknesses in the marketplace can guide where to put the emphasis in planning strategy. Having an idea of the buying and use process for your product helps to guide your analysis of these strengths and weaknesses toward actions to be taken.

Just as important as understanding your strengths and weakness is understanding your successes and failures. Do not just accept success—*understand why it happened.* It may have happened for different reasons than you suspect, so repeating a successful action may not result in a repeat of the success—the marketplace may have changed. Failures are even more important learning experiences. Too often, people like to forget their failures because they are painful. In business, shying away from analyzing and fully understanding failures can be disastrous. A venture capitalist once said that he thinks and talks more about his failures than his successes "Because they are more fun."—and more educational, too.

Understand Your Strategic Intent It is important to understand just what you want to accomplish in your marketing strategy, with very specific dollars and cents objectives and for overall strategic intent. Most entrepreneurs soon learn to set specific dollar goals and even market share objectives, but often the broader aspects of what is to be accomplished are not spelled out.

One important issue to address is whether you are attempting to build primary demand or selective choice. As we have seen, to stimulate primary demand is to create or demonstrate a need for your product category (regardless of brand). Promoting selective choice means generating a preference for your brand. Hertz may very well gain a lot of new customers for itself by promoting the use of rental cars among those who have never rented a car (new primary demand). But a smaller car-rental firm would be wiser to promote itself to the regular car renter on the basis of some product or service difference (selective choice). The small firm can let Hertz do the work of creating the market while it concentrates on getting its piece of that market.

Another question to answer is whether to promote the firm or the product. There are many pressures on both sides. Promoting the strengths of the firm has its advantages in that it can enhance overall visibility in an industry and form a stronger platform for many activities. The company reputation can carry new products, for example. On the other hand, concentrating efforts on a single product, selling the product itself, brings more power to bear on that product. It is easier to sell product advantages than to create a good corporate "image." Neither of these two directions is right for every company. But too often a company will not have a clear idea of whether to promote the firm or the products, and it vacillates from one strategy to the other. This weakens both efforts. Whatever the direction, a clear path should be taken.

Another important aspect of understanding your strategic intent is to have a clear idea of how and why you plan to move in the marketplace. For each product line, you should state one of five possible intentions in the market:

- *Penetration:* Remaining with current products in the same markets, concentrating on holding and increasing market share.
- *Market Expansion:* Taking existing products into new markets or new market segments, broadening the market potential for the current product line.
- *Product Expansion:* Introducing new products into existing markets, capitalizing on company strengths and opportunities in familiar markets.

- *Diversification:* Leaping over the existing business entirely and introducing new products to new markets, getting into a completely new business for the company.
- *Liquidation:* Pull a product out of a market where the company has a position. Often this is the best strategy to allow company resources to be concentrated on more productive ventures.

Along with defining these market/product intentions, it is necessary to state market-share objectives. Are you buying share, selling share, or defending an established market share? The new venture is interested in expansion, at least up to a point. If so, be prepared to *buy* market share; it does not come free. It is an investment, just like plant and equipment. Market share is a productive asset that produces profits like any other asset, even if it is not shown on the balance sheet. Therefore, if expansion of share is the objective, it should be recognized that it will take investment of short-term profits.

In established products, it is often more desirable to hold rather than expand market share. Some investment will be needed to maintain share, just as equipment must be maintained. But a defensive share posture is primarily to protect profits in a lucrative market. If too much is spent on maintenance, profits will suffer. If too little is spent, share will deteriorate. Thus, it is equally important to acknowledge and plan for a defensive posture as for an aggressive one.

And it may be desirable to bail out of a market—to sell market share. This is the liquidation strategy. But be sure to sell out at a profit. Often the only profit in an unsuccessful venture can be made while selling out of a poor market share situation. Cut costs and let market share decline. Stop advertising. In the short-term, this can increase profits substantially—until your share position is gone. But invest these profits in some other market/product opportunity.

Indeed, most mature companies have or should have a "balanced portfolio" of product/market ventures—some stable and profitable, some declining and selling out, and some expanding growth situations requiring the support of new investment. The investment objective should be spelled out for each product/market separately in planning the marketing strategy. It is usually unwise to have the same profit objective for every product line or market. It is necessary to invest for the future in some situations and cash in on others. There will almost always be different cash/profit objectives for these different situations.

There are many aspects to planning marketing strategy. Among these perhaps the most important is to understand your own situation and what you are trying to accomplish.

Understanding Your Competition

Almost as important as understanding yourself is to understand competitors. Unfortunately, many firms do not take the time and effort truly to understand their competition. Often, they do not even know who the competition is. The goal in planning strategy is to understand your competition as well as you understand yourself and to set up intelligence systems that will keep you informed about the competitor. A complete analysis should be made of all the major competition in just about the same way we have said you should analyze your own company. About each competitor, you should know:

- What are their major resources and skills?
- What pressures are on them, financial and otherwise?
- Where are their strengths and weaknesses in the buying process?
- What are the costs and profitability for their products?

- What are their successes and failures and why did they happen? What have they said they would do? Have they done it?
- Are they building primary or selective demand?
- Are they promoting the firm or the products?
- What are their apparent intentions in the marketplace—penetration, market expansion, product expansion, diversification, or liquidation?
- Are they buying or selling share? Investing or collecting?
- What is their product/market portfolio like?
- What are their fundamental strategies? State them.

These are the very things that are important to know about your own company and your strategy. If you can also know these things about your competitor, you may know more than he does.

Learning about the competition does not mean setting up a spy network inside their accounting department. Realistic market analysis such as we have been describing can tell most of what is needed. Financial data is available from the 10-K reports filed with the Securities and Exchange Commission. These go into much more detail than the annual reports. Also, your sales force can be turned into an intelligence gathering machine, using some very simple reports and a structure for piecing together the information. Competitive advertising and promotional materials can be collected and routinely analyzed for message content and changes in product positioning. Trade shows and news clippings can signal impending new product introductions (or failures). The point is to open up the lines of communication and observation to learn what the competition is up to and why.

Select and State Your Strategy

All of the information and decisions we have been talking about must finally be pulled together into a marketing strategy. It is extremely important to have an explicitly stated strategy, written down and agreed to by all elements of corporate management. A strategy is really a vehicle to pull all of the company resources together so they can work together to a common goal. This is how the maximum power can be brought to bear on the marketplace.

We have said that developing strategy consists of analyzing the marketplace and developing a conceptual "model" of how it works, shaping the product to fit the needs of the marketplace, and understanding your own situation and intentions and those of your competition. Writing down all of these things in a marketing plan will just about delineate all elements of the strategy. But to pull it all together is a creative activity. Only you can do it for your company. One key to synthesizing a strategy that will last over time is "keep it simple."

Giving a "name" to your strategy (and those of your competitors) is a good way to pull it together and to keep everyone operating on the same strategy. Here are some of the ones we have run into. Most industries have similar ones!

- *Pioneer:* This is the Polaroid strategy. Continually invest to be far out in front technologically. This is a very tricky strategy in that it involves high front-end investment and therefore requires high profit margins for a time long enough to recoup. It requires strong patents or other protection from competition.
- *Share Leader:* This is the Procter & Gamble strategy. Often they are not the first into a new product category, but when they decide to enter the market they shoot for the largest share position as quickly as possible. They develop excellent products and invest heavily in marketing to buy share quickly.
- *Slipstreaming:* Just as a race car driver will follow right on the tail of the leader, in his slipstream, this can be a marketing strategy. It involves copying every move of the market leader, allowing him to make the heavy investment in creating demand. The "me-too" follower can often

reap rewards with a lower investment. Private label brands, such as the supermarket brands, will often follow this strategy. It must be very well executed to work, and it can be dangerous.

- *Low Ball:* This is the price-cutting strategy often followed by small firms. It can work unless price is really of little concern to the market. The problem is that it cuts the profits and therefore squeezes the ability of the small firm to grow. Another danger is that the larger firms can often produce at a lower cost and can afford to meet the price.
- *Random or Irrational:* This is the strategy followed by many, many firms who have not consciously set out a marketing strategy. It frequently leads to weak marketing efforts because all parts of the company are not working in harmony for the same objective.

Once your strategy has been developed, agreed upon, and written down, it can and will be used by the various components of your company to guide their efforts. The advertising people will have a clearer idea of what they should accomplish. Finance will understand why there is a low profitability in some product lines. Sales people will know who to call on to maximize their efforts. And hopefully, your company will be in harmony—which will translate into increased profits.

Seven

Legal Aspects of Proprietorships, Partnerships, and Corporations as Business Forms

Thomas A. Skornia

WHY THE CORPORATE FORM?

I think the most important difference between corporations on the one hand and partnerships and sole proprietorships on the other is that nobody ever had his partnership or sole proprietorship listed on the New York Stock Exchange or publicly traded over-the-counter. Furthermore, very few limited partnerships are publicly held, and those that are seem generally restricted to tax-shelter kinds of investments in oil and gas and real estate. If you are going into a commercial or a financially oriented enterprise, the only way that you are going to be publicly held, in all probability, is to become a corporation. (Now there are some kinds of hybrid organizational forms—real estate investment trusts, for example—listed on the exchanges. However, I won't address myself to those topics in this brief discussion.) As I see it, the main difference between corporations and the other organizational forms is that the other forms do not lend themselves to the creation of public vehicles and the realization of supermoney

At the time this chapter was written, Thomas A. Skornia was a Senior Partner with the San Francisco firm of Skornia, Rosenblum & Gyemant, attorneys-at-law.

either by the outside investors or by the inside entrepreneurs. You may *start* as a proprietorship or a partnership; if you pursue the sort of business discussed in this book, you will no doubt end up with a corporation.

Thus, I will concentrate on the corporate form because I think that's the one entrepreneurs should, over the long term, be most interested in, and I will contrast it with the other forms.

Limited Liability

Let's look at the topic first from the standpoint of the advantages of incorporation: First and not to be easily dismissed—but not to be overplayed either—is the concept of limited liability. In other words, financial liability to people who are injured by your business (either by its products, by its premises, or by the conduct of the officers and management) will be limited to the assets which have been put in the corporation by you and by your investors. Thus, if the corporation is properly organized and capitalized, they will not be able to attach your personal assets and personal estate with their claims. For example, let's say that you have a corporation or small business that is capitalized initially at $100,000; and that you hold your directors and shareholders meetings regularly, keep minutes, books, and records; that you do everything according to the laws that set forth the organizational principles under which corporations must operate. Now let's suppose that somebody buys one of your products and suffers a severe and lasting injury for which they successfully make a claim for $1 million in damages. That judgment would be against the corporation only; and if it were in excess of insurance coverage, for example, the only entity from which the injured claimant could collect would be the corporation.

Now that is not a happy event in itself because it has, in effect, destroyed your corporation—bankrupted it. But if you have assets on the outside, the claimant at least has not reached those, and you can walk away from the business and go out and start another one without having been stripped of *all* your other assets. This is particularly important to those of you who have been through the entrepreneurial route once before and who may have substantial personal estates, all of which you do not want to commit to a particular new business. In order to insulate those outside assets from that kind of liability, you would want to have limited liability, preferably in the form of a corporation.

Now you can also get limited liability to a lesser extent by employing a limited partnership form of organization. The problem here is that, in order to enjoy the limited liability in the partnership form, you as a limited partner cannot participate in any significant way in the management of the business. If you do, you will be considered by law to be a general partner with general liability. Hence, you will not have any insulation between you and potentially very large legal claims which might be made against the entity. So if you want both to be an active entrepreneur and to have limited liability, a corporation is really the only way you can get it.

Public Visibility

There is, I think, a certain aura of status and prestige surrounding the corporate form. This aura can very easily be overplayed; but I think doing business in the corporate, as opposed to the sole proprietor or partnership, form may give you some public visibility that you would not otherwise have. Conversely, if you are interested in maintaining privacy, then you may want to *avoid* the corporate form.

Continuity

The corporate form makes transferring of your interest much easier; similarly, it makes more secure the future of the business. Let's assume your business manufactures a product with a long and virtually perpetual useful life. The outlook for stable, long-term growth of this business may be quite good. But, unfortunately, human life is not unlimited, and proprietorships or partnerships usually die with the proprietor or one of the general partners. Only the corporate form offers straight-forward continuity after the death of one of the principals. Also, from the standpoint of personal estate planning, the corporation gives you the opportunity to transfer interests to the next generation, to sell off interests to individuals in the family or other key employees, or ultimately, as I indicated earlier, to sell interest to the public at large. It is much easier to split a corporate form into pieces—shares of stock—than it is to split a partnership. Partnerships are inherently limited since they don't really have the possibility of infinite fractionalization in the same way that a corporation does. For example, a limited partnership may have up to 100 or even 200 limited partners if it is publicly held in a real estate or oil and gas syndicate. But you rarely get much broader ownership than that because the partnership form requires a fairly long document. It also places many constraints, specified in the partnership agreement, on each person who participates. However, in a corporation all you need are people who are interested in owning a piece of the equity, stock, which they may want later to sell, collect dividends on, or use in some other way. Corporate stock is much easier to deal with than partnership interests, and it is much easier for investors to grasp as a concept. It is a straightforward matter to split a corporation into 5 million different pieces, this meaning 5 million shares of stock, that can be held by as many as 100,000 different shareholders. It is all but impossible to break up a partnership into that many different pieces. Again, the ease and transferability of ownership of the corporation makes it the more likely vehicle for public ownership.

Now entrepreneurs or insiders who have basic control over the corporation may be interested in passing on that control, without further dilution, to the next generation in their families or to the next generation of key employees. The latter group may, indeed, be the best choice to uphold the interests of all of the stockholders because they are experienced and they have a stake in the business. Everything else being equal, such people make the best managers. It is much easier to pass along that interest through a trust, under a will, to the people you want it to go to than it is to pass along a partnership. The partnership form is highly personalized; and under the laws of most states, the death of a partner holding 50% or controlling interest will result automatically in the dissolution of the partnership. While you can draft into the partnership agreement provisions which call for virtually automatic resurrection of the partnership, there is a period during which the law may be uncertain and the relationships among the parties may be unclear. This is not so with the corporation. The shareholders always have the democratic ability to control the overall direction in which the corporation is going by electing a board of directors, responsible for establishing basic corporate policy, to represent them. The rest of the management, which runs the corporation from day to day, stays in place through the death of the principal owner so that, with proper planning, the transition is almost unnoticeable.

In a sole proprietorship, by definition, there is only one owner. When he dies, getting a successor and making the transition may be extremely difficult if it can be done at all. The good will that that decedent owner has built up over a period of years may be dissipated instantly with his death so that his family and successors are basically unprotected. Since the value of the business was inherent in his continuing life, with the end of his life, the value of the business is gone. In the corporate form, by providing for proper succession, you can readily avoid such loss of value and maintain, for the benefit of the successors, widows, and orphans, that value which has been built up at great cost and great energy over a period of years.

Tax Protection

The corporation form enjoys tax protection from ordinary income. Now if you are one of the fortunate entrepreneurs who has a significant estate outside this particular business and has what is known as "preference income" under the Internal Revenue Code of 1954, as amended by the Tax Reform Act of 1969, you may be in a tax bracket as high as 70% on some of the income you earn. If you enter into a partnership or sole proprietorship form that throws off income—presumably this is your objective—and you don't have a corporation which can retain the income and pay the somewhat lesser corporate rate of 48% plus the state tax, the income may come directly to you, chargeable to you at the 70% rate. Hence, your total share of equity and estate value is reduced by the difference in tax rate between what the corporation would pay if you left it there and what you pay by reason of its being taxable to you as an individual, proprietor, or partner. Thus, there can be an aspect of tax protection by operating in the corporate form. However, if you don't have preference income and your highest income bracket is 50%, maybe you are better off not to operate in a corporate form. That is something you should consider carefully with your accountant and counsel before you make any decision on shifting from one form to the other.

Variety in Financing

The corporation is a vehicle for public ownership, and there are a great variety of financing methods available in this form of business organization. Not only can you split up the ownership of a corporation into several million shares, if you want to; but in addition, you can offer some fairly fancy financing packages to the investment community. Contrasting, in the case of limited partnership interests, there are only two classes of partnership interest available. Those that you would offer to the public are classified as "limited." Those which are held by the basic operators of the company are "general." In the case of a sole proprietorship, you have only one interest—your own sole ownership of the business. With a corporation, then, things are quite different. For the insiders and management, you can use common stock, which offers the big equity rise. For outside investors, especially for a start-up situation where those investors want preferred treatment if anything goes wrong and there is ultimate liquidation of the business, you can use preferred stock, which gives them the first claim to the assets before the common stockholders participate. You can also make that preferred stock convertible, if you wish, so that the preferred stockholders may enjoy the same up-side potential and equity growth as the common stockholders by reason of a presumed one-for-one convertibility ratio of the preferred into the common. At the same time, these preferred stockholders are protected in their down-side risk because, if there is a liquidation, they are the first stockholders to participate in the distribution of assets. In the event the preferred stockholders don't get paid 100 cents on the dollar, the common shareholders will get nothing.

Another financial instrument is the convertible debenture, which offers an even stronger claim against the corporation assets than preferred stock because the investor is then in the position of being a creditor then rather than an equity holder. An important advantage to the company offered by the use of debentures is that interest paid on the debentures is a deductible business expense of the company. Dividends paid on preferred or common stock are not deductible. Thus, if you have a tax objective in mind and you want those dollars that you are going to pay out to those owners to be deductible for tax purposes (it's going to be includable by them in any case), you want to use convertible debt. In this way, you will give them the possibility of the up-side rise in equity because of the conversion feature while limiting the down-side risk by reason of preferred distribution of assets. On top of that, you will enjoy the benefit of a tax deduction to the corporation because this is debt rather than equity financing.

Now you can be even fancier and put some warrants with the debentures or with the stock or offer some other options. It is possible to get so sophisticated—like Jimmy Ling did in the late 1960's—that you come up with such hybrid securities that the New York Stock Exchange won't even list them for trading because they don't know what the hell they are. (Ling had about five or six different classes of securities, and the New York Stock Exchange finally just cut them off entirely because they couldn't tell which were preferred over which. There seemed to be no way to make an adequate disclosure so that anybody other than Ling himself could understand what was going on. In fact, there was reason to believe occasionally that he didn't either.) But, anyway, in the corporate form, you can be very flexible with your financing.

WHY NOT THE CORPORATE FORM?

Now, as with most things in life, there are always trade-offs. You pay for those benefits and goodies in the corporate form by giving up certain other things that may be of value to you and which, if they are of sufficient value, you will want to realize by going into a partnership or proprietorship.

Alternatives or Subchapter S Corporations

First of all, in a corporation taxed as a corporation, you will have a lockup of start-up losses. One exception to this is an organizational form known as a Subchapter S corporation. The advantage of operating as a Subchapter S corporation is that any losses experienced by the company may be passed along to the stockholders directly on a pro-rata basis. If the corporation loses money in its first fiscal year but has not elected to operate as a Subchapter S corporation, it will have a nice loss to show on its Form 1120, Corporation Income Tax Return; but this loss will not do the investors any good for tax purposes.

Thus, if you are selling stock in your new company as a tax shelter and you have wealthy investors who have ordinary income that they want to shelter through this vehicle, then you should either be in a position to employ a Subchapter S corporation or a limited partnership, so that the losses during that first year can be used to offset ordinary income on your investor's Form 1040. For instance, assume they put in $100,000 on January 1st; the company loses $95,000; and on April 15th of the next year, they have a loss of $95,000 to use against presumptively $95,000 in other income. They may be able to pay no taxes for the year and still have their full equity position in the corporation. Now that's a very attractive deal if you have high-income, high-tax-paying investors who want that kind of benefit. But you either do it through a limited partnership or through a Subchapter S corporation.

The Subchapter S corporation is governed by some very stringent legal requirements. It is limited as to the number of shareholders, and quite restrictive as to who may be shareholders, it cannot receive more than 20% of its income from so-called passive investments; and it is limited in some of the fringe benefit programs for the key insiders because the test for allowability of deductible contributions to pension and profit sharing programs is far less liberal than it is in the standard corporation form. All of these things tend to hem you in and limit what you can do with the Subchapter S corporation. However, if you do have a small number of shareholders, if they are all high-income individuals who find the ability to take a tax loss in the early year or years appealing, then the Subchapter S or limited partnership form may be the appropriate vehicle. Then, after you have used up the ability to take those front-end losses against your investor's ordinary income, you can switch to standard corporation tax practice.

Now notice, that you can't have this thing two ways. If the individual shareholders of a Subchapter S corporation have taken losses against their income on their Form 1040's, you cannot use that loss again as a net operating loss carry-over against the corporation's later profits. If you want to accumulate corporate loss to minimize corporate taxes in the future, you can't have a Subchapter S election. In other words, you can't use it twice.

My general feeling about limited partnerships and Subchapter S corporations in the commercial or manufacturing area is that they usually make a very bad sell. Venture capitalists don't want to hear about your losses. They want to know that you are being realistic and they understand that you are likely to lose some money, at least initially. But to emphasize the advantages of loss is, I think, reverse psychology—you really want to sell them on the potential for supermoney and long-term capital gain. People who tend to be interested in a tax loss are the wealthier professionals—physicians, for instance—who have substantial ordinary income and who, by and large, make the worst possible shareholders because they suffer anxiety early in the game. Even though you have told them how much you are going to lose, they become hysterical when you actually start losing it. If they have any control over the company, they are likely to want to take active part in that control, whereas the more sophisticated venture capitalists will not intervene if you are on plan, even if you are losing money. Therefore, you should be very careful both about the psychology of selling a loss and the kind of investors you get if you do sell it. Again, I recommend that you lean toward the corporate form.

Disadvantages

The corporate form demands extra energy output and some extra costs because you will have to do additional accounting. In addition to your own personal records, you'll have a corporate set of books to keep, extra tax returns to file, and other filings to make with state and federal agencies in addition to records, meetings, and other formalities attending the corporate form that are not present in a sole proprietorship or partnership.

Confidentiality is also affected by the corporate form. If you are a sole proprietor or a partnership, the only place you have to file information is with the tax authorities; they are, by statute, obligated to keep it confidential. There are sometimes leaks—and very celebrated ones—but the statute *requires* confidentiality. Now in order to set up a corporation, you have to file a set of proposed Articles of Incorporation with the Secretary of State, and you have to name your directors. Shortly after you set up the corporation, you have to file a statement naming your officers. When you issue stock, you have to make at least a minimum filing with the Department of Corporations indicating who your principle shareholder or shareholders are. All of that causes you to expose information that you might want to keep to yourself; California statutes involving the Department of Corporations and the Secretary of State, for example, *require* that such information be on public record. If you can make a good case showing that some of the information in your business plan, such as financial statements or the identities of the founders, should be held in confidence to protect you from unfair competition, sometimes the Department will agree to set up in your file a confidential section with a big red cover on it. This section is not supposed to be delivered to the front desk when people ask to look at your folder. Sometimes it is delivered anyway; of course, that is the first place people look. Obviously you have to be careful since this represents a potential leak. Furthermore, you have to remember that Dun and Bradstreeters and other professional snoopers show up with great regularity at the Department of Corporations to check out whether what your controller has been telling them is complete and truthful. Usually it is the truth, but frequently it is not very complete. Often you will be appalled at your own Dun and Bradstreet report because it will have more information in it than your controller gave *you* last week.

Now to minimize disclosure, you can begin, as I indicated, by requesting a confidential portion in your folder at the Department of Corporations. Also, if you wish to avoid naming your directors, you can set up the corporation with so-called "dummy" directors, such as your lawyer, accountant, or insurance man. "Dummy" is not in reference to their intellectual capacities—the term is used because these are not the people who are really going to be interested in the corporation in an ownership sense. Shortly after incorporation you can hold a meeting and elect the *real* directors and officers. This confidence, however, will only last for 90 days; within this time period, you are supposed to file a statement of *real* officers and directors of the corporation with the Secretary of

State. Again, when considering whether or not to incorporate, this lack of privacy may be important to you.

Doing Business Out of State

Private firms and corporations also receive different treatment when qualifying to do business in other states. Actually, individuals do not have to qualify at all, although they may have to take out licenses such as peddler licenses, city licenses, etc. If you are a proprietor and want to set up a warehouse in Nevada and a sales office in Chicago, you can do it without obtaining any special permission; all you have to do is pay the different state taxes. You, as an individual, function under the "Priveleges and Immunities clause" of the U. S. Constitution, which permits you to enjoy throughout the U.S. the same privileges and preferences that you enjoy as a citizen of the state in which you reside; and one of these privileges is doing business with minimum licensing regulations. But a corporation, not being an individual, is not entitled to that constitutional guarantee. As a result, every corporation generally has to qualify to do business in other states, which requires another filing; probably a fee to go with it; probably an advance payment of franchise or corporate income tax to go with the filing; and then periodic updating of your capitalization, changes of capitalization, amount of sales, and all the rest of that. Clearly, there is additional cost in each state you do business in. If you are going to have a branch office or if you are going to warehouse products in that other state, you are almost surely going to have to qualify.

Now what happens if you don't? The state may have daily penalties for every day in which you do business without qualifying. These can mount up rather fast. In addition, the state will prevent you from using its courts to sue—for example, to collect bills. If you make sales in Illinois and you are not qualified to do business there and some guy there owes you $50,000, you go into court and they will throw you out because you, as a corporation, were not qualified to do business. Now that can be remedied at the time you bring suit by qualifying after the fact; as soon as you qualify, you can bring suit on the earlier transaction. The problem is that a lot of businessmen and a lot of lawyers procrastinate and wait until the last damn minute to file the suit—maybe only two or three days before the expiration of the statute of limitations. Then they find out they weren't qualified. The court throws them out; and before they can complete the qualification process, the statute of limitations has run out on the debt. This can be very serious—possibly a matter of malpractice for the lawyer who let it happen or malfeasance for the management who made it happen by failing to qualify. These "extras" concerning a corporation operating out of state must also be considered when deciding whether or not to incorporate.

Double Taxation

If you do not use the Subchapter S election, you may realize income which potentially goes through the tax sieve twice—once when the corporation earns it and a second time when it is received by the stockholders as dividends. Now young companies, by and large—and even many publicly traded growth companies —don't pay any dividends. But eventually they do; and this may be one of the reasons for buying the stock—sooner or later even widows and orphans will own it because they want to receive the dividends. What happens is this: You ultimately end up paying corporate income tax at a roughly 50% rate. Then, when the dividends are paid out, the stockholders pay personal tax on them. For example, let's say that the corporation makes $1 profit. It pays 50¢ in taxes. There is 50¢ left to pay out to a shareholder who is in the 50% tax bracket and thus pays another 25¢ in taxes, leaving a realized net income of 25¢. Thus, a total of 75¢ out of the corporation's $1 profit went for taxes. That is a pretty fierce bite! Not only that, if you liquidate the corporation, you are hit with a similar element of double taxation. In contrast, a partnership, a Subchapter S corporation, or a sole proprietorship is only taxed once. Thus, in considering whether or not to incorporate, you must discuss the double taxation problem with your accountant and your lawyer.

PARTNERSHIPS AND PROPRIETORSHIPS: SOME ADVANTAGES AND DISADVANTAGES

The partnership form offers favorable tax characteristics similar to those of a Subchapter S corporation. If you have losses, investment credits, or other tax characteristics favorable to a high-bracket taxpayer, they will pass through automatically from the partnership tax returns to the individuals' Form 1040 and be usable by them as offsets against other income. Thus partnerships can offer a favorable tax structure.

On the subject of privacy: If you have a limited partnership, you will have to file and publish a certificate naming the partners. If you have a general partnership (i.e., you have no limited partners) you don't even have to do that. Thus, there is more privacy in a general partnership than in the corporate form.

In the case of partnerships, financial liability can be of critical importance. Limited partners in a limited partnership usually enjoy the same kind of limited liability as do the shareholders in a corporation, assuming (as in the case of the corporation) that it is properly organized and capitalized and that the certificate of limited partnership is properly filed and published. One of the first things we do when we are representing a creditor of a limited partnership gone bad is to determine whether or not a certificate of limited partnership was filed. If it wasn't, the partnership is technically a general partnership, and everybody is regarded as a general partner. Now usually the general partners tend to be judgment-proof. The people who were intended as *limited* partners are the ones with the money. If you can turn the limited partners into general partners, you can go after them for the liabilities of the entire partnership. The one thing to be *very* careful about if you are participating in limited partnerships is to be sure that the thing is done right and that the certificate is both filed and published in a timely fashion. Only if it is will your liability be limited to the amount that you voluntarily invest.

In any partnership, limited or general, there always has to be at least one general partner who has general, unlimited liability. Thus, as in the case of the corporation, a partnership should carry insurance against this risk. If you are able to *obtain* insurance at reasonable premiums, the concept of limited liability may not be material. If you don't have insurance, then the concept of limitation of liability by reason of the form of business organization becomes most important.

Another disadvantage of the partnership form of organization is that the partners have no tax protection in the case of ordinary income. If this tax shelter suddenly turns into a "cash cow," you may have problems because you have received unexpected income taxable at a rate potentially as high as 70%. You may encounter difficulty at that point in converting quickly into a corporate form and modifying the tax shelter aspects.

The final disadvantages of the partnership form, as I indicated, have to do with the difficulty of creating a public vehicle, the lack of flexibility in financing, and the difficulty of providing for continuity of ownership. With proprietorships these things, I think, simply go in spades. However, it seems to me that the main problem with a proprietorship is the lack of continuity when the sole proprietor dies.

Eight

The Role of the Accountant in the New Enterprise

Charles A. Walworth

My department at Haskins & Sells is designed specifically to help small businesses, especially new enterprises. We assign one staff member to each client; this person is responsible for all of that client's needs: audit, management advice, tax, etc. Rather than having the client work with different people in the organization, we provide him with one staff member who works closely with him all the way from the development of a business plan until the operation is well underway.

STARTING A BUSINESS

I would like first to give you an idea of how the accountant can be of help in starting a business.

Governmental Requirements

There are a vast number of details imposed on any business by various government agencies. The entrepreneur needs an accoun-

Charles A. Walworth is a partner with Deloitte, Haskins & Sells, an international accounting firm.

tant and an attorney to make sure that everything necessary is done. Here are just a few of the requirements:

1. You have to register with the state if you will be collecting sales tax.
2. You have to arrange to collect withholding taxes and F.I.C.A. taxes and to pay unemployment taxes and disability taxes.
3. You have to obtain an employer identification number from the Internal Revenue Service. This number is analogous to an individual's Social Security number—it identifies your business.
4. If you are located in certain cities or counties, you may come under local zoning ordinances; and of course, you are also subject to local business taxes based on payroll or sales.

The accountant is familiar with these and other requirements.

Form of Organization

The accountant quite often will be called in by the attorney when it comes to setting up a corporation or deciding whether or not a corporation should be formed. From the standpoint of the accountant, there are several different forms of organization for tax purposes:

1. If you operate as a proprietor, you show your business income statement on Schedule C of your Form 1040. All the income is thus included in your personal income tax return.
2. In the case of partnerships, there is only an information return filed. A percentage of the partnership income proportionate to their ownership in the partnership is reported by the individual partners on their own tax returns. The partnership itself pays no tax.
3. The corporation is a separate entity. It pays taxes on its own income after deducting all of its expenses, including salary to the owner. An

advantage in operating as a corporation is that allowances for certain payroll benefits, such as pension plans, profit-sharing plans, and other fringe benefits, are much more liberal than they are for an individual or for a partnership.

The form of the enterprise can have a significant tax effect. Your accountant will show you how the tax rules can affect you.

Accounting System

The next thing that an accountant does is perhaps the most obvious—he sets up the accounting system. First he devises a chart of accounts. That is, he discusses your business and your informational needs. Then he will help you decide how much detail is appropriate for your business because it is possible to have too little or too much. If you have too little, you may have to go back through all your basic records at the end of the year to accumulate the information you need for your tax returns and financial statements. On the other hand, sometimes those clients who want to have an account for everything become lost in the detail, making preparation of financial statements excessively complex and time-consuming.

As a minimum, you should keep track of sales in terms of meaningful categories. If you have different gross margins for different types of sales, break down sales according to these divisions. Then, knowing the margin for each type of sale and the sales volume, a little arithmetic will tell you what the cost of sales should be and what the gross profit should be. You don't have to wait to take inventory at the end of the year to see where you stand.

An accountant can also help in setting up the "chart of accounts" by helping you decide which are meaningful departments. That is, you want to break up the accounts so that each responsible individual in your organization has the information he needs, and you also want to be able to judge his financial performance. Thus, you are faced with allocating costs among departments. Certain costs will fall naturally into one department or another—the sales manager is responsible for sales expense; the production manager, for production labor. But there are a number of overhead costs that are difficult to allocate. Probably the important thing is to avoid getting carried away with the allocating. Each supervisor should be responsible for his own operation and the costs he can control; you as the manager are the one who controls the overhead costs.

Bookkeeping

An accountant can be of help in recruiting and training bookkeeping personnel. There is an important distinction between assisting in recruiting and training bookkeeping personnel and in providing bookkeeping services. Many CPAs and public accountants do keep books; our firm does so upon occasion. But the type of professional services I am suggesting here are those that start once the bookkeeping is complete and the financial statements are prepared.

Recently I gave a talk to a group of businessmen about the services a CPA can provide. Afterwards, one man came up to me and asked, "Is there any ethical prohibition against an accountant's giving advice and talking about my statement with me?" Apparently his accountant would produce the statements and simply mail them to him at the end of the month. The businessman would have preferred some interpretation and advice based on these statements. As I see our job, the smallest, least professional part is putting the numbers together. The professional work starts afterwards—it is a matter of how you use the numbers and what action you take based upon them.

Now, of course, I realize that the client must get his statement put together; we are able to recommend service bureaus and bookkeepers if we do not provide the service ourselves. However, when a company gets to a certain size, it is important that it have its own internal bookkeeping. At that point, we help to hire and orient the bookkeeper.

Financing

Probably the most significant assistance an accountant can render his client is in connection with obtaining financing. The accountant is familiar with the various sources of capital and can offer advice about which will fit the needs of the enterprise. He knows the criteria used by various lenders and investors in placing funds and can steer the client in the directions offering the greatest potential.

Once a specific request for funds has been made, the accountant can assist in the negotiations. His role is to gather and interpret the financial data needed to evaluate the request, often by preparing pro forma financial statements.

Pro forma financial statements project over some future period the effect of estimated and assumed financial trends and data on the financial statements—on an "as if" basis. The projections might be prepared quarter by quarter for the first two years and annually thereafter for the next three years. Or they might be month by month and then quarter by quarter, depending on the type of operation. An accountant's report on pro forma statements would indicate that he has checked the compilation of the pro forma statement and that, in his opinion, it has been properly compiled on the basis of the estimates and assumptions furnished by management (*not* by the accountant).

In preparing the pro forma, the accountant will go over with the manager or the prospective business owner each of the assumptions, starting with estimates of sales. The accountant may question whether the production facilities are adequate to service the sales projection or whether the cost of additional production facilities needs to be factored into the projection. He will question which expenses are fixed and which are variable. Certain items are going to be about the same regardless of the size of the business, while others are going to climb as the business volume increases. He will inquire as to seasonal pattern: a retail business starting up in January may be out of cash before its heavy November and December sales clear out inventories and bring in cash.

He will then take these estimates and assumptions and put them together into an income statement, a balance sheet, and a cash flow statement. Then he looks at the results. Do they make sense? If it looks as if profit is too high, there is probably something wrong. Maybe some costs have been overlooked. Maybe the sales projection is overly optimistic. On the other hand, let's say that projected income is not as great as the manager expected. Maybe his planned profit margin is too low, and he must consider whether to charge a higher price. If necessary, new information is factored into the projection, and the pro formas are reworked until the accountant and client are satisfied. As a practical matter, we find it most efficient to prepare a model of the operations using our time-sharing system so that the calculation is done automatically.

ACCOUNTING SERVICES AFTER START-UP

Once your business is started, there are many other services an accountant can perform.

Income Tax Returns

Preparation of federal and state income tax returns doesn't sound very glamorous. It is not fun, as you know, to fill out your own income tax returns. But the point I would like to make is that the accountant does more than simply enter the numbers in the slots. There are a number of very important tax elections to be made when you start the business or when you enter into a new type of transaction. It is in advising as to these tax elections and in submitting the proper paperwork for each that the accountant makes his contribution. For example:

1. One very significant election for a corporation is what accounting period to use. You should use a period that fits your natural business year. Don't automatically take the calendar year. If you are busiest in January and if receivables and inventory are high then, it is better to wait until March or April to end the fiscal year. This important election is made on the initial return; to make a change thereafter, you have to get permission from the Commissioner of Internal Revenue.

2. Another election is accounting method—cash or accrual. Most of you in starting a manufacturing business would probably choose the accrual method. But there are a number of service businesses in which it may be to your benefit from a tax viewpoint to report on a cash basis. Again, you do this by filing initially on the method elected. If you want to make a change later, you have to get IRS permission.

3. Another is organization expenses. You can elect at the time of filing your initial return to write them off over a five-year period, but you have to attach a statement to your tax return stating the election. Once you do this, it is an irrevocable election.

4. You can also elect methods for deducting bad debts and computing depreciation. Once you make an election, you are pretty well locked in. It is not impossible to change, but to do so can be difficult or costly.

Payroll Tax Returns

We recently had one of our tax specialists gather for us all the various payroll tax reporting forms. We came up with a stack an inch thick. Our conclusion was to recommend that our clients use a service bureau or a bank payroll system and let them worry about the complications. I know that many companies in the past have avoided using a bank payroll system because they felt that they would lose the use of the payroll money and the payroll tax funds in the interim. This just isn't the case any longer because the trend is to require earlier deposits of withholding tax. In fact, if you withhold more than a couple of hundred dollars in a month, you have to make a deposit. You just can't depend on tax funds for operating; the IRS takes a dim view of the practice. In making projections, incidentally, we usually assume that payroll costs and payroll tax costs are paid during the month in which they are incurred.

Tax Planning

Tax planning to save or defer income taxes can be very important, especially to accountants. If we didn't perform such service, we'd all be working a hundred hours a week during January through April and not at all the rest of the year. If nothing else, we encourage tax planning because it is good for our business. And hopefully, our tax planning is good for your business.

For instance, consider the president (who may also be the controlling shareholder) of a small corporation. He wants to maximize his salary, which is deductible for the corporation, so that there is only one tax paid. His object is to avoid payment in the form of dividends and to leave as much in earnings in the corporation as possible. The IRS, of course, is well aware of this desire and is always on the alert for unreasonable salaries and unreasonable accumulation of earnings. Your accountant, once he has finished your return, should discuss with you your salary allowance for the year, whether you can justify a higher one, whether you should reduce it, the level of earnings that have accumulated, and whether there is adequate documentation to show the need for such accumulated earnings.

Another possibility is that of switching to a Subchapter S corporation. Here the income of the business goes right through to the owner, eliminating one layer of tax; in effect, the corporation is treated as a partnership. This possibility must be considered well in advance of the time of filing your returns.

AUDIT SERVICES

Another, if not the most, important service provided by an accountant is the audit. When you get to a point where your company goes public, you are going to have to have an audit. The Securities Exchange Commission and the stock exchanges require it. You may also find that your bank will require it. Even if you don't go public, once the company reaches a certain size, it is required to file audited statements with the SEC. This applies if you have $1 million in assets and over 500 shareholders.

Distinction between Audited and Unaudited Statements

There is another class of services that we refer to as "preparation of unaudited statements," which should be distinguished from audited statements. The difference, essentially, is that unaudited statements do not require the accountant to perform all the independent verification demanded by audited statements. However, an unaudited financial statement can be very useful to the individual businessman. You may feel that you can trust your employees, that your receivables don't need to be verified with the customer, or that your inventory is on hand and you don't need an accountant to observe it. But still, you may want statements drawn up that are in accordance with "generally accepted accounting principles," and that make all the necessary disclosures. If so, ask your accountant to prepare an unaudited statement from the books. In doing so, he would exercise due care to see that there is proper disclosure and that the principles used are appropriate.

SEC Requirements

If you ever go public, you will come under the scrutiny of the Securities and Exchange Commission. Their interest is that the prospectus has in it the necessary disclosures to avoid misleading the investing public. In the prospectus, the SEC will require audited financial statements of your last three years of operation. In other words, when you are ready to go public, you have to be in a position to furnish audited statements for the last three years, so you should look ahead. In many cases, an accountant can go back and audit retroactively. That is, he can go back, test your books in the last two years before this one, and properly state that he has audited for three years. The only thing he cannot audit retroactively is inventory.

If your business has significant amounts of inventory, the accountant is required by his profession and his own good judgment to observe these inventories to see that they really exist and that your inventory-taking procedures are appropriate. This, of course, he cannot do once the inventory has moved—he cannot observe an inventory that was there three years ago. Therefore, if you are planning to go public in a few years, make sure you have an auditor come in once a year and observe your physical inventory-taking.

A last point about going public: Before they go public, most businessmen see minimizing taxes as their main goal. Once they go public, this objective changes to maximizing profit. For instance, when you are struggling to get started, you want to keep your taxable profit low, so you try to place as low a value on inventory as possible. When you go public, then you would like to have a higher inventory valuation. Ordinarily, the accounting profession does not look kindly upon your having the best of both possible worlds—it certainly would not approve a change that has the effect of increasing reported income. In this one case, however, when you go from privately held to publicly held, there is a one-time "dispensation" in recognition of the fact that your accounting needs are now different. You can expect at this point to make some changes in accounting method; your accountant can advise you as to what might be considered. His only concern is that you stay within the bounds set by the profession and his own good judgment.

MANAGEMENT ADVISORY SERVICES

There are a number of areas other than tax or audit where the accountant can aid the businessman. These are commonly termed management advisory services. Some of the more typical services of interest to the new enterprise are mentioned below.

Information Systems

The accountant can help in devising internal reporting forms and methods. The degree of formality of these internal reports and their frequency depends very much on the layers of management. If the business is a one-man operation, the proprietor doesn't need a report every month. But if there are a couple of layers of management, the top man may want formal statements every month or at least every quarter. Management reports that are needed to plan and control operations are not necessarily those that should go out to the shareholders.

Budgeting

The accountant can stress to you the need for an operating budget, having seen circumstances where companies floundered because they did not have operating and cash budgets. Even where budgets are used, all too often the objective becomes shaping the facts to fit the budget rather than vice versa. With proper planning and a positive approach, the budget can be a working tool to assist you rather than hamper you.

The accountant can analyze your cash flow and relate it to the capital needs of the business—that is, the working capital for sales expansion, new equipment, etc. From this analysis he can point out needs for short-term borrowing or permanent capital or, on the other hand, the availability of excess cash for investment or dividends.

Other Services

An accountant can help in analyzing your profit structure and in helping to decide prices—that is, he helps to define what your full costs are and what your marginal costs are. You must know how low a price you can put on a product and still recover out-of-pocket cost. You also need to know what price you have to sell it for in the long run in order to make a profit.

An accountant can help you in evaluating data processing methods. For many a medium-sized company, an elaborate data processing installation may be as much of an extravagance as a corporate jet may be for a major company. The accountant can look at your needs objectively and see what makes sense in your situation.

An accountant can help you in deciding whether your inventory and your receivables are in line and reasonable for the size and scope of your business. He can help in isolating those few inventory items which account for the bulk of the inventory and should be carefully controlled. He can help in setting minimum sizes of orders and optimum reorder points, and he can evaluate whether you should lease or buy equipment.

PLAN A LONG TERM ASSOCIATION

Use your accountant. Once you retain him, take advantage of his skills. Get somebody with whom you feel comfortable, someone you will call when you have a decision to make. Keep your accountant involved. Have him meet your banker and your attorney.

Recognize, however, that all this takes his time and that his fee is based on the time he spends. An important point when you're working with an accountant is that, although his time is money, he has the time available to invest just as you are making an investment in your business. The risk-reward ratio of your business is not the same for him as for you. You have higher risk, higher reward. His reward cannot be so high. He cannot, if he is going to become your auditor, hold stock in your company. The most he can hope for is to obtain a valued client. If you can convince him that you've got a potentially successful company, he will be willing to invest a lot of his time in you. And if you can sell your accountant on your prospects, then you are in a good position to sell investors, suppliers, and customers.

Nine

Bank Financing

Harry Goodfriend

DEPOSITORY FUNCTIONS

A bank—any bank—has a very restrictive area within which it may make loans. Under present U.S. laws and by traditional practices, a bank is a lender and may not assume an equity position—an ownership interest—in its borrowers. It will not and cannot become a partner with the businessmen to whom it makes loans.

Furthermore, the funds available to a bank for lending purposes are limited with regard to source. Primarily, loanable funds come from deposits received from the bank's customers. These funds are very simply divided into two types: checking-account deposits and interest-bearing accounts, more commonly known as savings accounts.

In recent years, bankers have been innovative in acquiring additional funds for loan purposes. This has been made necessary by the rapid expansion of our economy and the diversion of depositor funds to investments in the stock market, mutual funds, governmental securities, and the like. Thus, traditional savings-deposit sources have been disappearing. To offset this diversion of funds, banks have begun encouraging the purchase of large—in

Harry Goodfriend is the President of the Bank of Santa Clara, California and former Senior Vice President of the Crocker National Bank.

amounts of $100,000 or more—certificates of deposit. These are offered at interest rates substantially higher than is permitted by regulations governing conventional savings accounts.

This is in direct competition with the government securities market, the commercial paper issuers, and other relatively high-yield but short-term investment instruments. Also but to a lesser degree, the largest banks have sold their notes directly to investors. This really is little different from commercial paper as used by the larger corporations except perhaps in the manner of marketing. Banks are able to sell their notes directly to investors. For the most part, corporations sell their commercial paper through specialized brokers.

The handling of deposits by banks is subject to very rigid regulations designed to protect the depositor. Most of these rules are an outgrowth of the problems of the 1930's and the revised banking laws of that period, including creation of the Federal Deposit Insurance Corporation for the protection of bank deposits to a maximum insured amount for each depositor in each bank. Presently, banks must maintain a reserve requirement of 16% to 17%, depending on where the particular bank is located, on each dollar of demand (checking) account balance. If a bank holds a federal charter making it a national bank, this reserve is carried on deposit at a Federal Reserve Bank without interest and earns the depositing bank nothing. If the bank is a state-organized institution, the required reserve may be in the form of specified bonds, usually national or state issues, and may earn whatever the particular bond investment yields.

In addition to this reserve on checking-account deposits, the bank must have cash on hand to meet its depositors' daily needs —for their pocket money or business requirements. This varies from 5% to 7% of all demand deposits. Thus, we find that from 22¢ to 25¢ of each $1 deposited in a checking account is set aside for either reserves or till cash.

Savings deposits, because they are less likely to be withdrawn for day-to-day needs, have a substantially lesser reserve requirement and, of course, a lesser till cash need.

This means, very simply, that a bank has only about 75¢ out of each $1 on deposit available for loans or investments—the exact amount depends on how much of the total deposits are in each category of account (checking or savings). From such money handling, the bank must realize the income necessary to pay interest on its savings accounts, wages to its employees, and all the other normal expenses of any business. Hopefully, there will be something left over; if so, the bank then has to pay income taxes as well as dividends to its shareholders since they are entitled to a return on their investment. If the bank is to grow, it must retain some part of its earnings to enable it to keep pace with a growing economy and the demand for increased services.

I believe you can now appreciate that banks operate on a very narrow margin of income over expenses. Truly, we bankers can say ours is a business of high volume and narrow profit margin. Therefore, it is plain to see that a bank cannot undertake much risk when it makes loans; there just isn't any possibility of offsetting more than a fraction of 1% of income against losses.

THE LENDING FUNCTION

This narrow profit margin we have been discussing has a positive effect not only on the lending of funds but also on the low rate of interest charged for the loan.

Lending is the primary business of a bank. Loan interest is, after all, the principal source of bank income. The types of loans made by a bank are related very directly to the types of deposits it holds. For example, a bank with a high proportion of savings balances will make more real estate loans than a bank having a high proportion of checking account deposits. And a bank having a large number of individuals as depositors will make more personal installment loans than will a bank with a large number of business depositors.

Fundamentally, banks make loans to businesses for their short-term seasonal or cyclical needs—to supplement the capital investment of the owners of the business. To a banker, a short-term loan is for a period of 90 days, possibly up to six months. The time for which the loan is written is important and is related wholly to the use of the borrowed money. Let me illustrate. In every business, there is a normal cycle between the time raw materials are acquired and the finished product is made and sold. A football program salesman buys programs Sunday morning and sells them before game time for cash; he has completed a full cycle from purchase to sales and collection in a few hours. On the other hand, a manufacturer of umbrellas buys raw materials—the steel, plastic, and other material—in the spring and manufactures these diverse raw materials into umbrellas for delivery to retailers in early fall for sale at retail when the rainy season starts. This cycle could be as long as nine months.

When you buy raw materials in the marketplace, a part of the cost depends upon when the buyer pays for the purchase. In every such transaction, there is a fee charged, directly or indirectly, for the time between purchase and payment. Customarily, the terms are stated as 2% tenth day, meaning if the invoice is paid by the tenth day of the month following purchase the buyer may subtract 2% of the total. This can add up to a lot of profit in a year, even when it is necessary to borrow from a bank to take advantage of the 2% discount as offered. The same thing occurs when we, as consumers, use our credit cards. If we pay promptly, there is no added charge; if not, we pay up to 1.5% per month on the money owed on the purchase.

No bank is going to lend money unless the use of such borrowed money is profitable to the borrower. That is to say, the discount taken must equal a larger amount than the interest charged by the bank for the loan. This might be described as Rule Number 1 of lending.

Review of Types of Loans

Bank loans are as varied in type as the needs of the borrowers they serve. In the space allocated here, we can attempt to characterize loans only in some basic, rather generalized terms.

First, most bank loans are unsecured. It is not customary for a banker to make a loan simply because it is secured. Rather, loans are made because the borrower is assumed to be honest, intending to repay the debt from profits earned in the normal conduct of his affairs, without necessitating the sale of the security.

As stated earlier, most bank loans for business purposes are for short periods of time—three months or so in length. Such loans suit the needs of most businesses for meeting peak periods of activity—the Christmas season for the toy merchant; the summer vacation season for the lake resort operator. As long as the borrowing period is of short duration, neither the lender nor the borrower has much difficulty in projecting the probable repayment date. But as the seasonal aspect or need period gets longer, the ability to forecast repayment accurately becomes less certain. Obviously it is easier to know what is going to happen tomorrow than to know what is going to happen six months or a year from now.

On the other hand, economic conditions that have existed almost since the end of World War II have resulted in increased demand for working capital as well as for owners' investment in business—both small one-man operations and large corporations with thousands of employees (and probably thousands of shareholder-owners as well). This financial demand has created a need for increased borrowings and for longer maturity periods than had previously been considered normal. Thus, a new type of loan arrangement has come into use—a "term loan." This is exactly what the name implies—a loan for a specified period of time with specific arrangements for repayment.

Term loans, whether in large or modest dollar amounts, require more formality of arrangement between lender and borrower because verbal or informal understandings are often forgotten in a short time. Thus, the lender is likely to demand a written agreement. In the case of a sizable loan, the agreement may be a very complex legal contract. For a smaller loan, the agreement may be a brief memorandum which both lender and debtor sign. However, whether the agreement is formal or informal, the purpose is the same—to document the conditions under which the loan is made and to avoid future misunderstandings. All such arrangements will include stipulations covering the ownership and management of the borrower's business, the repayment arrangements, other borrowings, major expenditures, capital withdrawal, and the like. The purpose is to substitute exact agreements to compensate for the inability of accurately predicting future happenings.

The usefulness of term loans is particularly apparent when the borrower needs to expand his facilities, buy expensive capital equipment, take on new activities, or respond to exceptionally rapid growth in sales volume. In many instances, term loans have merely become a form of installment lending; but they do provide a workable solution to many inflation-related problems and are widely accepted by both bank lenders and borrowers.

Certain types of businesses—typically those with easily identified, easily handled, and readily marketable inventory—borrow on a "secured" basis. For example, a dealer in gold or other precious metals, furs, sugar or grains, and the like could easily borrow on a secured basis. In other words, if a lender can refer to a national market quotation in the daily newspaper to learn the value of a commodity and if he can repossess the goods and arrange their sale in an open market should such drastic measures prove necessary, then this type of inventory is generally acceptable as security for a loan. Since the risk involved in making secured loans of this type is low, interest rates tend also to be low. In many industries, such borrowing is regarded as a tradition of the trade.

The third and final basic type of loan is the installment loan most of us use when we buy an automobile for personal use. The most common example of this type of loan in business lending is in financing the purchase of new equipment, whether it be a passenger car, truck, or machinery. The equipment so financed must be standard, not custom made-to-order for one application only, and it must be easily identified by manufacturer's serial numbers or other means. Most loans of this type are for the purchase of new equipment. Frequently, it is the seller who arranges the financing through the lender as a convenience to the buyer in order to facilitate closing the sale. However, a borrower may also refinance existing, owned equipment on an installment basis. Loan terms may run as long as seven years when larger sums are involved. Customarily, the lender advances only a part of the resale value of the equipment; seldom if ever is the cost of the equipment fully financed.

While on the subject of secured lending, let's not overlook the fact that frequently the owners of businesses have assets in the form of marketable securities such as stocks, bonds, life insurance with cash surrender value, or other readily valued assets which they may not wish to sell but which they may use as collateral in order to borrow money for their business. Strictly speaking, this is not a business loan; but the purpose is the same and repayment is expected to flow from the profits of the business and not from the sale of the pledged collateral.

HOW TO GET ALONG WITH YOUR BANKER

In developing relationships with other people, particularly business relationships, one of the things you must do is sell—you must sell *yourself* as well as your products or services. So we apply our understanding of salesmanship to selling ourselves to our banker. This need not be difficult if we remember that the banker *wants* to do business with us. In fact, the banker *needs* to do business with us if *he* is to succeed.

Now let us look at the banker from his side of the desk so we can understand what he is thinking while he looks at us. A banker deals in very definite patterns; and with the use of specific tools, he makes his judgments about us as prospective borrowers. The criteria are the same irrespective of the nature or size of the business he is looking at. They are very simple and extremely practical things with which each of us is familiar.

The first thing a banker considers is character. He must judge above all else the honesty of the person across the desk. If in his opinion you are not honest, he won't lend you money. That is simply common sense. Next, he wants to be assured of your capacity to perform. That is, he wants assurance that you can handle profitably the funds you and he are talking about. Ability is something we do not have in equal quantity. Then he must consider the size of your dollar investment in your business activity. Remember that the banker is not allowed to become a partner with his borrowers. Thus, he has to know that your investment is adequate so that he can retain his position as a lender. Finally, he must decide whether business conditions justify the reasons you give for wanting to borrow. His decision is based on economic considerations, and an important part of his job is to keep in touch with the market conditions. He may very well know reasons why an expansion or other development in your affairs at that particular moment may not be in your best interests.

There you have the banker's judgment tools: character, capacity, capital, and conditions. These are known as the four "C's" of credit. There is another "C" which may be considered under some circumstances, as we discussed earlier. It is collateral. Is this a loan which should be secured?

Your job as a borrower in this series of judgments is to supply the input which permits intelligent decision-making. Therefore, let us look first at what goes into the banker's thought processes. Character is judged on two bases: what your paying record has been in the past and the overall impression you make on others as seen through the keen eyes of an observant banker. He gets this input from you by what you tell him about yourself: what you have done, how you did it, what you are doing and why, and what you plan to do. He will check references directly from names you give him and through credit-reference sources. During these revealing conversations, he will be judging your honesty as well as your abilities. In addition to conversation and credit checking, he will want financial information in the form of balance sheets, income and expense statements, a reconciliation of surplus (what happened to earnings), and cash flow projections—a three-word way of saying "budget."

The first of these, the statement, is like a photograph. It gives your financial picture at a given moment. The second, the income and expense exhibit, is more like a moving picture showing your progress from some point in the past through the present time. The reconciliation of surplus tells very simply what happened to your profit—did you spend it all, did you give it away, or did you reinvest it in the business? That old hateful budget—accountants call it the cash flow projection—indicates what you plan to do with your funds and the to-be-borrowed funds in the future and when you plan to do it.

I hope this discussion has persuaded you that you have a sales job to do when you approach your banker. You must be prepared to reveal much about yourself, your background, your present activities, and your aspirations. Also, the banker needs factual and current financial information, which you should be prepared to volunteer to him.

When you have done your homework, rehearsed your opening remarks, gotten together your financial exhibits, and are ready to approach the banker, don't overwhelm him. Be cool and calm; let him lead you into answering questions he has prepared himself to ask you. But don't be timid; or worse yet, don't let him intimidate you! Invite him to visit your place of business to see what you do and to meet your associates. If he is a good banker, this visit is important because he is a trained observer and will notice housekeeping, inventory control, and employee attitudes toward you. He will be getting acquainted.

Having done these things and having decided that the banker is someone with whom you can do business, you are ready to talk directly about borrowing. Tell him you need so many dollars to use for such and such purpose, and you will pay the loan back on a named date from monies received from collection of receivables or whatever the source may be.

Once the loan is made, all is sweetness and light—up until the time when the loan is about to become due and you haven't quite made your objective. Don't panic; and worst of all, don't stay away from the banker. Proper handling is quite the opposite. Get yourself together, go see the banker and tell him you can't pay on time because . . . . But within a week, a month, or whatever time it may take, you will be able to pay up. Ask for an extension and, if you need more money, say so. If you do this before your debt is past due and worrying him, what else can your banker do but smile back and say "yes"?

These sales tips are so very simple it would embarrass me to suggest them to you if years in the banking business had not taught me that all too frequently they are forgotten. Salesmanship! Such a glorious endeavor and so fundamental to all we do, whether it is wooing a bride, convincing a clerk to increase production, getting the other poker-players to stay in the pot—or convincing the banker he should lend us money.

We live in a complex and changing world socially, politically, and economically. To survive, we need to put our very best efforts into all we do and to work together. Whenever we find our efforts being thwarted—by a banker who doesn't listen or who doesn't understand—we must go elsewhere to accomplish our objectives. Remember, bankers are human with all the good and bad faults of all men. In some states, they are on nearly every street corner. Take your pick.

Ten

Accounts Receivable Financing

Julius Lustig

Transactions in the factoring and accounts receivable financing industry represent an annual volume of well over $40 *billion,* a level exceeded only by the commercial banking industry. On the basis of this volume, it is readily apparent that factoring and accounts receivable financing constitute a sound and practical means of providing the capital that is so vital to the success of small business and the growth of our economy.

Although the annual dollar volume represented by these transactions is enormous, a disturbingly large number of businessmen remain unfamiliar with the industry. Its vast potential resources, available to provide the liquidity of working capital to an endless variety of businesses, go untapped by those very businesses that most need these resources.

Ignorance of the industry is so widespread that Clyde W. Phelps of the University of Southern California made special mention of the problem in his book, *The Role of Factoring in Modern Business Financing* (Commercial Credit Co., Baltimore, 1956). He stated that the query "Exactly what is factoring?" would be a very

Julius Lustig, a financial consultant based in San Jose, California, has been active in the financial industry for over twenty years. The founder and former President of Business Factors, Inc., he is also a former Vice President of the Amfac Commercial Finance Corporation and a former Director of the National Commercial Finance Conference.

safe question to use on a quiz program if the sponsor was reluctant to give away too much of his prize money. Further, the term *factoring* is often confused with the term *accounts receivable financing.* It is therefore appropriate that the difference in the commercial usage of these very important terms be made clear at the outset.

FACTORING

Factoring started in American colonial days when shipments made by manufacturers (mostly textile mills) from the old country created worrisome credit and collection problems due to the slowness of transportation and communication. The factory salesmen and representatives in this country originally supplied the necessary credit information and often would guarantee the accounts. The term *factor,* derived from the Latin verb *facere,* to make or do, literally means "he who gets things done." These colonial factory salesmen were the first factors. In the late 1800's and early 1900's, the selling function was gradually discontinued, and the factor became a specialist in providing credit information and actually buying and financing manufacturers' invoiced shipments.

Thus, when a producer supplies goods or services to a customer, the factor actually buys the customer's invoice or other evidence of an obligation to pay (usually referred to as an *account receivable*). The factor then becomes the owner of this account receivable. The client's customer (the account debtor to whom the invoice is billed) is then notified that the invoice has been assigned and is payable only to the factor. Thereafter, the factor does the bookkeeping and, if necessary, the collection work. The factor thus relieves his client of the chores and expenses involved in maintaining credit, bookkeeping, and collection departments.

Factoring charges customarily are based on credit risk, dollar volume, number of invoices, and overall work involved.

ACCOUNTS RECEIVABLE FINANCING

Accounts receivable financing differs from factoring in that the lender does not *buy* the accounts. Instead, he accepts them as security—collateral—for a loan with full recourse to the manufacturer or client if the client's customer fails to honor the obligation. Whereas the factor usually notifies the client's customer that the accounts have been assigned, the lender providing accounts receivable financing does not. Depending upon the terms of the lender/client agreement, the lender may or may not perform credit checking, bookkeeping, and collection services. Usually these functions remain the work of the client.

While an increasing number of banks now provide loans where accounts receivable are offered as security, the bulk of this type of financing is handled by commercial finance companies.

From the preceding discussion, it may be seen that factors and commercial finance companies are organizations engaged primarily in the business of making loans and advances to manufacturers, wholesalers, and distributors where accounts receivable are pledged as collateral. The role of the factor and the commercial finance company are very much alike in that they are both in a position to make more operating cash available than may usually be obtained through unsecured bank credit. Now that we have clearly defined the differences between factoring and accounts receivable financing, let's move forward with our discussion of accounts receivable financing since that is the subject of this chapter.

Who Uses Accounts Receivable Financing?

Business firms of all sizes find accounts receivable financing useful and profitable when the available capital and cash flow are not adequate to meet their operating and growth needs. This is often true when, for whatever reasons, the business may not meet the qualifications for unsecured bank credit or may need funds in excess of the authorized line of bank credit. Capital for the financing of company growth is the touch-stone of a successful business operation. Cash is as important an ingredient of manufactured products as are production methods and materials. Just as new methods and processes must be found to meet the demands of modern technology, cash must be found to supply the requirements of industrial growth when the money supply is tight.

Who Qualifies?

Generally, the lender prefers a manufacturing company with a tangible product rather than a service business where disputes with the customer are more likely. Also, firms in the construction industry may not qualify because of progress billings, lien rights, and retentions which may affect the lender's security interest. Lenders do not arbitrarily decline these accounts, however, but usually consider each applicant on its own merits.

Banks, as custodians of public funds, are strictly regulated by federal and state governments in making loans. To qualify for bank lending, a business must generally demonstrate a record of profitability plus a reasonable net worth indicating the ability to repay loans out of future profits.

While the commercial finance company likes to see a healthy net worth and profitability, it is able to look beyond the client's financial statement in order to establish the credit worthiness of the client's customer, for the loan will be liquidated by the customer's payment of the account.

A banker always reviews a loan applicant in terms of the three "C's": character, capacity (management capability), and capital. Since a commercial finance company frequently undertakes higher-risk loans than are involved in bank financing, character is the criterion of primary importance. Presumably, the commercial lender is secured by the legal protection provided by the assignment of the accounts receivable. He is, nevertheless, extremely vulnerable to the issuance of fraudulent invoices should the client prove to be dishonest.

In evaluating a potential client, a commercial lender also considers the size of the business, the average dollar amount of the invoices issued, the payment terms of the invoices, the credit standing of the potential client's customers, seasonal variations in business volume characteristic of the industry, bookkeeping and accounting procedures employed, tax problems, and other matters that may have bearing on the credit worthiness of the business.

Invested Capital and Cash Flow

Cash flow is the life blood of a business. However, money utilized for cash flow must be differentiated from invested or equity capital, which is put into the business from savings, borrowed from friends and relatives, or acquired through the sale of stock. As a business grows, equity capital is normally invested in machinery, inventory, and goods already shipped to customers where these goods have not yet been paid for (accounts receivable). While these items are assets of the business, they obviously are not as liquid as cash.

Cash flow involves the turnover of capital. The cash flows from liquid reserves in a bank account into raw materials inventory into finished goods inventory into accounts receivable and, finally, back into cash in the bank. This constantly revolving cycle is perhaps the most important element in assuring the survival of a business. Any business in the process of maintaining sustained growth will require more and more working capital to meet its cash flow needs.

How is Additional Working Capital Acquired?

A businessman has several options available to him to satisfy his need for additional working capital.

1. He can take on a partner. However, partners often create more problems than they solve.
2. He can sell stock (assuming, of course, that the business is incorporated). This can be a very difficult, time-consuming, and costly procedure; and in addition, the founder's equity will be reduced.
3. He can borrow from a bank. However, he may not be able to meet the banker's standards to qualify for a loan; or he may need more capital than the banker is willing to provide.
4. He can borrow from a commercial finance company, pledging his accounts receivable as collateral for a loan.

Next to cash, the accounts receivable are the most important liquid asset the business has. Therefore, in a tight money situation, it makes good business sense to consider the services of a commercial finance company and turn these receivables into cash.

The basic service provided in accounts receivable financing is to increase the supply of operating cash available to a firm by speeding the turnover of working capital—particularly that working capital represented by an investment in accounts receivable.

The Security Agreement

The detailed terms and conditions of the relationship between the lender and the client, or borrower, are specified in a *Security Agreement.* The heart of the agreement is the requirement that the client will not present any invoice for payment unless the merchandise (or service) so billed has been completed and delivered. In addition, the agreement specifies the rights of the lender: he may verify accounts, set credit limits, require periodic financial statements including a monthly aging of the accounts receivable, audit the client's financial records, and initiate other reasonable actions to protect his loan.

Under the terms of the agreement, the borrower is required to make certain warranties regarding the financial status of the business and the validity of his invoices. Also, the borrower is typically required to guarantee such warranties personally. The most important warranty is that all payments received on accounts pledged to the lender will be forwarded promptly to the lender. In order legally to validate the assignment of accounts receivable to the lender, a notice must be filed in accordance with the regulations of the Uniform Commercial Code.

The Lending Process

The lender usually will advance up to 80% of the outstanding current receivables. (Accounts past due 90 days and over are not eligible.) After the initial loan is made against the existing accounts already on the client's books, loan payments are made to the client on a daily or weekly basis as new invoices are billed. Payment to the client is usually made within 24 to 48 hours after copies of the invoices are received by the lender.

At any given time, a reserve amounting to 20% of the outstanding receivables is held as an allowance for contingencies such as returned merchandise, disputes that may arise regarding quality of the merchandise, invoice terms, or nonpayment of the account by the client's customer.

In our earlier discussion of factoring, we indicated that the true, "old-line" factor buys accounts receivable at a discount and *without recourse.* In other words, if the client's customer fails to pay, the factor suffers the loss. However, in the case of accounts receivable financing, money is advanced to the client *with recourse.* In such a situation, the reserve in the client's account is charged if one of his customers becomes delinquent by more than 60 to 90 days after the due date in accordance with the terms of the Security Agreement.

What Is the Cost of Accounts Receivable Financing?

The lowest interest rate charged by a bank is the rate extended to its most favored customers. This rate is referred to as the *prime* rate. The interest rates charged by commercial finance companies are usually higher than the rates charged by banks and may run 6% or more above the prime rate. However, the overall interest paid by the borrower may prove to be very little more—or even less—than the cost of conventional forms of borrowing. In particular, banks usually lend money on the basis of 60- or 90-day notes and may require the maintenance of compensating balances of 15% to 20% of the amount borrowed, thereby reducing the actual loan funds available to the borrower and, in effect, increasing the interest paid. In financing accounts receivable, loan interest is computed on the actual daily loan balance outstanding; and of course this balance will change with the ebb and flow of advances and collections. For example, let's say that a firm borrows $50,000 from a bank for 90 days at the prevailing interest rate. Quite possibly, the loan funds will be placed on deposit in the firm's checking account a week or more before they are actually used. Later, a week to ten days before the note is due, the firm may have sufficient money on deposit to pay off the loan. Rather than do so, the firm may wait until the note matures before paying. Many variations of similar circumstances occur in practically all business firms during the course of a year.

In financing accounts receivable, the firm usually assigns invoices and draws funds only when money is needed. Furthermore, the daily loan balance is automatically reduced when incoming checks in payment of assigned accounts are transmitted to the lender daily as received. (Remember, this transmittal is a primary requirement of the Security Agreement!) This daily transmittal enables the firm to maintain a minimum loan balance, thereby resulting in lower interest charges.

Depending on the needs of the client, there are many case histories proving that the overall cost of accounts receivable financing can be less than the cost of borrowing from a bank on a fixed-term basis in spite of the fact that interest rates charged by commercial finance companies are generally higher than bank rates. The comparatively higher interest rate for receivables financing is due to the higher cost of administering the loan:

1. The collateral (invoices) must be systematically processed, recorded, and controlled.
2. Daily shipments and payments received on prior receivables make for numerous changes in the loan balance.
3. A specialized staff must be maintained to conduct credit checks and analyze the aging of accounts.
4. Periodic audits and account verifications are costly.

When any businessman is comparing interest rates, he does well to determine exactly what he is comparing. John L. Glaros, Vice President of the First National Bank of San Jose, had this to say while speaking at a seminar on the subject of comparative interest rates: "Perhaps the highest price any businessman ever pays for money is the price he pays for lack of it . . . for the amount of money obtainable may often be a more important consideration than the mere rate paid for the money."

FINANCIAL DEPARTMENT STORE

In addition to financing receivables, commercial lenders have come to be known as "Department Stores of Finance" because of their flexible loan policies. In fact, an article on receivables financing in the November, 1962 issue of *Dun's Review* bears the title "Department Stores of Finance." Combination or "package" loans are often made which include loans for inventory or advances to purchase inventory in seasonal businesses; loans for equipment; and funds for mergers, acquisitions, or special situations. Generally, bankers can provide just about every type of funding possible—and certainly you should use bank credit lines to the utmost—but in almost all of the above situations the commercial lender can provide more funds than can be made available by a bank.

SUMMARY

Now let's summarize the advantages of accounts receivable financing:

1. Cash available as fast as merchandise delivered.
2. Continuous source of capital to meet day-to-day operating overhead.
3. Cash for special buys, inventory, and equipment.

4. Take advantage of cash discounts. (This alone can often offset interest cost.)
5. Protect and improve credit rating.
6. Increase volume by carrying more and larger receivables.
7. Extend longer terms when necessary to obtain desirable business.
8. Flexibility-borrowing capacity increases as sales increase.
9. Avoid taking in partners.
10. Avoid equity dilution by sale of stock.
11. No long-term fixed debt—loan is self-liquidating.
12. Pay only for funds as needed and in use.
13. Better projections of sales and operations because cash available as needed to meet projections.
14. Devote time to profit-making ideas instead of to money problems.
15. Increase cash flow turnover—profits made on turnover of working capital, thereby increasing profits on invested capital.

FINANCING TOMORROW'S GROWTH

William M. Stocker, Jr. and Robert N. Sheets in "How to Find Money for Your Business" put it this way:

"As business faces a period when money is the tightest in twenty years, and when capital reserves are thin as consumer demand and industrial growth are on the upswing, it is important to know where dollars are found and the cost of obtaining them.

"What causes tight money? The main trouble is that there just are not enough workmen and materials to go around to build all the projects businessmen think up in our present growth economy. Thus, businessmen bid higher and higher for the materials and services that are available—and borrow more and more. Demand for capital exceeds the supply of capital. To prevent a serious inflationary price spiral, the Federal Reserve Board has recently raised the cost of borrowing. Now banks must either charge their customers higher interest or themselves cut down on borrowing from the Federal Reserve. Businessmen must re-evaluate their projects in terms of the higher cost and lenders must look more closely at ability to repay loans and charges. Industry makes heavier demands on the money sources other than banks and this money supply is reduced. Thus the market tightens; the pinch is on credit.

"Today the stigma of borrowing is gone. The reason is simple: Few firms can avoid it. Also, both borrowers and lenders recognize that it is a business transaction in which the borrower is paying an agreed fee, "rent" if you like, for the use of the money. Loans are rarely given as a favor begged. Provided only that the borrower can show an acceptable ability to repay the loan, or is willing to compensate the lender for the risk involved, there is no reason why he should hesitate to ask for money.

"If you need funds, call the lender you select and make a date to meet. He'll be glad to see you."

You will note that the above quote appeared as an editorial in *American Machinist* on November 19, 1956!!

REFERENCES

For more information on this subject, the following books and articles are recommended:

1. Clyde W. Phelps, *The Role of Factoring in Modern Business Financing* (Baltimore: Commercial Credit Company, 1956).

2. Monroe R. Lazere, ed. *Commercial Financing* (New York: The Ronald Press, 1968).

3. "Department Stores of Finance," *Dun's Review*, November, 1962.

4. William M. Stocker, Jr. and Robert N. Sheets, "How to Find Money for Your Business," *American Machinist,* November 19, 1956, pp. 138-39.

5. Milton P. Kupfer, "Accounts Receivable Financing: A Legal and Pracçtical Look-See," *The Practical Lawyer,* November and December, 1956.

Eleven

Equipment Leasing

Robert P. McGrath

Starting your own business can quite possibly be one of the most exciting events that you will ever experience in your lifetime. If it is done correctly, it can be just one hell of a lot of fun.

BACKGROUND OF OUR COMPANY

Now before I get into my comments on leasing, I'd like to give you a little background on our own company and how we started in business. A few years ago, we decided to become manufacturers' representatives for a line of electronic test instruments. This was a good business; we made money. In fact, we made more money than we would have made had we been working for someone else. But we knew that over the long haul, this was not the final way to go. We knew that we eventually had to put a capital base under our corporation. So we investigated the various possibilities—manufacturing or services. We chose services; and we chose a new aspect, which was the short-term rental of electronic test instruments.

Robert P. McGrath is the former President and founder of Metric Resources Corporation, a nationwide equipment leasing organization.

Our company has grown rapidly over the past five years. We now have offices and warehouses in some eight or nine cities throughout the U.S. We have become one of the major forces in the industry. We operate primarily under the name of "Leasametric." At the same time, we have moved into full pay-out equipment leasing.

TWO ASSUMPTIONS

Now I am going to make a couple of assumptions about you. Assumption Number 1: Probably you either have a technical background or will be involved in a corporation that we would define as a technology corporation. Assumption Number 2: You are going to need capital equipment in the operation of your new business. So I am going to talk about two aspects of leasing: leasing as a general aspect and the significance of leasing from a specialized company that deals in the commodity you happen to be interested in.

WHY LEASE?

When you get down to it, there are really only three ways that you can get the equipment you want. Way Number 1: You have lots of money that is burning a hole in your pocket and you lay out cold hard cash. Way Number 2: You go to the bank and borrow the money. Way Number 3: You lease the equipment. Let's examine each of these.

Cash Purchase

First of all, let's assume that you have plenty of money in your pocket. Borrowing is not a problem. Cash purchase is, of course, the cheapest way to get the equipment. It's a luxury that probably few of us can afford, and it isn't necessarily the smartest way to do things. If you have that much money, you should probably be going after your business objectives more aggressively by putting your money into research, product development, or marketing instead of tying yourself down with physical assets. It is also important that you reserve a certain amount of cash as long as you can because you don't know when or if you may need it in the future.

Bank Loan

The second way, of course, is to borrow money from the bank. A lot of people do it this way; in fact, it's probably the most common way. There is one distinct advantage to borrowing from the bank money with which to buy equipment—you may repay the loan over a long period of time. Now there is nothing wrong with this; in fact, it's pretty good. But there are a couple of things you should be aware of.

First of all, understand the real expense involved. If you are going to borrow money from the bank, the bank may require what is called a "compensating balance." For instance, if you are going to borrow $1,000 from the bank, it means that you may have to maintain something like $200 on deposit in the bank at all times. This has the net effect of raising your interest rate.

Secondly, when you wish to borrow from a bank in order to buy equipment, they invariably say, "Well, we think you ought to put 20% to 30% down; we'll finance the rest of it." That, again, has the result of raising your effective cost. What's even more important is that the bank may not want to lend you the money at all! That is not necessarily because you have a bad business plan or because you are a bad credit risk. It may simply be the nature of the bank. You remember that banks are primarily involved in short-term lending, and they refer to "resting the loan, cleaning it up once a year." Now after you have made and retired a number of short-term loans, you may qualify for what is called a "revolving line of credit." But often, you will find as a new company that this is impossible to obtain.

Lease Financing

The third way to obtain your equipment is by leasing. Leasing is fundamentally different from the other ways because the lessor is more concerned with the *use* of the equipment than he is with the *ownership* of the equipment. Similarly, *you* are concerned with using the equipment, not with owning it. Furthermore, through a combination of bank borrowing and leasing, you can have more cash available to you than you might otherwise. Then you can use the available money for the real things that you are concerned with—research, product development, marketing, etc.

ADVANTAGES OF LEASING

The philosophy of leasing is to bolster your cash and credit lines so that you have more money available for the things necessary to make your company grow. In other words, you are going to earn a higher return on your invested dollars by putting them into research and product development than you are by tying them up in equipment.

Expense Accounting

There are some traditional advantages in leasing. One is in "expense accounting." A lease is a business expense. In other words, it is like paying the electric bill, the telephone bill, even the garbage bill. It's a monthly expense; and therefore, it can be written off for business tax purposes very nicely.

Inflationary Hedge

Leasing is an inflationary hedge, as is borrowing. In other words, you're paying off the leased equipment in tomorrow's dollars and not today's, just as in the purchase of your own home, where you pay off the mortgage with tomorrow's dollars. That is the best inflationary hedge you can have.

Simplified Accounting

Another advantage of leasing is simplified accounting. It is very much simpler to have one lease payment than it is to worry about such things as depreciation of equipment, determination of its useful life, evaluation of the appropriate investment tax credit, and other accounting problems.

Footnote Financing

The next advantage of leasing is what we call "footnote financing." This comes back to what I mentioned earlier—that your overall borrowing power may be improved when you lease. Money borrowed in order to buy equipment appears on your balance sheet as a liability. I remember that the banker always looked at my balance sheet and played off ratios one against the other. It used to be that evidence of leasing did not appear on the balance sheet at all. Now good accounting practice requires that it should appear, but not in the figures. Leasing commitments appear in what we call "footnotes." Therefore, since it appears down in the footnotes, your operating ratios still remain the same; and you are able to borrow more money.

Cash Flow Control

Leasing can provide great flexibility in cash flow planning. A leasing company may arrange the terms of your lease in such a way as to schedule payment to coincide with your projected income. Let's say that you have a government contract requiring certain equipment. The leasing company can structure your leasing agreement so that a majority of the obligation is paid off over the period of the government contract, with much smaller payments later on.

Payments from Profits

Another feature of lease financing is what we call "payments from profits." The equipment that you lease is used to generate profits —that is, it is used to produce products the sale of which will generate profits. Therefore, you are paying for the equipment with part of the profit that you generate from its use. You are not paying for the equipment in one lump sum at the beginning, and you do not have to make a down payment. You are simply paying for the equipment as you use it.

Flexibility

Lease financing generally provides considerable flexibility in financing your capital equipment needs. If your business suddenly finds itself with a surplus of cash as a result of windfall profits or shrewd management, or let's say the XYZ Company wants to buy you out, there are many ways of terminating your lease. You can usually do this in ways that would not have been possible had you financed the equipment by borrowing money from the bank or had you bought the equipment outright.

Attractive Terms

As a general rule, the time period over which equipment may be leased can run as long as five years. Were you simply to purchase the equipment outright, making use of a bank loan to be paid off on the installment plan, the maximum loan period would typically be three years. Therefore, by using lease financing, you have a longer period of time in which to pay for the equipment. As a result, your monthly payments are lower. In other words, your business requires less cash to secure the use of the equipment it needs to operate.

Cost of Leasing

I'm often asked, "How do leasing charges compare, interest-wise, with bank borrowing?" Leasing does cost a little bit more; but when you consider the bank's compensating balance and shorter financing periods, the real overall cost is probably not much greater. If, by having equipment available to you at a low monthly rate, you can make cash available for more productive use elsewhere, leasing is probably a very good way to go.

LEASING LEXICON

Let's say you have decided to lease. You have considered the alternatives in equipment financing; you feel that leasing best suits your needs. Let's look at some of the terms involved so they will be familiar to you.

Renting

First of all, most people get hung up on the difference between "renting" and "leasing." There are two ways of looking at it: From a legal standpoint, they mean exactly the same thing. In your leasing agreement, the words "monthly rental" are used all over the place. However, in practical usage and not in the legal jargon, "renting" and "leasing" are different. A "rental" normally involves a quick-reaction, short-term requirement. Someone rents an oscilloscope from us, for example, to solve an immediate problem. They need it for just a month or two. Of course, the short-term rental rate is somewhat higher than the monthly lease rate since we have to maintain an inventory for this purpose.

Leasing

"Leasing," on the other hand, normally refers to a longer-term arrangement, such as three to five years. The maintenance of leased equipment is your responsibility—just the same as if you had purchased the equipment. Remember that leasing is a dedicated commitment to make X number of payments over a period of Y years regardless of what happens to the equipment. You can't come back later and say, "Well, this really isn't the type of equipment I needed after all." As I said, a lease is a *commitment* to make X number of payments. Now there are ways out of it, as I indicated earlier; but you must remember that you are making a long-term commitment when you sign a lease.

Term of the Lease

There are a number of different variables within the lease contract. The first variable is *the term of the lease.* That is simple—it means the period of time covered by the lease. It may be three years, five years, or what have you. Remember, the term of the lease can be selected at the time the leasing agreement is drawn up to take into consideration your particular needs.

Rate of the Lease

The next consideration involves *the rate of the lease*, or monthly charge. What goes into determining the rate? In leasing, we never talk about interest or anything like that because that is suggestive of a conditional sales contract. What we're doing, in effect, is simply renting that equipment to you for the term of the lease. The monthly charge is based on the original cost of the equipment, which is by far the bulk of the lease expense, plus the interest rate that we have to pay to finance our operations, the physical handling, the billing, and a modest allowance for profit. One other very important thing goes into the rate—the risk. What is our risk in dealing with you? If we feel that the risk is great, we probably won't deal with you at all. However, there is a huge gray area in evaluating risk. That is where dealing with a specialist in a particular type of equipment can be very advantageous.

Consider a situation where the equipment to be leased is of a type with which we regularly deal. In this particular case, the risk may be high that we will have to take the equipment back from the customer due to nonpayment. Even so, we may go ahead, recognizing that one of our other customers might be interested in the same piece of equipment if we got it back. Clearly, a bank would regard such a situation as being for more risky than we would since the bank wouldn't know what to do with the equipment if they got it back. In our case, we have a pool of rental equipment worth several million dollars. Therefore, we are not as worried as a bank might be about getting the equipment back. Specialization can sometimes mean the difference between your being charged what you might consider to be an outrageous rate and a somewhat lower rate.

Residual Value

The last term that we will talk about is confusing to a lot of people. The term is *residual value.* When you have completed your 36, 48, or 60 monthly lease payments, what happens? What is the value of the equipment at the expiration of the lease term? Clearly the equipment has depreciated, although it probably still has some value left. We call this remaining value the "residual value." Typically, residual values are in the range of 10% to 15% of the original cost.

At the expiration of the lease term, you may exercise one of three options:

1. *Return the Equipment.* You can return the equipment to the lessor, and there is no further obligation on your part.
2. *Buy the Equipment.* You can buy the equipment for its residual value, which, coincidentally, just happens to be its basic market value as well. Thus, you are buying that equipment for the value of its remaining usefulness. Often, when a lessor talks about an "option to buy," he means the option to buy the equipment at its residual value.

3. *Re-Lease the Equipment.* You may re-lease the equipment for an additional one, two, or three years. Since the residual value of the equipment is quite low at this point, the monthly rate is quite low also.

LEASING FROM A SPECIALIST

Now let's consider the advantages of meeting your leasing requirements by dealing with someone that specializes in the type of equipment you need.

Selection of Equipment

Today there are so many different types and models of equipment being made that it is virtually impossible for anybody to be an expert on all of it. Impossible, that is, unless that person or company deals solely in that type of equipment. At our company, we have saved some of our clients thousands and thousands of dollars simply by suggesting the equipment ideally suited to do the job they needed done. At times, customers have requested certain types of equipment. Based on our analysis of their requirements, we have recommended a different model, not only saving them money on the cost of the equipment but also providing them with equipment that much more closely matched their needs.

Substitution of Equipment

When most people start a company, they want to have exactly the same type of equipment—right down to same manufacturer and model number—that they used in the company where they were previously employed. However, technology changes, and the leasing company may very well have newer and better equipment made by the same manufacturer available at a much lower cost. It helps to deal with a company that knows the entire equipment industry that serves your market. A leasing specialist can provide these services free of extra charge.

Used Equipment

In dealing with a specialized leasing company, it may be possible to obtain a piece of used equipment. If the leasing company has its own repair and maintenance facilities, it may be able to provide a piece of used equipment matched exactly to your specifications, completely calibrated, traceable to the National Bureau of Standards, and fully guaranteed to perform "like new." Drawing from our own multi-million dollar inventory of rental electronic test instruments, we are often able to supply new companies going into business with equipment that is just two or three years old at a substantial savings. There is really no reason not to do this. Interest in used electronic equipment has become very common in recent years, and this interest will continue to grow. Used equipment is very popular in some industries; for example, roughly 14% of automobile sales today are used automobiles. However, despite increasing interest, sales of used electronic test equipment or production equipment still account for only .5% of all sales.

Volume Discount

Another advantage in dealing with a leasing specialist results because many types of equipment are purchased in quantity. Thus, the unit cost is lower than it would be if a single piece of equipment was bought. The equipment secured in this way can frequently be offered to the customer on a very attractive basis.

Fast Delivery

Since a leasing specialist buys in quantity, there is generally an existing inventory from which to draw. In the case of a start-up company, equipment needs must be met *fast.* Leasing may be the ideal way to get this kind of delivery service.

Marketing Your Surplus Equipment

Small companies are usually too cash-poor to be able to afford the luxury of having an expensive piece of equipment sitting around gathering dust. In some cases, a leasing company may be able to help you sell serviceable equipment that your company no longer needs.

Perhaps your company has a piece of expensive equipment that is used only infrequently. A leasing company may be able to help you rent this equipment when it is idle.

Early Lease Termination

Finally, you may find that a piece of equipment you leased last year for a period of five years is no longer needed. From a strictly legal point of view, you're hooked. *But,* if you're dealing with a leasing company that regularly handles that type of equipment, the chances are very good that they can re-lease the equipment to someone else for you. That can be a very valuable service.

SUMMARY

In summary, leasing can be an important and economically sound means of financing your equipment needs. Fundamentally, a lease is a simple, long-term rental agreement that permits you to use the equipment you require in the conduct of your business at a relatively low monthly cost. Dealing with a specialist can provide many advantages not readily available when alternative methods of equipment financing are used.

Twelve

Objectives of the Venture Capitalist

Burton J. McMurtry and Donald M. Dible

OBJECTIVES OF THE VENTURE CAPITALIST

Our subject is "Objectives of the Venture Capitalist." You may say, "Gee, that's a dumb topic because there are so many different venture capitalists, and their objectives are so different." That's quite true. On the other hand, there are some things that venture capitalists have in common. The first is that they are all interested in making money. But again, that sounds rather unspecific unless you ask, "*How* do they want to make money? Do they want to take a lot of money out of a company two days after they put it in? Or do they want to make an investment in a company, participate in the growth of that company, and see something really substantial come out of it?" The answer to that question is that most venture capitalists whom I know are interested in realizing *capital gains* on their invested dollars.

When venture capitalists invest in a company, they usually receive what is called "letter stock" in return. This is stock that has not yet been registered with the state and federal governments

Burton J. McMurtry, Ph.D., is a General Partner with the west coast venture capital firm of Institutional Venture Associates in Menlo Park, California. At the time this article was written, he was President of the Palo Alto Investment Company, also a venture capital firm.

for public sale. In fact, lettered stock is often so bound up with governmental restrictions that it is sometimes referred to as "funny money." The venture capitalists understand these restrictions and make their investments in spite of them. They hope that the company in which they invest will eventually achieve significant growth, resulting in a public market for the company's stock and offering the investors the opportunity to sell their stock—hopefully for more money than they originally paid for it. Because the investment will have been over a long period of time, the investor's profits will be taxable at the preferential, long-term capital gains rate.

Actually, if you are able to maintain the confidence of your venture capitalists, they may maintain some level of investment in your company for as long as it is around. In some cases, venture capitalists have held stock in a portfolio company for more than ten years because of the continuing growth and profitability of that company and investor confidence in its management.

START-UP FINANCING

The balance of my remarks will concentrate on start-up financing—that is, financing at the very earliest stage of a business. It is this type of financing with which I have had the greatest amount of experience as a venture capitalist, and it is the area of business financing on which I am best equipped to comment. On the other hand, I do not plan to address myself to a discussion of the "downstream financing" of a business that is already off the ground and in need of incremental financing—say just prior to a public offering.

Appreciation of Value

Start-up investors are interested in capitalized earnings. They are interested in substantial gains. Exactly how much are they going to be interested in? That depends on the investor. This is where the greed factor and the realism factor, which are important to both the venture capitalists and the entrepreneurs, really come into play.

I'm on record as having said that most venture capitalists who do start-ups look for *at least* ten times appreciation of their investment over a three- to five-year period. In fact, that is perhaps an understatement about a real start-up financier. In most of the deals that we go into, we like to think that there is an opportunity for a twenty- to forty-times appreciation in the value of our investment over, let's say, a five-year period. That does not mean that we expect to take twenty to forty times our initial investment out in cash during that period. However, we certainly would expect to have some liquidity after five years. That is, we hope to be able to sell *some* of our stock for real dollars, which we can then reinvest in other companies. In other words, the appreciation in value that start-up investors are looking for is *very* large. The reason for this is obvious. Venture capitalists aren't any smarter than anyone else; in fact, a lot of us are quite a bit dumber than many of you. There are so many, many factors that may prevent a business from becoming truly successful that the risk inherent in start-up investments is enormous—there simply are not going to be that many real winners that become major corporations. So the potential appreciation has to be very large.

Liquidity

In addition to the problem of substantial return on our investment, we must also confront the problem of liquidity. Let me try to summarize what I mean. It might be possible for a venture capitalist to put, say, $100,000 into a company. The company might have good management and, with that $100,000 plus some money from the founders, the company gets off to a good start. Soon it may become profitable and achieve positive cash flow. At this point, it should be able to finance its accounts receivable, secure a line of credit, and continue its pattern of profitable growth. After a couple of years, it may be a $1 million or $2 million company in terms of sales. It might, perhaps, also be very profitable. Now that may sound like a real success story; and for the guys who run the company, it is. Many businessmen would be very happy to build a company to this level so quickly. If such a company continues to grow at the rate of 15% to 20% a year, no one will deny the merit of the accomplishment. There is absolutely nothing wrong in having as your objective a plan to start and build such a company. More power to you.

On the other hand, such an objective is totally inconsistent with the investment objectives of a venture capitalist. Why? Liquidity. This kind of company is what we call the "living dead." Such an investment can lock up money for a very long period of time, leaving the venture capitalist in a very inflexible position. The investor must be able to see the day when he can sell at least part of his original investment (hopefully at a substantial profit) in order to have money available for investment in *new* and promising companies.

Despite the profitability of this little company, who wants to buy stock in it? How do you value it? The shares are privately held, and there are a limited number of stockholders. Only one American business in a thousand has stock that is publicly traded at least once a week. You can get into a lot of trouble with companies that have not grown sufficiently to become legitimate objects of a public offering. We have a bias which says, "Don't take a company public until it has reached at least $10 million a year in sales and has a solid history of profitability." Some investors disagree with us. However, we think it's tough enough to run a business and get it moving well without burdening the management with the extra administrative problems of being a publicly held company. There are some counter-arguments to this position. But nevertheless, liquidity is a major problem. In general, the venture capitalist wants to see a business plan for a company that really has an opportunity to grow to be a substantial company—like at least to $10 million in sales volume in a matter of three to five years. If your plans don't call for that, you may find yourself being turned off by a lot of venture capitalists for reasons that may not be clear to you. Your problem is the absence of potential for liquidity.

Initial Capitalization

One of the most perplexing problems in evaluating a venture capital investment has to do with assigning a value to the start-up company in relation to the initial amount of venture capital required. In other words, what percentage of the equity does the investor take in return for the money he puts into the company? Let's go back to the question, "What is the venture capitalist looking for?" He wants to make money. How does he make money? He makes money by investing in a company and having that company do well. Does he want to own all of that company? Unless he is just a "Super-Greed" without any consideration—and in fact, doesn't really expect good things to happen at all—he *doesn't* want to own all the company. He simply wants to own an "appropriate share" of the company. That's a nice weasel-word way of putting it. What do I mean by that? It means that every investment really is a fresh deal. The way you try to evaluate a company at the time you make an investment in it is very, very subjective, indeed. I don't think there is anybody in the venture capital business who will say, "We've got this exact formula that we apply when the guy walks in the door, and it cranks out a number that says what that company is worth and how we are willing to invest." It's *terribly* subjective! What most venture capitalists will try to do is the following: They will look at your business plan, and they will see what your projected performance is in terms of sales and net income after taxes. They will look at what the growth rate is, the kind of industry you are in, and a lot of other things that we will get to later on. They will try to say, "Well, if we made an investment in that company today and if the projections are net three to five years out, the company will be earning $1 million after taxes. That means that the sales revenues are substantial also. It's in an industry where, with our crystal ball (which frequently is almost opaque), we can project that the stock market at that time will anticipate a fifteen times price-to-earnings multiple on that stock. (Understand, we're not trying to be stock promoters.) Then you could say that the stock in the company might be worth $15 million at that time. Or you might say, "Gee, that stock will sell for twenty times earnings because of the glamour of the industry and the quality and capability of the management."

For discussion purposes, let's say it's a $15 million company. Let's suppose that the company required $1 million in start-up cash. Let's suppose that you, the entrepreneur, decided you *really* need $1 million in cash at the outset to get that business going. What you have really said is that you think your company will be worth roughly $15 million five years from now *if* you meet your targets. You really feel that you need $1 million now.

The venture capitalist then says, "That's $1 million. If my $1 million in cash bought the *whole* company and if I still owned the whole company five years from now, I would only realize a fifteen times increase on my money!" You, the entrepreneur, have a problem! There is no way for both of you to do what you want to do; namely, for you to own enough of the company to make it worth your while and for the venture capitalist to feel that there is potentially a worthwhile return in it for him.

If you are smart, you will try to structure your deal so that the amount of capital required at the outset will get you to some very, very significant milestones. This initial capital does not necessarily have to provide for all of your downstream financing for inventory, receivables, and other things. You could finance these requirements through other channels if you have proven the viability of your business before you need the additional capital.

The start-up venture capitalist will also ask you, "What do you think the company's worth?" (Here I sympathize with the founders because my own background is in the area of operations.) A typical answer from an entrepreneur is: "Well, I think the company ought to be split 60/40. Sixty for the entrepreneurs and forty for the investors." And the venture capitalist says, "Why is that? And how much money is required?" The entrepreneur says, "Well, I'm not sure." The capitalist thinks about that for a minute. How could the entrepreneur arrive at the split of 60/40 if he is not even sure how much money is required? He is focusing on the wrong problem. He is really getting ahead of himself.

I think one exercise you should go through before you see a venture capitalist about financing your own business is the following. Ask yourself what the investor is going to ask himself. Suppose you come in; you have a reasonable plan; you've got a bright team of guys; you make a good impression; and you have defined fairly well what it is you are going to do. You say, "I need half a million dollars to get this business going, and that is going to buy 50% of the company." What have you told the venture capitalist? You have said that you need half a million dollars for 50% of the company. You have made a very simple statement to the venture capitalist; namely, that your company today is worth $1 million. If you are selling half of it for half a million dollars;

the other half, wherever it is, is also being valued at half a million dollars. Make sense? Of course it does. Now it is hard to raise that kind of money right now, even for the most attractive deals. But regardless of conditions in the financial marketplace, that is really what you are telling the venture capitalist. He will automatically do some thinking. If he is really interested, he will do quite a bit of thinking about what constitutes a fair basis on which to go into this thing. Most venture capitalists want to go into a deal as partners, and a bad way to start a partnership is to argue from extreme positions. If you are not reasonably close and comfortable from the outset, if the deal doesn't sort of come together in a comfortable way, you may be in for some real trouble and not just in trying to build your business. You may be in for trouble with that venture capitalist because, at the first sign of problems (which are bound to happen), he may say, "Oh, I paid too much money for that company." Then he may be harder on you than he should be. When you are down, he may jump on you instead of trying to build you up.

In sum, consider the start-up value of a company in several ways: What are the projections? What kind of capital appreciation can you expect? How much money would it take to reproduce that team and that company if you went about doing it yourself—not that you are going to?

Confidentiality

Apparently just about every entrepreneur is concerned about the confidentiality of the information that he transmits to a venture capitalist. He is afraid that the investor is going to run out and set up a company to steal his concept or pass on the idea to one of the companies in which he has already invested. Rest assured that this is extremely unlikely. I can't see inside all the other venture capital companies, but I am really very impressed with the discretion that characterizes the industry. Actually, I shouldn't be surprised at it because I personally experience enormous pressures to be super-discreet. Without discretion, our ability to operate in this business would be severly impaired. I can't prove that venture capitalists are any more honest than anyone else, but I am confident that most of them are far less likely to run around with your idea than you might think.

Investors' Motivations

In addition to the obvious desire to make money, many venture capitalists genuinely want to *participate* in new business growth. Investors motivated by this desire generally make excellent partners for start-up companies. But the chemistry of the relationship between a venture capitalist and the founders of a company in which he has made an investment is highly variable and greatly depends on the background of all parties concerned.

Currently, profits made from venture capital investments are generally taxed at the preferential capital gains rate. But changes in the tax structure are now being considered. These would ultimately eliminate this preferential tax treatment—in the name of "closing loopholes"—and capital gains would be taxed as ordinary income. Clearly, removal of the tax incentive will have an enormous impact on the venture capitalist and his willingness to invest in the risks represented by start-up companies. The nature of the venture capital industry as we know it will change as a result. Many investors simply will no longer be willing to consider investing in start-up companies. In my opinion, the effect of such changes in the tax laws could be *disastrous* for the economy.

In spite of the gloomy picture, some of us venture capitalists will still be around. It's not that we're *dumb*, we just have peculiar values. I know at least half a dozen venture capitalists, including me, who would still be in this business even if our capital gains were taxed at twice the rate of ordinary income. I personally find that the desire to participate in this new business growth, the excitement of being where the action is, simply overpower judgments as to what is and is not a smart way to make money.

What to Look for in a Venture Capitalist

When you start looking for venture capital, I think it's *extremely* important that you check out your investor. You can be darned sure that he is going to check you out very, very thoroughly if he gets serious about your deal. You should *really* do the same with him.

Ask him about some of the successful companies in which he has invested. Who are the guys running those companies? (You should contact them and talk to them.) What about some of the companies that are simply doing O.K.? What about some of the companies that haven't done very well at all? Also, is there a company that did so badly that the president was thrown out? Is there one of those ex-presidents available to talk to? There is always somebody in each of these categories. You ought to look them all up and talk to them. You will wind up with a whole spectrum of views, but you *want* to hear them. They can help you to decide whether or not you want to work with that investor. This kind of check-up can be very useful.

Check, for example, on the degree of the venture capitalists' participation in a new company. It can vary a great deal. Some try to act like management; that can be very, very bad. In particular, you have to be especially careful about people who have extensive operating backgrounds. The other key man in business with me and I, as well as several other people close to the company, come out of operating backgrounds. In the very early investments that we did, I think we got much too close to the founding teams. In some cases, we were so close to management that we became a crutch. In one or two cases, we actually interfered with the management in those companies. On the other hand, in one or two cases, we helped in situations where a typical venture capitalist wouldn't have bothered. He would have let the company die and said, "If you guys can't make it on your own, that's your problem. We're betting on you; *you* run the company." We have come to much more of a middle ground.

You want to be sure that the venture capitalist you deal with understands who runs the company—namely, the president of the company. Running the company is not the venture capitalist's job. Once the investment is made, there is, honestly, a very limited amount that your venture capitalist is going to be able to do for you. If you have some good investors, they can serve as a sounding board. That can be very useful because the president of a small company often doesn't have anybody to talk to much of the time about the things that really scare him. Unfortunately, a lot of venture capitalists try to make a case as to how important they are to the success of a company. Naturally, you get a lot of vicarious satisfaction out of seeing companies do well. But I think, if you are realistic, you realize what a trivial role you really play outside of making the founder comfortable with you. When something happens that causes him to panic, he may call you up and say that he would like to talk to you about something. When you come over, it is clear he is panicked. You may be able to help him through a crisis, but what's that worth? I don't know. It gives you some satisfaction, but it is not a major thing. It's the guys who run the company—and the operating people in the company—who make it go or kill it.

It is also necessary for the entrepreneur to be careful about relying too heavily on his board of directors. We were minor investors in one company that had gone through a lot of trouble. We invested in it after it had started up in what was supposed to be a turnaround situation but actually wasn't. It was a turnaround in a sense; it turned around into bankruptcy. Then it came out of bankruptcy and got going, but it was still a very small company with $25 million in sales. It had a lot of investors, a situation which in itself can be bad. It had a nine-man board of directors, two classes of stock, and convertible debentures. The board spent all of its time fighting each other and fighting management. The guys in the company were trying pretty hard, but it wasn't really going anyplace. That kind of thing you really want to avoid. You *can* correct it, although I'm not sure the one in the example really got corrected. The board got cut down from nine to five, and some new people and different management were brought in. The company has since become viable, but you shouldn't have to go through such things. Life is too short!

What Happens After the Investor Says Yes

One of the worst things that can happen in a venture capital deal is for the new company founders to fail to recognize that getting the money is just the *beginning,* not the end, of a long journey. True, raising the money may have been awfully difficult. But it is *just the beginning.*

Of course, we all recognize that if you don't get the money, you can't get the business off the ground. On the other hand, we try to help the founders get the company off the ground with as much of their own money as possible. Clearly, they are going to own a lot more of the company if they do. There are all kinds of strengths in starting a company on that basis.

Once the money is raised, the time has come to implement the business plan. It is not the time to take a vacation or to build castles in the air with all that money your share of the company is going to be worth in three to five years. Now that you've convinced the venture capitalist and your team of co-founders that the idea has real potential, the time has come to start building a business. It's time to find out for real if those projected sales and profit figures in your proposal were worth the paper they were written on.

How the Investor Says No

Some venture capitalists ultimately finance only a tiny percentage of all the deals that get submitted to them, so an awful lot of would-be entrepreneurs are going to get turned down. Now believe me, it's no fun to say, "No!" But it has got to be done—hopefully in such a way that some measure of good will is retained. The trick is to say "No" without having the guy go away mad and bad-mouth you to all of his friends, some of whom may have just the kind of deal that you've been looking for all these years. Keeping good will when saying "No" and at the same time being perfectly direct about your reasons for declining to invest is difficult. Unfortunately, many investors are often less than direct when turning you down because they are afraid you'll get mad. Here are a couple of stock responses that you may encounter. They can waste *months* of your time.

"We don't take the lead." One of the standard responses is, "Gee, you've got a good team of guys. That's an interesting plan. We would really like to put some money in that, but we don't like to take the lead in venture deals. We prefer to have somebody else take the lead role, and then we like to put money up with them. So if you can find somebody to take the lead role in this deal, let us know. Then we might be very interested." You go out the door thinking, "Gee, that guy really liked my deal. Except for the fact that they don't take the lead on start-ups, or whatever I'm doing, the guy is really interested." So you are encouraged; you go out and try to find some guy who takes the lead. You call guys up and say, "Who takes the lead in things?" You go to talk to those guys. You may receive the same answer again. More often than not, the answer is a polite turn-off that can be *terribly* misleading. What the guy is really saying to you is, "No way am I going to go into this deal. But if some other venture capitalist looks at it and finds something in it that makes more sense than I think it makes, I want to keep the door open so I can stick money into it." Such a direct answer is unpleasant to give and to receive. Yet we try to be direct, and so there are a few people around the San Francisco Bay Area who are very mad at us, even though we told them that our answer was just our opinion. Then again, there are some people who only *used* to be mad at us because they have since discovered that we were the only people who told them what we really thought.

"Conflict of interest." Another response is: "Gee, we *really* like this deal, but we are already invested in a company where we have a potential conflict of interest." Now that is another beautiful way to get rid of you. The investor has told you what a great guy you are so that you will go out and tell other people that those venture capitalists are good guys to deal with because they said you were a good guy. That is the problem in our kind of business and in any service business. You don't want people out there saying, "Those guys told me that I was an idiot, that my plan was all wrong." You're not going to recommend that your friends go and see those investors unless the turn-down was explained in a reasonable way.

In sum, *try* to get somebody in the venture capital organization to level with you because you can waste an inordinate amount of time not getting money while you bounce off walls getting told what a neat guy you are and what a neat plan you've got. There's always lots more money around than there are deals.

SUMMARY

Understand your motive. This is vital to the venture capitalist. He wants to know what you want. Frequently, *you* don't even know what you want. That's not uncommon. But *find out!* It is really important that the venture capitalist knows what your objectives are. Do you want to run a proprietorship or do you want to build a truly substantial business? Be ready to answer this question rather specifically.

Search for an investment partner. Look for a venture capitalist who wants to work *with* you, not someone who wants to run your business.

Expect trouble. You are going to have it. You are going to have it in some of the areas where you anticipated it would occur and in *lots* of areas where you didn't. If you are not the kind of guy who is really at his best under pressure, then you probably shouldn't try to build a substantial company. In my limited experience, the guys who are good at taking pressure are really special. They're guys who, when everybody else panics, are cool because there is something *important* going on—like we are about to go out of business. Almost every start-up that we have been through—possibly because of us—gets to that stage. So expect trouble.

Finally, *be direct and open.* If the venture capitalists would do that, it would save you time. And if you will do it, both in trying to get your investment dollars and particularly once you get your company going, everyone benefits.

Thirteen

Selecting Your Investors and Structuring the Deal

Russell J. Robelen

In raising funds for a new business, there are a considerable number of preliminary matters that must be resolved before you can even begin to talk about structuring the deal. During your first meeting with your potential investors, they will be formulating opinions as to your capabilities. They will also want a fairly precise indication of the amount of financing you will need and a rough idea of the percentage of the equity you expect to retain as founder's stock.

THE BUSINESS PLAN

Certainly a business plan will have to be prepared. I'm confident that almost every contributor to this book has mentioned this point, and I can't emphasize it enough myself. Surely you can appreciate that venture capitalists look at an enormous number of situations. If I had to sit down and have each entrepreneur verbally present his deal to me, the number of opportunities that I

Russell J. Robelen is a San Diego-based technical and management consultant. At the time this article was written, he was a General Partner with Idanta Partners, a west-coast venture capital firm.

could consider would be very greatly reduced. Therefore, I insist that a man first present a written plan. Then, assuming I like what I read, I will have him elaborate orally on the details. If there are several investors—and this is generally the case—all of them will study the plan.

FOUNDER-INVESTOR COMPATABILITY

It is wise for the founders and investors to spend enough time discussing each others' objectives so that each can evaluate compatability. It is not only important that your investors approve of you; you must also be able to get along with them. Together, you will probably experience some trying moments, and you want to be able to survive them without having to contend also with founder-investor problems.

Now let's assume that a number of discussions have taken place. The investor is beginning to grasp your business concept. He has met all the principals involved and has probably asked for a set of references with whom he can discuss your capabilities. In addition, he'll probably talk to a few people that are not on your list in an effort to arrive at an objective evaluation of your experience and the experience of the people you are bringing into the organization with you.

INITIAL FINANCING

Also before structuring the deal you should arrive at a clear understanding of how much money is to be raised initially. A common mistake made by entrepreneurs is to think that seed capital should include all of the funds required to see them through to the point of positive cash flow. If you are trying to create a major business, such complete financing at the outset is quite rare. More typically, what happens is that you will raise only part of the necessary financing. This seed capital should not be much more than is necessary to carry your organization through to a point where you will have something to show—the achievement of some important but intermediate milestone. This accomplishment should enable you to raise a second round of financing. In fact, you may go through two or three rounds of financing before you finally become profitable.

There are a number of reasons for this. The most important and obvious is that you can raise money on much more attractive terms if you have something to show for it. For example, let's say we have to raise $2 million in total to start a business and bring it to the point of profitability. If you try to raise all $2 million at the front end, you will have to pay a substantial portion of your equity to get it. Alternatively, suppose that you initially raise $500,000. Then, six months later, when you have made some progress, you arrange additional financing. Later you may arrange still another round of financing before achieving profitability. I stress this because a lot of entrepreneurs seem to feel that it's too risky to think about trying to raise money downstream. Undoubtedly, the most risky thing you can do is to start a business. It is unwise to think that you can minimize this risk by trying to raise all of the money at the point of start-up. If you are really trying to build a major business, you should plan your financial needs in several stages.

FINANCING INSTRUMENTS

When you get right down to it, the number of financial instruments that are suitable for structuring a seed capital situation are really quite small. Starting and financing a new business is risky;

therefore, the types of instruments that are most commonly used are those that lend themselves to high-risk, high-reward investments. Without qualification, the most common financing instrument is common stock. In most cases, the management group is permitted to buy common stock at one price while the investors buy the same class of common stock at a higher price—perhaps higher by a factor of three to five times. I have even seen deals where a factor of ten was negotiated.

Now where everyone owns common stock, the investors and the entrepreneurs both have the same long-term interests. Such a situation is more desirable than one where the investors have their money committed to the business in the form of preferred stock. Holders of preferred stock generally receive dividends on their investment. However, the payment of dividends will prevent the company from using all of its profits to finance new growth. Since growth is usually the primary objective of most new companies, preferred stock requiring payment of dividends is not recommended as a financial instrument. By providing both the founders and the investors with common stock, you can do much to insure that the objectives of all parties are the same.

Still another advantage of common stock is that it is simple. Believe me, when you are trying to structure a deal, there are all sorts of complications to worry about. Talking about various classes of stock adds further complexity to the deal. It may also be very difficult to explain the different classes of stock to the entrepreneur.

Another reason for limiting your financial instruments to common stock has to do with your investment philosophy. As professional venture capitalists, we expect that we are going to make a sizable return on our money or that we will lose it all. These are far more likely outcomes than some in-between situation where, after two or three years, the business is essentially in limbo. If you go into a situation where you later want to liquidate, it is unlikely that there will be any money available anyway, so ownership of preferred stock would simply mean that you would be first in line to draw water from a dry well.

So although having a preferred stock position at the front end allows you first crack at the assets of the business before the common stockholders, it is unlikely that such a situation will develop. Therefore, there really isn't much point in providing the investors with some sort of preferred stock position. To sum up this point, I think you will find that in most seed capital situations—and I emphasize *seed capital*—financing is usually provided in exchange for common stock.

FOUNDER INVESTMENT

We have already indicated that the amount of money needed to start the business should be determined before you talk about "structuring the deal." You should also decide on how much money you, the entrepreneurs, are prepared to invest. Now in any situation, the management group or the entrepreneurs are going to have to put up some money at the front end. The amount required will usually vary according to the investor's desires.

Let me tell you our position on this point; I think it's similar to what you will find in dealing with most venture capitalists. We obviously want the management to have something at stake. We want them to put up some money. I'm not saying that we want them to have their entire net worth at stake. We don't want the would-be entrepreneurs to go out and sell their houses and move into an apartment or sell the family car and mortgage everything they have. There are an awful lot of pressures brought to bear on the entrepreneur by the demands of the business. If he is a married individual with a family, the pressures will be even greater. So we don't really want him to have to change his standard of living to the degree that it creates domestic problems. For example, a wife who suddenly finds her standard of living dramatically changed may create morale problems that can have a very adverse effect on the outcome of the whole proposition.

In determining the degree of founder investment, we try to strike a reasonable balance, and it's very hard to do. We always talk to the founders and attempt to get an idea of what their net worth is; and then we talk about how we can "structure the deal" around the amount of money that they feel they can comfortably put up. This amount of money should include investments by all of the people in the founding group, which will usually be on the order of four or five.

Another thing that we would discuss with the founders would be the distribution of the founders' stock. We would talk to the president-to-be to determine his views. If he says: "I have a team of five guys, and I'm going to take 90% of the management stock. I'm going to distribute the other 10% among my other four people" we get the feeling that this isn't going to be much of a team effort. In other words, the president is really going to run the show as a one-man company, and he's got a few other people on board for "window dressing" to make the business look like a complete organization. On the other hand, we would frown on a situation where all of the founders have the same stock position because it appears that they are going to try to manage the business by committee. Committees don't seem to work. One person *has* to be the head man, and his position in the company in terms of stock ownership *has* to be consistent with his role because there are going to be a lot of tough decisions that one man *has* to make.

STOCK-OPTION PLAN

We also ask the president-to-be how many people he feels he can bring into his business using the initial amount of stock as an incentive. The management's stock might well be distributed among as many as 15 or even 30 people; a stock-option plan of some sort could be used to attract people beyond the initial founding team.

The stock-option plan is not ordinarily a part of the initial deal. Typically, by the time you get to the point where you want to initiate a qualified stock-option plan for attracting future employees, the amount of stock that is already outstanding will be substantial in relation to the amount that you are going to set aside for use in your stock-option plan. Since the people who participate in a qualified stock-option plan are paying for the stock at 85% of the fair market value, it's really just another way of raising capital. Although such plans are sometimes discussed with your initial investors, I don't think that this is really a significant aspect of "structuring the deal."

INITIAL EQUITY EVALUATION

Now the last question is the most difficult. It considers who gets what after you have resolved all these other matters. Most entrepreneurs consider this to be the most important point in "structuring the deal." It is probably the hardest point to resolve because there really is no quantitative way to evaluate it. There are many factors involved.

Fashionability

From the venture capitalist's standpoint, one of the first considerations has to do with whether or not the industry that the new company is planning to go into is considered "fashionable." Strange as it may seem, there are times when the venture capital community is as fashion conscious as Madison Avenue. Remember that, downstream, your investors are going to want to sell their stock in the public market, and they want to be reasonably sure that the public will regard their stock as a glamour issue. This was certainly the case in 1968 and 1969 when there was a flood of computer and computer-related companies being started. If you had the word "computer" in the name of your company at that time, your chances of raising money were enormously increased. As a matter of fact, you could even go to the public market to raise start-up capital. Many companies received their initial financing from public offerings during this "hot market" period. Whether or not your particular industry is in vogue at the time you need financing will significantly influence the structuring of your deal.

Whether "start-ups" are in vogue is still another consideration. For example, 1970 was a bad year in which to raise money for *anything.* Judging from all my sources, the era we are now going through is characterized by an abundance of venture capital. As a matter of fact, my colleagues indicate that they are aggressively looking for investment vehicles. The current problem is a lack of good deals—not the availability of money.

The Majority Control Hang-Up

A lot of entrepreneurs really get overly concerned with the question of control—the idea that they should own 51% of the business. A lot of unsophisticated investors I have seen also get very concerned about this fact. They think that *they* must have 51% in order to control the business and protect their money. This sort of deadlock is avoided only if there is a feeling of rapport between the entrepreneur and the venture capitalist. The two really have to understand each other, like each other, and be able to work with each other. You can't have harmony with one group saying, "Well, if I have 51%, then I can make these people do whatever I want them to do. I'm in control."

Let me demonstrate the fallacy of "control." Take the investor who owns 51% of the company. Let's say that, three to five months after the company has started, the money has been completely used up. At this point, the founders may decide that they really don't like their investor after all, saying, "This venture capitalist really gave us a raw deal. We're supposed to be running the company, but he's constantly interfering by exercising his 'control.' Let's pack up and go start another company—with a different name—somewhere else." That certainly leaves the investor out in the cold. Although he's got 51% of the business, he's got 51% of nothing.

On the other hand, let's say that the management team has 51% of the stock, and they become disenchanted with their investors. If the founders decide that they really don't like the investors and if the investors get really unhappy with the founders, you can imagine what chances the founders will have in trying to raise second-round financing when the first investor group—a professional venture capital firm—has decided not to put in any more money. As a matter of fact, when called for references, the investors may indicate that the founders are a bunch of bums that no investor could work with. The chances of raising second-round financing in that situation are reduced enormously. In fact, it may not be possible to raise additional financing at all. The point is that you really shouldn't get overly concerned about the question of control. We maintain that we neither seek nor avoid controlling situations. I think that control is really just one parameter of the deal.

The more money the outside investors put up in relation to the founders' investment, the more likely it will be that the investors will own the controlling interest. This is particularly true when the total dollar amount put up by the investors is large. As an example, my partner was once involved in the start-up of a cement plant in Bakersfield, California, where the initial capital raised was $21 million; $5 million was put up by venture capitalists, $16 million by insurance companies, and a very small amount by the management. Not surprisingly, the management's percentage of ownership in this business was very small. As a matter of fact, it was less than 5%. Contrast this with the more typical deal where the initial capital required is on the order of $300,000. Let's assume that the members of the management team have left their former employers, have prepared a good business plan, and have gotten the company started on their own funds. In such a situation, the founders may be able to arrange financing while retaining 60% to 70% of the equity.

Dilution of Equity The final point I would like to make on the subject of control has to do with dilution of equity. If you plan to start a major business and if the initial financing is accepted as being just the first in a series of second, third, fourth, fifth, etc. rounds of financing, it will probably not be very long at all before you have a great many different investors, none of whom is likely to own more than a small percentage of the business. In such a situation, the matter of majority ownership is simply not relevant.

A RECENT EXAMPLE

To illustrate many of the points I have been trying to make here, let me cite an example from the Fall, 1972 Special Issue of the magazine *Corporate Financing* [pp. 9ff.]. This issue was devoted entirely to the financing of small to medium-sized businesses. One example that was discussed had to do with a fellow named Schneider, the founder of a company called Instapak Corporation. His product is a special dispenser that discharges a liquid that hardens into polyurethane foam. Before it hardens, this foam can be molded to fit around almost any product. The foam is used to cushion the product during shipment.

Schneider decided that he had to raise $100,000 in seed capital to get the company underway. He indicated that he had set out consciously to prepare the company for its second round of financing. "We knew we would get the money," he said, "but we wanted to get it at the lowest possible price in terms of equity. Price is equivalent to the percentage of ownership you give us." Schneider knew exactly what point he wanted to reach before he showed the new company to a venture capitalist. In other words, he decided to try to run his business for six months until it achieved the following four criteria:

1. He could demonstrate that a major customer was using the product. At the end of six months, the processing machinery had, in fact, been leased to IBM, the Air Force, and General Electric.
2. He could show that the company had good management. He wanted to demonstrate that the founders were not just a bunch of engineers. In fact, he had worked previously for a bank and had run a business. He also demonstrated that he could assemble a team of people to do the job.
3. He could show a trend in which he could identify cash flow several months out and project a break-even point in the near future.
4. He could establish the credibility of his projections by showing that he had met previous projections.

Having demonstrated those things, he then went out to talk to four investment organizations about his deal. He showed them his business plan; all four wanted to invest. He decided to team up with the Sprout Capital Group, a venture capital subsidiary of Donaldson, Lufkin & Jenrette in New York. He chose them because of their record of highly intensive tracking and assistance to portfolio companies.

RECOMMENDED FINANCIAL ASSISTANCE

Any growth company really needs two types of financial assistance. The first is the financial nuts and bolts guy who can keep track of things—figure out how to finance inventories and so forth. He is seldom hard to get. The second is the experienced financial planning guy who can go into the money markets and wheel and deal. A small company can't afford him, and yet he is extremely important. Schneider felt that Donaldson, Lufkin & Jenrette would provide that sort of assistance; that was the reason he chose them. Similarly, it is our stated policy not to go into a deal where all we have to contribute is money. We only go into situations where we can contribute something more than just money. What we are really saying is that we think we have a body of knowledge that will enable us to help our clients avoid many of the pitfalls that so frequently cause young businesses to fail. I know that most professional venture capital firms that regard themselves as active investors operate under the same principles.

One area where we feel that we can certainly be of help is in raising subsequent financing. When it comes to dealing with banks and other financial sources, we have many established relationships that we can draw upon. It is extremely rare for a start-up company to have a knowledgable corporate finance man on the team at the outset. For one thing, people with qualifications such as this are usually employed by large corporations. They typically receive compensation far greater than a small company can afford to pay. For this reason, we feel that you should rely on your venture capital partner to provide this kind of assistance. You really ought to look very carefully at the investors whom you are considering to see that they are active investors who will work closely with you and really try to help you in a variety of ways.

Now I use the word "assist" here because a lot of management people confuse that with managing the business. As venture capitalist, we have neither the time nor the inclination to manage the business. If, when we are evaluating a potential investment, we think we may wind up having to run it, our decision is simple. We won't make the investment.

When we make an investment in a management team, we expect that team to run the business. However, we stand ready and able to assist them in any way that will help them build a successful company. I think the difference between "managing" and "assisting" is a most important distinction.

A Mini-Computer Start-Up

One of the companies that we were involved with typifies some of these points. A group came to us in December of 1971, shortly after we started our firm. They were formerly with Honeywell and wanted to start a company to build mini-computers. Not only did they have an idea for a product, they also had a well-formulated business plan for exploiting that product and building a promising company. These fellows saw a situation developing in the market on which they could really capitalize. We had several discussions with them and satisfied ourselves that their plan had merit. Eventually, we put up $300,000 to get the company started. When these people first came to us, they said that they knew they needed a first-rate financial man; but they didn't know what qualifications he should have. They asked us if we could help them in trying to locate that financial man. We said that we could; and in fact, we helped them write an ad for some of the leading newspapers to try to attract the right person. We also interviewed the respondents to the ad. As I said earlier, that's one area where I think a venture capital organization can be of real assistance to a new, up-and-coming business.

INVESTMENT PREFERENCES

People frequently ask us, "What sort of businesses do you like?" We always say that we like all kinds of businesses—high technology or low technology. As I said earlier, we have even invested in a cement plant. We look at your company from the merits of the overall business concept and not the particular field that you are going into or the product you have. People also ask us, "What sort of things don't you like?" We usually decline to answer that question as well. However, we came close a couple of times to saying that we didn't like the mini-computer field because there were far too many people in that industry. It was too easy a business to get into, and it seemed to be glutted with companies run by a lot of engineers who thought that they had a better way to develop a mini-computer and, having done that, the product would sell itself. Surprisingly, the first business that we financed was a mini-computer firm, the group from Honeywell about which I just finished telling you.

FINAL NEGOTIATIONS ON EQUITY DISTRIBUTION

The last point I want to make is that there will come a time when you finally decide how much money you are really going to ask for and what percentage of the business you really think you ought to keep. The venture capitalists presumably have been thinking about the same question. Finally it comes to a point when one group will make a specific proposal to the other. Sometimes it will be the venture capitalist who will make a proposal to the entrepreneurs; sometimes the entrepreneurs will make the first proposal. If you are reasonably close—by that I mean within 10% or 20% of each other—then you may have a negotiable deal. If you are 30%, 40%, or 50% apart, you may never be able to negotiate a final deal.

In the event you do agree on a deal, the last thing you must do is sit down with your lawyer, the venture capitalist, and his lawyer and put your agreements into a document that may be referred to as a stock-purchase* agreement or some other name. Essentially, the document will describe the nature of the deal: how much money is being put in, what the percentage of ownership is, and all of those things. This document, based on my experience, will vary depending on the law firm and not according to interests of either party. It seems that the written agreement is designed more to protect the parties against the SEC and the IRS rather than to protect one party from the other. The compatibility of the founders and investors should be resolved long before you ever get to the final legal documents. The success of the deal depends far more on the people who participate in it than it does on the documents that record the manner in which it is structured.

Fourteen

Financing through an Investment Banker

Edward C. Reed

As I see it, investment banking is a broad term. It involves the raising of money for corporations, generally, on a long-term basis, either through debt or equity securities. Investment bankers are most often known for raising money through the sale of common equity issues; but they function in the market by raising money through the sale of debt issues as well. Generally speaking, commercial bankers (the people with whom you have your checking account) prefer short-term loans. They really don't like to get into long-term financing, and so this has become the real job of the investment bankers.

THE INITIAL PUBLIC OFFERING

First, let me discuss public offerings, particularly as they relate to equity issues. In particular, I'm going to address myself to the subject of the initial public offering—the first time a company

Edward C. Reed was the President of Schneider, Bernet & Hickman, Inc., a Dallas-based investment banking firm, until his death on June 18, 1977.

offers its securities for sale to the public. This can be broken down into three general areas:

1. The criteria we use in evaluating a company.
2. A review of the services an investment banker can offer his clients.
3. A brief analysis of the investment banking industry and some thoughts as to what you should consider if you plan, someday, to go public.

When we look at a company, we look for a well-established business. If we're considering taking a company public, we're not interested in the man who comes in today and says, "Boy, I've got a great idea. Why don't you raise me a couple of million dollars and I'll be in business tomorrow. It's going to be the greatest business going!" Generally, we're looking for an established record. In the prospectuses that are filed prior to a public offering, the offerer is usually required to provide three years of audited financial statements. This means, obviously, that the business should be at least three years old.

We're also looking for a competent management group. If you've been in the business of selling shoes in a retail store and then suddenly decide to go into the electronics business, we're going to wonder about it. We're looking for people who have a proven background in their chosen business if we're going to raise money for them from the public.

Generally, we won't look at a company that is a one-man show. We're looking for a business that has a good qualified management group. I'm not saying that you have to have a *large* group but we'd like to see that there are two or three people on board who know what's going on in the company. If one of these people dies or if he leaves the company, there will be other people who can take over and run the company. I realize that you can't always get a qualified potential successor at the start, but I think you ought to have some people who can run the company on a day-to-day basis if necessary.

While these criteria may seem excessively difficult to meet, you must consider them through the eyes of the investment banker. When we offer securities for sale to the public, we are not always in a position to determine the ability of the buyer to undertake financial risk. In a public offering, there is nothing to prevent individuals unable to handle a financial loss from buying stock. Therefore, on the front page of the prospectus, we may go out of our way to indicate that the proposed offering is speculative in nature and that it represents a high degree of risk. In spite of these warnings, many people who can ill afford to lose their money will buy the stock. Therefore, the investment banker takes it upon himself to do his best to protect the investing public by applying rigorous standards in evaluating any company whose stock he has been asked to consider for sale to the public.

Next, we look at the earnings record of the company. Here you will find many different criteria, depending on the size of the investment banking firm. If you go to a national underwriter, you undoubtedly will find that their earnings requirements are much higher than ours. We are a regional firm and employ about 130 salesmen in twelve cities throughout the southwestern U.S. We look for companies that have at least $400,000 in earnings after taxes.

If you're starting your own business for the first time, that may sound like a lot. However, many people find that they can get to this level in two or three years' time, depending on the kind of industry they go into and how aggressive they are.

We also like to make a public offering involving a minimum of 200,000 shares of stock. This figure is based on the recommendations of our traders, the traders of other regional and national brokerage houses, and the independent traders. They all indicate that they want to have enough shares available so that the stocks can be readily bought and sold. If you have a very small number of shares in the hands of the public, there will be very few shares sold daily and you lose marketability. Most investors want to be able to buy or sell around 500 to 1000 shares without materially affecting the price. If you don't sell a large number of shares at the time you make your offering, you will then find that you have a limited "after-market." In that case, you may only be able to buy or sell a few hundred shares before affecting the market price of the stock. Therefore, one thing we try to achieve in our public offerings is a good after-market, where you, some of your employees, and the public can buy or sell stock in your company without materially affecting the price of the stock.

Generally, we try to establish an offering price above $10 per share. We've done some offerings at $8; we've done some at $12, $15, and $17. But we prefer to have the offering price be at least $10 per share. The reason has to do with the image you want to establish with your potential investors. We think that a very low-priced issue gives the impression, whether right or wrong, that it is a speculative issue. I think this attitude resulted from the days of the penny oil stocks and the nickel uranium stocks. We think that $10 to $12 stocks suggest to the potential investor that they're buying stock in a quality small company.

Now let me mention a couple of things about underwriting costs before I give you some specific examples. Your company's out-of-pocket costs should run from $50,000 to $75,000. These costs include things like fees for your lawyers and accountants, your bill for the prospectus printing, state Blue-Sky fees to get your stock registered so that it can be sold in various states, and other miscellaneous expenses. For accounting purposes, these costs have to be treated as expenses; you can't capitalize them over a long period of time. As you can see, making a public offering of stock can involve a considerable expense to the company.

The investment banker and the brokers who offer the stock are compensated on the basis of what is called the "spread" (or "discount") in stock price. The spread is the difference between the public offering price for the stock and what the company receives from the underwriter. In a $2 to $3 million public offering made in the early 1970's, the spread would typically be around 8%, possibly even as high as 10%. The amount of the spread depends to a certain extent on the kind of business you are in, your growth record, and the size of the company. If you have a company with $75 million in sales, the spread will be smaller for a $2 to $3 million public offering. If you get up to a $6 million offering the first time, the spread may drop down to 6% to 8% of the total amount of money that is being raised.

Warrants

Sometimes, particularly on an initial offering, stocks will be sold with warrants. A warrant provides the underwriter with the right to buy stock at a fixed price at some future date. The terms on the warrants are negotiated at the time the underwriting is arranged. If we are able to obtain warrants for the stock, we will generally be willing to lower the spread. For instance, an underwriting where the spread would normally be 10% could be done at 9% if warrants were part of the package. The warrant customarily provides for the purchase of additional stock at 120% of the original offering price within a five-year period following the offering date; customarily, the warrant cannot be exercised in the first year. While the number of warrants issued will vary from offering to offering, in one case the underwriters received the right to buy 8% of the total issue. Thus, the company seeking to go public can save some of its underwriting costs by giving the investment banker an opportunity to participate in the growth of the company.

EXAMPLE OF A PUBLIC OFFERING

Consider this example of how a public offering might be structured. Let's assume that you own all of the common stock and are prepared to sell 50% of the ownership of your company to the public. (We find, in most cases, that the management of the company wants to retain at least 50% of the ownership for itself.) Let's further assume that your after-tax net income for your last fiscal year was $400,000. If the company is valued at ten times earnings, the total company value would be $4 million. Since you are selling half of the company, this half should bring a total of $2 million from the investing public.

For simplicity, let's assume that you are going to offer stock at $10 a share. Since you are going to sell $2 million worth of stock, you will sell 200,000 shares. If you allow a 10% spread, the people who sell your stock will receive payment of $1 per share and you will receive $9 per share. The $1 per share goes to pay the underwriters (the people who take the risk in underwriting the shares) as well as the salesmen and brokers who actually sell the stock to their customers.

HOW LONG DOES IT TAKE?

If your company is ready to go public and we meet you for the first time, it is highly unlikely that we could arrange a public offering in less than three months from the time of that initial meeting. It takes roughly a month to prepare a prospectus—and that depends a lot on how fast the accountants and lawyers can work and how quickly the printers can get the prospectus printed. After filing, it will take about 40 days before you get your first response from the Securities and Exchange Commission regarding their suggestions on how you should revise your prospectus. It may take you two or three weeks more to incorporate these revisions into your prospectus and refile.

Occasionally it is possible to reduce this waiting period. However, on the first public offering, it doesn't happen very often. One of the exceptions to the rule happened last year. We had a very large company with about $80 million in sales. When we took the company public for the first time we received very fast treatment from the SEC, and we were given approval in about 25 days after our initial filing. As I said, however, that was an exception, not the rule.

HOW WE FIND OUR CLIENTS

Investment banking is a competitive business, and all of us in the industry are constantly looking for promising growth companies. We get many leads from our own brokers and salesmen who may serve you by handling your personal stock transactions. They get to know you and your company, and that is one way in which we get leads.

We have a full-time staff of corporate finance people who continually check the Dun and Bradstreet register of million-dollar companies. Here in Dallas, we have a large number of million-dollar-net-worth companies. It is a great environment with a lot of good competition among investment bankers that I think is a very favorable climate for companies desiring to go public. There are now approximately 55 New York Stock Exchange member firms in Dallas, so you have a lot of choice and variety.

We also rely on lawyers and accountants for leads. We look at 200 or 300 companies a year, and we select 6 or 7 out of those that we take on as clients. We tell companies what they need and what our criteria are. We try to turn down companies as quickly as we can if we don't see any possibilities. Therefore, if you come to us or people like us, you will receive a pretty fast answer. On the other hand, we spend a lot of time with the companies that we think have good potential.

WHAT SERVICES WE PROVIDE

After we have accepted your company as one of our clients, what services do we provide in arranging the financing?

First of all, our primary function is to coordinate the public offering. We coordinate the lawyers, the accountants, the company management, and even the printers in order to complete the financing on schedule. After we have decided to proceed with the public offering, it is very important to have everybody involved meet together to discuss potential problems.

As an example, one of my good friends told me that he wanted to go public. He said, "I've really done everything right. I've got the best lawyers; they've all had previous dealings with the SEC. I've got the best accountants; in fact, here's our audit for the last five years. I specifically told the accountants to make the financial statements look just as if they were going to go into the prospectus. Everything is all set. This is going to be an easy deal for you. You can take us public and it won't take you any time at all."

Later that week, we called in the lawyers, the accountants, and the company management, who I thought were the only people that we'd need in this deal. After some discussion, it came to light that this company held large oil reserves. It just so happened that one of the people from the reservoir engineering company they used—an independent firm that would have to render an opinion as to just how large the reserves were—had offices in our building. We asked him to come to our meeting. We started exchanging ideas, trying to decide what information we needed and what we needed to look into, when the reservoir engineer said, "I was looking over this company's books and we, as independent people, can't give any credit to the secondary reserves." The company had been allocating their costs to both the primary reserves and secondary reserves. When this problem came to light, it dramatically changed the evaluation of the company's earnings per share. As you can see from this example, it is important to get *everybody* involved who is going to have to give an independent opinion. We suggest that wherever possible, these people have had prior dealings with the SEC. Very often you'll run into problems; but once you get competent people working on them, you should be able to resolve them. It just takes time and coordination.

In a few cases, we have even tried to help the company change their image. One company we took public had primarily been involved in the factoring business until they had a chance to make a very large acquisition in the mobile home financing field. It was in the mid-60's, and we thought that the idea of getting into the mobile home business, even into mobile home financing, would change their image significantly and would result in a higher price-to-earnings ratio on their stock.

We also took another company public that was in the engineering field. They got involved in pollution control; and as a result of this emphasis, significantly raised the price-to-earnings ratio at which they went public.

From these examples, you can see another service that the investment banker can do—be a little creative by helping to design and tailor companies. We tell clients that, if they have more of this kind of business and less of that kind of business, their stock would be better received in the marketplace.

HOW MUCH STOCK TO SELL

Another point I would like to make has to do with the maximum percentage of the company that should be sold in public offerings.

No company should sell a larger percentage of additional stock than the annual growth rate of its earnings. If you're growing at the rate of 20% a year, don't sell 30% of additional shares to the public because, the year after, your earnings per share will probably go down 10% and you will have a number of unhappy stockholders. We're very conscious not only of having you show a good growth picture in the past but also of having one that will look good in the future.

PRICING

Now I'd like to get into one of the more interesting sides of this business—the pricing of securities issues. Basically, we use very standard guidelines of the kind you would learn in any college course in finance. We don't have a "secret formula." For example, if you had a $10 million company—let's say a small chain of retail stores—we'd like to find two or three other retail store operations in the same geographic area that also had sales of $10 million. Assuming that they were already public companies, we would look at the price-to-earnings ratio on the stocks of those companies and at their growth records over the last four or five years. We'd also look at the return on invested capital, the book value, and the total market value of the companies' stock. We would compare earnings growth, size of the company, areas of distribution, market to book value, and profit margin ratios. We would then determine a statistical average on which to base a decision on the stock price at which your company should sell. There are always pluses and minuses in making these evaluations. Maybe you've got a stronger management team and you're growing faster. But basically, we're going to compare your company to other companies in the public marketplace in order to come up with a realistic value for your company. You probably think that your company is the greatest in the world and that your stock ought to sell at twice the price-to-earnings ratio of your competitors. That would be a tough thing for us to accept and justify to potential investors.

I grant you that there is a lot of subjective judgment involved in this. One factor is how well you sell yourself. Let's say that the president of a competing company is a poor public speaker. He'll probably get a few minuses on this. Maybe you're a super salesman and can effectively communicate with the analysts, stock brokers, and investors. Then we'll give you a little higher price. These are the kinds of things we're constantly weighing.

We have one other requirement in our firm. Let's say that we evaluate your company and decide that it is worth $11 a share in the public market. Then we would tell you that we'd like to sell your stock to the public at $10 a share. We would sell your stock at slightly below market value because we want the public to make a little money, too. If we could price our deals perfectly, we'd price them at approximately 10% below the level at which we think they're going to sell. Then we'd hope that, immediately after the offering, this company would sell at $11 so that the initial investors would make some money and the stock wouldn't drop below the offering price. The next time you want to raise money from the public, you'll have a lot of shareholders with whom you have created substantial goodwill who will want to buy more of your stock. If you don't structure the offering in this way and your initial price is too high so that your stock starts to go down, it will be extremely difficult to sell additional shares in the future.

We've turned down quite a few deals because the management of the company involved wanted $11 per share instead of the $10 per share that we recommended. We need investors that constantly want to buy stock in new companies. If they buy the stock and it doesn't go anywhere, they've got stale money. Then they're not going to want to invest in other companies that we bring public.

As I said earlier, it usually takes a minimum of three months to prepare and market a public offering. One of the really tough parts of this business is in predicting what the stock market conditions will be three to four months from now. When we discuss the proposed price of your stock, we'll ask you for some estimates. Then we'll say, "Okay, if your estimates hold up, we'll take you public in three or four months at this kind of price based on the current conditions in the stock market." With the gyrations of the stock market, predicting what's going to be happening in three to four months can be a really difficult job that involves a lot of judgment.

A year or so ago, we took a company public. Prior to the offering, in the summer of 1971, I went to talk to one of the company's directors. He said, "I don't think we really want to go public right now. What if we wait?" Bear in mind, the company was doubling its sales and earnings every year. "How much more would you pay if we didn't go public this fall, but waited until next spring?"

After swallowing hard, I suggested a price that seemed reasonable for next spring. I had to make a decision in a hurry, and that was it. In the spring of the following year when they wanted to go public, we told them, "We are ready." At that time, Presidential candidate McGovern was doing quite well in the polls, and we thought that he had a chance to get elected. We felt that, if he did, we'd have higher taxes, which would have an adverse effect on the stock market. For this reason, we told the company, "Ok, we'll take you public. But if it gets too late in the summer, we may either reduce the price or not take you public. We think it is of paramount importance that you go public now. We don't want to get into the middle of the election and find out that we're bringing your stock public in a bad market."

Actually, the company went public about a year after I first talked to the Director of the company, at the price per share I had discussed a year earlier. Our earlier judgment happened to be pretty good.

PREPARING TO GO PUBLIC

In getting a company ready for a public offering, there's one thing I can't emphasize too strongly—you must have accountants and lawyers who have had previous working experience with the Securities and Exchange Commission. For your routine corporate financial and legal requirements, you may continue to use the same firms that you have used in the past. However, in preparing for a public offering, you should bring in outside, SEC-experienced help if your present accounting and legal firms don't already have this kind of experience. We feel strongly enough about this point that we won't consider a deal—no matter how attractive it may otherwise seem to be—if the people preparing the prospectus and the supporting documentation don't have prior SEC experience.

For one thing, the SEC has at its headquarters in Washington, D.C. people who specialize in various industries. It is important that your accounting and legal people know their SEC counterparts so that when registration problems arise—and they will—they can be resolved quickly and amicably.

OTHER SERVICES OF INVESTMENT BANKERS

In addition to helping companies make their first public offerings, investment bankers provide a number of other services. We can arrange secondary offerings. A secondary offering means the registration and sale to the public of privately held but previously unregistered stock. Such stock may originally have been acquired by the management of the company when the company was first incorporated. Investors may have bought unregistered stock in a private placement, or a consulting firm may have provided some of its services to the company in exchange for unregistered stock. When the holders of unregistered stock want to sell part of or all of their holdings, the process is called a secondary offering. For example, let's say the president of your company has been drawing a very small salary ever since the company started in order to make the earnings look as good as possible. Now since his stock is worth a lot of money, he might like to buy a new car or a new house. This takes cash. He can get cash by selling some of his stock in a secondary offering.

Investment bankers also can be of great help in developing your banking relationships. Also, we do some in-depth evaluations on privately held companies for estate tax and related purposes. We can help you in preparing your quarterly reports and in making presentations to various analysts' societies. We write reports; we help get your stock listed in the paper and in Moody's and other financial publications. We are helpful in getting our own institutional specialists to call on mutual funds and banks in an effort to get them interested in your company. When you desire to hold annual meetings and make investor presentations, we'll listen to you make two or three dry runs and give you some suggestions on how you can make your talk more meaningful to the potential investors, institutions, or analysts that may come to hear it.

PRIVATE PLACEMENTS

Raising money on a private placement basis can take several forms. It can be straight debt; it can be debt with equity kickers; or it can involve letter—unregistered—stock. We use many of the same criteria that we use in the case of a public offering. We want a company with a good record. We want qualified management—competent people. I think our investors would also like to see that the company has a management team—not a one-man show. On the earnings aspect, you can probably cut the requirement down to around $200,000 in after-tax profit. The cost of raising money in this way is much lower than it is in a public offering. You don't have to write a formal prospectus; and while you may have to have an audit, it probably doesn't have to have the same detail as would be required for a formal prospectus. It will take a great deal less time for the lawyers to write up the contract, resulting in lower legal fees. The legal costs will probably run around $10,000 or $15,000.

In addition, you will pay your investment banker on a sliding scale, depending on the size of the financing. It gets a little difficult to project the exact cost when you get into small private placements. There are a lot of financial people who talk about a formula of five-four-three-two-one, which means that they will charge you 5% for the first $1 million, 4% for the next $1 million, 3% for the next, and so on. In fact, however, the fee is almost always negotiated. To give you an illustration, we did a private placement in the early 1970's of $6 million. We charged the company $125,000 as our fee, which represents about 2% of the $6 million. If that $6 million were raised in a public offering, the fee would have been 6% to 8%. As you can see, the cost of private placement financing may run one-third to one-quarter of the cost of a public offering.

I think it is fair to say that most stock brokerage houses are more interested in public offerings than in private placements. One reason is that we are able to use all facets of our company in a public offering. We involve our corporate finance people—the people who talk to the officers of the company. We also involve traders; we get the salesmen interested; and we get our research and investment counseling people involved as well. Most of our service departments get to participate when we have a public offering.

Also, it is a fact that there are more types of financing available to a company that is publicly held than there are to a private company. Naturally, we'd like to have as much repeat business as we can get. It costs us a great deal to locate and investigate a company; and if we can do more pieces of financing with that company, our costs are cut.

If you expect to go public some time in the future, it is a good idea to work with your investment banker once you are earning $100,000 or so after taxes. He doesn't usually charge anything for this unless there is a lot of work that he has to do; and he will give you many helpful ideas. Before you achieve this level of income, it may not be a bad idea to send him your annual figures once a year and let him look them over; he may give you two or three good suggestions that will be helpful to you later on.

SUMMARY

In summary, I'd like to list four principle reasons for going public:

1. To get liquidity in the company or reduce the amount of debt.
2. To help raise cash for management who have stock options or investors with private stock (secondary offerings).
3. To raise funds for company expansion or acquisitions.
4. To satisfy the ego. I think a lot of people go public because the guy next door is public.

In addition, here are four points that I think summarize what you need to know in structuring your company if you do plan to work with an investment banker:

1. Have growth in sales.
2. Have growth in net income.
3. Have growth in earnings per share.
4. By far the most important: have *steady* growth in earnings per share. I can't emphasize enough the word "steady."

Fifteen

Money for Your Business—Where to Find It, How to Get It.

DONALD M. DIBLE

One of the recurrent problems that plagues most owner-managed businesses is the shortage of adequate capital. In the case of new businesses, this problem can be severe.

Promising small businesses traditionally have relied upon such sophisticated money sources as investment bankers, venture capitalists, and federally licensed and leveraged Small Business Investment Companies (SBICs) for their equity capital needs. In today's market, these sophisticated investors have many options from which to choose. Regardless of market conditions, their objective continues to be the maximization of return on investment, consistent with intelligent risk analysis.

Their first option is the purchase of securities in publicly traded companies at bargain basement rates. Their second option is the private placement of *growth* capital in young, but already established, companies of demonstrable merit. In a tight money market, the terms of such an arrangement may be very attractive for the investor. The investment option representing the highest risk, obviously, is in financing the start-up company. Given the first two op-

Donald M. Dible is the founder of The Entrepreneur Press and author of Up Your OWN Organization! A Handbook of How to Start and Finance a New Business.

tions, a private placement with a start-up company is, I think you'd agree, a most unlikely choice as an investment vehicle.

What about banks? Surely, you can get a personally endorsed loan for your business from the friendly loan officer at your commercial bank. Not necessarily. In evaluating the financial statement of any business, a banker will pay particular attention to the ratio of debt to equity capital. A general rule is that you cannot borrow more money than has been invested as equity capital. Furthermore, most bankers are not eager to lend money to new businesses at all, preferring to wait until there is at least some history of profitable operation.

How, then, can you assemble the resources you'll need to get started and to keep you going until you begin to turn a profit? Take heart; there is hope. There are, in fact, four different money sources that can now help you stretch your business dollars: 1) personal financial resources, 2) trade credit, 3) customers, 4) economizing.

PERSONAL FINANCIAL RESOURCES

Many of us significantly underestimate the value of our personal resources when taking a financial inventory. Let's look at some of the more obvious (and not-so-obvious) resources you may have:

Home

In the recent inflationary period, the value of practically all residential real estate has appreciated substantially. If you have owned your own home during this period, you are indeed fortunate. The difference between the current value of your home and the balance outstanding on your mortgage may represent an equity asset of between $20,000 and $50,000. You might consider converting this asset to cash by 1) taking a second mortgage in the amount of your equity, 2) refinancing your mortgage, 3) subdividing your lot and selling part of it, or 4) selling your house and moving into an apartment. Every year tens of thousands of people go into business using "house money" to bankroll their ventures.

Life Insurance

A loan based on the cash value of your life insurance policies can be a low-interest source of money. Many policies provide for automatic loans from the insurance carrier at interest rates far below the prime rate charged by commercial banks.

Stocks and Bonds

You may own stocks and bonds that, for a variety of reasons, you do not wish to sell. Such instruments make ideal collateral for loans, and you can borrow anywhere from 40% to 60% of their current value, depending on the lender.

Credit Cards and Personal Credit

When you prepare your financial business plans, you will surely want to take the fullest possible advantage of your credit worthiness. At the same time, you will want to minimize the amount of money that you have to take out of the business to meet your personal financial needs. This is particularly true when the business is just getting started and every dollar in the treasury is needed to finance business growth. During this period, personal credit cards of all types and descriptions can give you just the extra leverage you need. Instead of drawing a heavy salary in the first year of operation, supplement your modest cash draw with the judicious use of credit cards.

Credit cards come in a great variety of classifications: bank cards such as Master Charge and Visa, travel and entertainment (T & E) cards such as Diners Club and American Express, as well as cards for department stores, oil companies, airlines, and so on. With a good credit record, it should be no great feat for you to secure enough credit cards to give you a personal line of revolving credit in excess of $30,000.

Now, obviously, you can't buy a carload of raw materials for your business with your bank credit card, but you can cover a lot of your *personal* expenses with it—as well as such business expenses as transportation, food, and lodging. With a little thought, I'm sure you can come up with a variety of ways to employ credit cards in financing your particular business.

While we're on the subject of personal credit, you should give serious consideration to arranging for the installment purchase of an automobile and other major consumer items *before* you start your business. You'll find it a lot harder to qualify for this kind of financing after you've started. Lenders tend to worry a great deal about the financial stability of new small businesses and their founders. Your credit application looks a lot better when, under "Current Employer," you show that you have been employed with "Solid as a Rock, Inc." for the last six years instead of with "Shaky at Best" for the last six weeks.

Relatives and Friends

I happen to consider relatives and friends to be extremely valuable personal financial resources. Where else can you find lenders who, simply because they like you, will advance money on anything as risky as starting a new business? However, do yourself and your lenders a favor. Document their loans. Draw up a formal note showing interest charged and the dates on which principal and interest are payable. You never know when a personality problem may arise that could precipitate calling the loan. That can become awfully messy.

Take the case of the young man whose rich aunt loaned him $100,000 with which to start his business. The formality of a loan agreement was ignored. Six months later the aunt died. The heirs then forced the entrepreneur to liquidate his business so that they could each get their share of the aunt's estate.

Relatives and friends can also come in handy as cosigners. Let's assume that you apply for a loan and the lender decides that your qualifications are marginal. The availability of a financially strong cosigner can swing the balance in your favor. Your relatives and friends can prove to be very important personal assets. Don't overlook them in your financial planning.

TRADE CREDIT

According to a U.S. government study, trade credit constitutes a 33% larger factor in financing the business community than that represented by bank loans. Clearly, every company treasurer should give serious consideration to trade credit in financing a small business.

Customarily, suppliers provide trade credit as an inducement to their customers to do business with them. Although credit terms in most industries are extended on a net 30-day basis, overall averages may stretch this to 45 days, 60 days, or even longer depending on the condition of the overall economy and the particular industry involved. Under the guise of "cash management," many companies make a habit of vigorously enforcing their collection policies while simultaneously treating their accounts payable with cavalier disregard.

Just how you handle your payables is your own business. But you should be aware of the fact that not everybody in business makes a habit of paying bills the day the first invoice arrives.

When it comes to making use of trade credit as a tool in financing your business, I recommend that you establish with your suppliers, in advance of purchase, the best extended credit terms you can negotiate. Depending on how hungry your suppliers are for your business, you may be able to arrange extremely attractive terms. Securing competitive bids will greatly improve your bargaining position. However, once you have agreed to terms of payment, honor your commitment if you value your credit. Nothing is more difficult than trying to operate a business when your suppliers will ship to you only on a COD basis.

CUSTOMERS

There are many ways in which customers can be induced to help you finance your business. The degree to which they are *willing* to do so depends on the extent to which you enjoy a monopoly on the goods or services that you offer. In other words, no one will pay in advance if he can get essentially the same goods or services from another supplier under more liberal credit terms. However, if you have the only game in town, you may be in a position to get your customers to finance your business.

As you know, the telephone company, electric and gas companies, the post office, and a host of government monopolies require deposits in advance (independent of your creditworthiness), so that you may enjoy the benefits of their services.

The same kind of policy may be applied in the operation of certain small businesses and selected industries.

A San Francisco Peninsula electronics company, which sells a patented device available nowhere else, provides a good illustration of customer financing. The company's customers are required to make a deposit of one-third of the purchase price when the order is placed. Another one-third is payable on delivery, and the balance is due in 30 days. As a result of these favorable terms of sale, this company has been able to finance a highly satisfactory growth rate while experiencing almost no problems with cash flow.

An extreme example of this type of financing is the case in which the customer is required to pay the full purchase price at the time the order is placed. You may be surprised to learn that you have been financing certain of your own personal suppliers on this basis for years. I am referring, of course, to magazine publishers. If you take a three-year subscription to a magazine, you may get the first one or two issues on credit based on your promise to pay. However, in order to continue receiving the magazine, you must pay the subscription bill, even though you won't receive your final shipment for almost three years.

Hugh M. Hefner, publisher of *Playboy* magazine, played this customer-finance game with admirable success when he initially offered lifetime subscriptions for $100. Obviously, he needed the money to finance his growth. Had the subscribers to some of the early issues bought $100 worth of *Playboy* stock instead of a subscription, they could have picked up a tidy profit.

In many industries, including a number of the construction trades, it is usual for the suppliers to receive progress payments when previously agreed-upon levels of project completion are achieved. Highway construction, aircraft assembly, and other large-scale projects are often financed in this way.

A special form of customer financing occurs in a number of service and manufacturing industries. Here the customer provides raw materials that the vendor transforms into finished goods. In the book printing trade, a publisher may supply the printer with paper; in a machine shop, the customer may provide the metal to be worked; and in a tailoring service, the customer may provide the cloth to be fashioned into a dress or a suit. In each case, the vendor avoids the expense of financing the purchase of raw materials.

Another way of getting the customer to pay in advance for goods or services is to establish some kind of "membership" arrangement. Here the customer may pay an annual fee for the privilege of attending meetings. Using a similar membership approach, some discount department stores require customers to pay a membership fee for the privilege of shopping there.

A novel twist on this customer-backed approach to business finance is seen in physical fitness spas, dance studios, and other contract service organizations. Customers sign an agreement to purchase the service offered for a period of one or more years. In most cases, the intentions of the customer are honorable and sincere at the time he executes the contract. However, many people lose interest in fitness and other self-improvement programs after a short time, and the incentive to pay the installments on the service contract may falter. In anticipation of these long-range collection problems, the original holders sell the contracts to finance companies at a substantial discount. While the average individual may balk at paying the original contractor for services not used, he is more likely to pay a finance company when notified that it has taken over his contract. The result is that the original contractor gets a handsome chunk of cash almost immediately after the customer signs the contract, whether or not the customer continues to use his facilities. Once again, the customer has financed the business, albeit indirectly.

ECONOMIZING

In preparing your pro forma financial statements, you probably allocated quite a bit of money for office equipment and other capital expenditures. If you figured on buying new equipment, figure again. Used equipment is what you want. That way, you may find that you need a lot less cash than you originally thought. Forget the rosewood paneled office with the Italian marble-topped desk, too; that comes later. And most financially strapped entrepreneurs quickly learn the delights of night coach and special tour package rates to save a few dollars when traveling. There are many other ways to economize in the operation of your business; we'll get to them shortly, but first let's concentrate on where to find used equipment.

1. Used equipment dealers may handle anything from office equipment to laboratory test equipment to cash registers to display cases for butcher shops and retail stores. You'll find these dealers listed in the Yellow Pages of your telephone directory under such headings as "Used Equipment Dealers," "Second Hand Dealers," and "Surplus Merchandise." You'll also find dealers listed under generic headings such as "Office Furniture—Used."

2. Dealers in new merchandise invariably find themselves stuck with a variety of goods that cannot truly be represented as new. "Demonstrator" and "loaner" equipment (provided for the temporary use of customers who are awaiting delivery of new equipment or who are having their own equipment repaired) fall into this category. These dealers may also have floor samples, warehouse- and freight-damaged goods, and obsolete-but-serviceable rental equipment available at a substantial savings.

3. Bankruptcy and liquidation auctions provide an opportunity to get some real bargains. To secure information on where and when auctions are to be held, consult the Yellow Pages of your telephone directory under "Auctions" or "Auctioneers." Many auctioneers

maintain mailing lists of interested clients and send out brochures announcing forthcoming auctions.

You may also obtain information on bankruptcy auctions by contacting the bankruptcy court in your area. You'll find this court listed under "U.S. Government" in the White Pages of your telephone directory.

4. Bankrupt companies that receive protection under Chapter 11 of the Bankruptcy Act are very likely to be interested in liquidating some of their assets. If you are lucky enough to learn about such a company in your own industry, you are in a unique position to fill your equipment needs quite reasonably. Bankruptcy filings are announced in the legal newspapers of record serving various communities across the country. Also, when a large company in a particular industry files for voluntary bankruptcy under Chapter 11, the trade journals serving that industry will usually carry mention of this fact. Upon learning of such a bankruptcy, don't hesitate to call the company involved to determine whether the owners are interested in selling some of their assets.

5. Now and then major corporations simply decide to get out of a particular industry and shut down one of their divisions. A friend of mine who has his own company read about such an instance in a trade journal. He purchased a $100,000 (price when new) piece of test equipment for a mere $7,000 cash. Then he called a leasing company and received $45,000 for the same equipment when he agreed to lease it back from them over a five-year period. He realized an immediate cash infusion of $38,000.

6. The United States Government is the single largest consumer of goods and services in the world. Not surprisingly, it also disposes of enormous quantities of surplus goods on a more or less continuous basis. For information on the sale of surplus government equipment at locations all over the world, write to the Department of Defense Surplus Sales Office, Box 1370, Battle Creek, Michigan 49016, and the Assistant Commissioner for Personal Property Disposal, Federal

Supply Service, General Services Administration, Room 926, Crystal Mall, Building 2, Washington, D.C. 20406. Local representatives of these agencies are listed in the White Pages of your telephone book under "U.S. Government."

7. Classified ads provide a simple, convenient, and inexpensive means of finding used equipment. You can consult the listings under the headings of interest to you, or you may want to advertise the fact that you are looking for a particular item. In some instances, trade journals carry classified listings, thereby permitting you to confine your search for specialized items to the more likely sources of supply.

Barter

Bartering your goods and services is a primitive-but-fun way to save money. It also affords certain tax advantages. I know of a carpenter who remodeled an orthodontist's home in exchange for having his daughter's teeth straightened. I also know of a plumbing contractor who paid for his appendectomy by plumbing his surgeon's vacation home. Radio stations have been known to exchange advertising time for consumer merchandise to use as premiums. The opportunities are unlimited.

Do It Yourself

When the cash supply is limited and the money for meeting a payroll is nil, you simply have to learn to do things yourself that you might otherwise hire someone else to do. You have undoubtedly heard that many small businessmen work 80 or more hours a week. Many of these companies are also husband-and-wife operations, where the wife works virtually without pay until the business starts turning a profit. This kind of toil may not sound like much fun, but it does save money.

Then, too, a lot of businessmen, in response to economic pressure, find that they have many talents and skills they never appreciated. A janitor used to empty their wastebasket when they worked for Big Business, Inc., but they now take care of this occupational specialty themselves. On opening a restaurant, they may find that they possess the dexterity of a short-order cook. The may learn how to write advertising copy, how to repair their machinery, or how to operate a typewriter and a ten-key adding machine.

In some cases where a specialist is needed but there is no money with which to hire one, the entrepreneur may have to take courses at a local college to learn the skill himself. It is often surprising what you can learn to do when your economic survival is at stake.

Free Publicity

Free publicity can do wonders for your business—and the price is right. You don't have to hire a public relations firm on retainer to get it, either. What you *do* need is guts enough to call a newspaper or trade journal editor, a radio announcer, or a television personality and explain your story. If you have something to say that will be of genuine interest, educational value, or amusement to the audience served by the medium you have selected, you have a good chance of getting publicity.

One businessman I know sent out new-product releases describing a $200 device to 12 trade journals serving his industry. He received more than 1,500 inquiries in response to articles carried in the two journals that printed his story. His total cost was less than $10.

I could doubtless catalogue dozens of other ways of saving money in your business, but I'd like to conclude by suggesting a different point of view. It is easy to become preoccupied with saving nickles and dimes instead of figuring out how to make dollars. Nothing succeeds like a company with the right product at the right price at the right time. The electronics giant Hewlett-Packard was started in a garage in the 1930s. The company grew rapidly with limited invested resources for a very simple reason: the founders were selling unique and superior products with high profit margins to a market eager to buy. Go thou and do likewise.

RECOMMENDED READING

Baty, Gordon B. *Entrepreneurship: Playing to Win.* Reston, Va.: Reston Publishing Company, Inc., 1974.

Brady, Frank. *Hefner.* New York: Macmillan Publishing Co., Inc., 1974.

Deiner, Royce. *How to Finance a Growing Business.* New York: Frederick Fell, Inc., 1965.

Putt, William D., ed. *How to Start Your Own Business.* Cambridge, Ma.: The Massachusetts Institute of Technology, 1974.

Sixteen

Debt versus Equity Financing

Donald M. Dible

This book was designed to help you understand the process of planning and financing a growing business. It is most important that you accept the notion that success in financing a business venture depends heavily on your ability to plan for the future of that venture and to communicate your plans to those who supply the financing.

A number of chapters in this book have dealt separately with planning the business and with various types of debt and equity financing. In this final chapter, the *interrelationship* between debt and equity financing will be discussed so that you may better understand how to apply the information in the various chapters to the operation of your own business. Let's start by analyzing debt and equity capital.

EQUITY FINANCING

Equity capital comes from either invested capital or retained earnings.

Donald M. Dible is the founder of The Entrepreneur Press and author of Up Your OWN Organization! A Handbook of How to Start and Finance a New Business.

Invested Capital

This is the cash committed to the business by the founders and their backers. The primary advantages in using invested capital to finance a business are that you don't have to pay it back to the investors, you don't have to pay interest on it, and you don't have to have collateral to get it. You do, however, have to give your investors a share in the ownership of the business in return for their money.

The individuals who invest money in a business are usually motivated by one or more of the following desires:

1. *Personal or emotional involvement.*

Often, relatives and friends put money into business ventures solely as a gesture of friendship and goodwill toward the founders. Not uncommonly, this is done with no reasonable expectation of recovering the investment. Just as some parents might give their son or daughter a new automobile as a graduation gift, others might buy a few thousand dollars worth of stock in the business started by their offspring because they wish him (or her) well. Should the business subsequently fail, they may console themselves by saying, "Well, I was afraid of that; but he was so enthusiastic about trying out his own ideas, I didn't have the heart to turn him down."

I have had friends invest in some of my own business ventures because doing so offered them the opportunity to participate in my firm without risking the security of their own regular job. One fringe benefit they enjoy is that I send them periodic reports on the status and financial progress of the business and describe some of the exciting projects that are underway. Thus, they are able to experience a vicarious form of entrepreneurship. It's a little bit like betting on a horse and then standing at the rail cheering the animal on, hoping it will finish in the money. Any race is more exciting when you have something riding on the outcome.

Most of the money invested for the purpose of getting a business launched—that is, started from scratch with little more than an idea—is furnished by investors motivated in this way.

2. *Capital gains.*

As the company prospers, the net worth of the business will grow. This produces an increase in the value of each share of stock. If the investor sells his stock at some future date, he will be able to sell it for more than he paid for it. Furthermore, under existing tax laws, he will have to pay capital gains taxes only on his profits; this special tax is at a rate just half that levied against ordinary income. It should be clearly evident that nearly all investors and venture capitalists are motivated by the desire for capital gains.

3. *Dividends.*

Whether or not a company distributes part of its profits to the stockholders in the form of dividends is a matter to be decided by the board of directors. (The board of directors is a group of individuals whom the stockholders have elected to represent their own interest in dealing with the management of the company.) Now if the stockholders desire long-term capital gains, they will instruct the board of directors not to declare any dividends so that all profits may be used to further the growth of the company. However, some stockholders may be in need of regular income from their investments. If the majority of the stockholders fall into this category, they will communicate their desires to the board of directors. Subsequently, if there are profits available for distribution, the board of directors will see to it that dividends are declared and paid. Stockholders must pay ordinary income tax on income received in the form of dividends.

4. *Alternative to Corporate Acquisition*

Sometimes large operating companies will merge with or acquire a small company. However, when the Dow Jones Industrial

Average is down, the value of any publicly traded stock is likely to be depressed far below its highest level. Given such circumstances, large corporations eager to expand through a process of merger and acquisition find great difficulty in persuading small businesses that they should sell out and become a wholly owned subsidiary or a division of the major corporation on the basis of a stock transfer (in which the founders of the acquired company would receive stock in the big company as payment). When such a situation exists, one of the increasingly attractive alternatives to outright acquisition or merger is the venture capital subsidiary division and/or department. By such means, the major corporation invests a part of its surplus capital in a promising new business. Later, if that business is successful, the company putting up the money will acquire it as a subsidiary or division. At a time when venture capital is increasingly difficult to obtain, a growing number of entrepreneurs are giving serious thought to accepting capital from some of these major corporations.

Retained Earnings

Establishing a profitable company and maintaining steady growth and profits over the long haul constitute the acid tests of management capability. According to government statistics, the vast majority of all new businesses fail within the first five years of operation. Most of these fail within the first *two* years of operation. It is my own observation that the failing businesses probably never did achieve profitability. That is, they survived for one or two years not because of good management but because it took that period of time to exhaust the original equity capital.

The businesses that survive over the long haul are well-managed businesses. They are run by capable managers who achieve and sustain a level of profitability that permits them to build a viable business by accumulating profits. Some of the largest corporations in America today were started at a time in our history when public investment and large private financings were simply not available. These companies were started with modest assets and were built up with retained earnings over a long period of time. The growth of these companies was financed through the retention of profits earned from the sale of goods manufactured and marketed by the company. (It should be pointed out, however, that federal and state corporate income and other taxes were a heck of a lot lower in those good old days, and it was much easier to hang onto profits once they were earned.)

In the final analysis, profits make or break a company. Profits determine whether or not a company can attract investment capital and inspire the confidence of the lending community.

DEBT FINANCING

In addition to equity financing and retained earnings, the only other form of business financing available is debt financing. When you borrow money, your lenders expect you to pay back the full loan amount plus interest. (The process of paying interest on a loan is referred to in financial circles as "servicing the debt." Interest paid in servicing the debt is a tax-deductible business expense.) While your lenders may not expect you to provide collateral for your loan, they expect you to have enough invested capital in your business so that, if you experience difficulty in realizing your profit forecasts, there will be a secondary source of funds available with which to retire the debt. As one of my banker friends says, "Fundamentally, banks make loans to businesses to *supplement* the *capital investment* of the owners of the business." Thus, you cannot rely exclusively on debt for the funds necessary to operate your business. Typically, people knowledgeable in business finance talk in terms of "debt-to-equity ratios" when analyzing the financial statement of any business. What they are referring to is the amount of debt the business owes in relation to the amount of invested capital and retained earnings. Every industry has a debt-to-equity ratio characteristic of typical businesses. Summaries of these ratios are prepared annually by a number of financial reporting service organizations such as Dun and Bradstreet, Inc.

The extent to which a business is able to secure debt in relation to its equity capital is referred to as "leverage." Thus, a highly leveraged business is one that has a high debt-to-equity ratio. Businesses that are highly leveraged in relation to the average for the industry in which they operate are much more vulnerable to downturns in the economy than are their better-financed colleagues. However, as long as the economy is healthy, a highly leveraged business stands to make more profits per invested dollar than a more financially conservative business. The extent to which you leverage your business depends on your attitude toward financial risk and the degree to which your creditors are willing to cooperate with you.

Five Loan Questions

When you decide to borrow money for your business, the typical lender will ask you five questions:

1. What do you plan to do with it?

If you are planning to use the money to undertake a highly risky venture, you will probably be turned down. However, if the reason given makes good business sense, you will probably get the loan *provided* you have the right answer to the remaining four questions.

2. How much do you need?

While this may sound like a terribly elementary question, you'd be surprised at how often businessmen go into their bankers with no clear idea of how much money they need. All they know is that they are having trouble paying their bills—possibly they can't meet tomorrow's payroll—and that they need help. The more precisely you can answer this question and the more information you can provide to justify the dollar amount you indicate, the more apt you are to get your loan.

3. When do you need it?

If you rush to your banker out of a clear blue sky and tell him that you need a substantial loan today or tomorrow, you have a problem. Right off the bat, you're letting him know that you aren't a very good planner—otherwise you would have given him more advance warning. (Lenders always give businessmen high marks if they are good planners.) After all, there's a lot of investigating, checking up, and other administrative activity involved in getting a loan approved. Therefore, if you need the money "yesterday," the chances are you won't get it at all. However, if you indicate that you'll be needing the money late next week, you are giving the lender the time necessary to process your application routinely. That makes him feel comfortable about you.

4. How long will you need it?

Most business lending other than real estate lending is done on a short-term basis—one year or less. Thus, the shorter the period of time over which you need the loan, the more apt you are to get the loan approved. However, the time at which the loan will be repaid should correspond with some important milestone in your business plan, such as receipt of payment from one or more of your customers.

That brings us to our final question:

5. How will you repay the loan?

This is probably the most important question in the lot. Presumably, you plan to use the loan for some business purpose that will produce substantial profits over the short term. And you plan to use the proceeds of that activity with which to pay off the loan. Fine.

What happens if something goes wrong? If the customers don't like what you are selling? If your customers decide not to pay you for one reason or another? If the union votes to go on strike? What then? Well, your lender feels a lot more comfortable if you can offer him a secondary source of repayment. In other words, if your original plans go awry, do you have other income or potential income that can be diverted to pay the lender? If so, you are in a position to list a secondary source of repayment, and the lender's fears will be calmed.

A Few Words about Collateral

Most borrowers simply can't understand why lenders are so cautious about lending money. "After all," they say, "I've got lots of collateral. If anything really serious happens, we can sell my fixed assets to pay off the loan." It is an unfortunate fact that one of the most commonly misunderstood concepts in any financial analysis is the valuation of fixed assets. This is particularly true when appraising fixed assets in terms of their value in a *going business* as contrasted with a situation where they're on the auction block in a bankruptcy sale. You can't *begin* to appreciate how little money is offered for very expensive equipment at a liquidation auction.

Once, at a Dallas seminar in which I was a panelist, I heard a banker describe the aftermath of the bankruptcy of a television station to which he had committed his bank for a $50,000 loan. The problem with most of the collateral was that it was specially constructed to transmit at *just one frequency.* None of the other TV stations within hundreds of miles could use any of that distressed equipment because it wouldn't work at the frequency at which they had to transmit their own signals. The whole kit and kaboodle was finally sold off at 5 cents on the dollar—a whopping loss to the bank. And the bank*er* responsible for making the loan wound up with his fanny in a sling.

When a bank offers to lend you money on a collateralized basis valuing your fixed assets at 80% of book value, *take it!* That's a lot more than the collateral is worth if anything goes wrong.

When I first started my business, I went to a number of bankruptcy sales. (Buying office equipment at 10 cents on the dollar is just one of many ways to supplement meager start-up finances.) I'll never forget the look of satisfaction in the eye of one successful bidder as he loaded his former boss's $1,500 custom-made rosewood desk and executive chair onto his own pickup truck. It cost him $145 for the lot. Clearly, the valuation of fixed assets for collateral purposes has to be done with a careful eye on the overall health and maturity of the business.

Lender Motives

Now it is clear that many lenders provide debt financing for a business with the expectation of receiving interest on the borrowings. However, there are a number of other motives for lending money, depending on the lender.

1. Increased deposits

Most commercial banks and other depository institutions give preferential consideration to business customers whom they feel have the potential to become highly successful. Successful businesses often have surplus cash which they may maintain on deposit in the bank at interest. Alternatively, they may maintain a large balance in their checking account that the bank may use without paying any interest. Also, big bank customers may maintain a large "float" in their checking account. (The float is those checking-account monies against which checks that have not yet cleared the bank have been drawn.) The bank has interest-free use of the float, also.

2. Competitive edge

In most industries, it is customary for suppliers to furnish trade credit to their customers. In fact, trade credit is the single largest source of debt financing used by businesses in this country. In order to qualify for trade credit, all that is required of a customer is that he persuade his suppliers that he is credit worthy. Depending on the supplier, this may merely involve a telephone conversation or it may require the completion of one or more credit application forms.

As a rule, if a customer is unable to persuade one supplier to extend trade credit to him (also known as shipping on open account), he will continue his search for a supplier until he does find one willing to extend credit. In a tightly competitive bidding situation, the supplier who extends the most liberal credit terms may be the one who gets the order.

3. Expand customer base

Many businessmen eager to expand their customer base may readily do so by easing their credit standards. In a business environment where business failures are commonplace, there are always plenty of marginally financed potential customers who will give their business to anyone willing to extend them trade credit —even if they have to pay a higher price and compromise on the quality of the goods and services they receive.

In addition, many manufacturers of expensive capital equipment routinely help their customers by selling them the equipment on an installment-contract or time-plan basis. This makes it possible for the customer to buy when he cannot pay cash or borrow large sums for purchases.

4. Personal and emotional involvement

In addition to the motives discussed above, relatives and friends may lend money to the business for the same reasons that they would invest in equity—because they like the businessman and want to help him succeed. In such cases, interest is always negotiated, and it would not be unusual for such a loan to be interest-free.

SHOULD I USE DEBT OR EQUITY TO FINANCE MY BUSINESS?

A great many considerations, including the long-term objectives of the founders, their personal goals, the financial characteristics of the industry in which they plan to operate, and the availability of money in the capital markets, will determine the extent to which debt and equity financing will be used in a business.

Long-Term Objectives The founder obsessed with the desire for control and ownership of his business may wish to limit the equity investment in his company to his personal resources. He will attempt to rely solely on loans, trade credit, and accumulated profits to meet any money needs that may exceed his personal resources. Under such circumstances, the growth of the business will be severely restricted. As has been pointed out in other chapters, profits are heavily taxed, and interest payment on borrowings will also serve to reduce profits.

On the other hand, if the founder wishes to build a major business in a short period of time, a combination of debt *and* equity financing will serve his needs ideally. As a practical matter, rapid, sustained business growth (as opposed to seasonal booms) is not possible using retained earnings and debt alone. Typical business profits, after taxes, amount to less than 10% of sales. Now let's say that you want to double your sales next year, which may mean that you'll have to double your plant capacity. Does it seem reasonable that in a typical business you can double your production capacity using a new investment in plant and equipment of just 10% of this year's sales? Of course it doesn't. At least part of the difference between the cost of expansion and this year's retained earnings must come from new equity capital. Then, with the judicious use of leverage on the new equity, the balance required can be handled with your increased borrowing capability. In other words, when more equity is invested, lenders are willing to increase the credit that they will make available to you.

Personal Goals The nature of the financing you plan to use in your business depends a lot on your own personal goals. Ask yourself why you really want to go into business for yourself. "To make a lot of money," you say. That's not necessarily the right answer. At least in the eyes of a sophisticated investor that's not the right answer.

When it comes to mere money, almost everyone has his own *comfort level*—the point where he's making enough money to do damn near anything he wants to do. Having achieved his comfort level, he runs out of incentive to do the things necessary to make even more money—such as making his company bigger and more profitable. For a lot of independent businessmen, this comfort level may be represented by a net worth of around $1 million and an annual income of $100,000 or $200,000. "Now that's not bad," you say. And you're right, that's not bad—as a personal objective. But when you stop building your company's sales and profits, you are bowing out of the competitive race. You must understand that an investor wants steady, never-ending *growth.* If you don't give it to him—and if he and the other stockholders can pull together enough votes to dominate the board of directors—you'll find that you are no longer welcome in the president's office. According to a recent survey, only about 8,000 of the 14 million small businesses in this country were publicly held companies whose stock was traded at least once a week. That's only about one-eighteenth-of-one-percent of the entire business community! The simple facts of investing equity capital in new enterprises is that sophisticated investors expect you to build a company that will join the ranks of this elite group. In order to get there, you have to be (or become) a manager! If that's not your idea of independence and success, I have only one suggestion for you: *Don't* waste your time trying to raise equity capital from sophisticated investors. Even in the unlikely event that you *do* get financing from such a source, you'll be on the outside looking in as soon as you show signs of approaching your *comfort level.* The prospect of raising millions in venture capital is alluring as *hell.* Remember, though, that the companies you read about in *Business Week* and *The Wall Street Journal* that grow to have tens of millions of dollars in sales in just a few years with the help of venture capital constitute a miniscule part of the total business community.

Financial Characteristics of the Industry As indicated earlier, every industry is characterized by a typical debt-to-equity ratio. Also, credit and equity financing practices tend to be standardized in every industry.

In the magazine industry, although subscribers might receive one or two issues of a publication prior to having to pay, they finally wind up paying—in advance—for magazines they may not receive for one or more years. When Hugh Hefner first started publishing *Playboy,* he sold *lifetime* subscriptions at $100 each in order to finance the growth of his enterprise. That's *really* paying in advance.

Many businesses operate on a strictly cash basis. Before the energy crisis, service stations commonly accepted a variety of credit cards in order to compete with other stations. When gasoline supplies fell and a lot of stations closed, competition was reduced and many independent dealers stopped honoring credit cards.

Many commodities such as farm and other food items are sold to store owners and restauranteurs on a cash basis. That's simply the way the industry functions.

In many construction industries such as aircraft and highway building, it is commonplace for the customer to make progress payments to the contractor. This eases the contractor's financing burdens.

In the automobile and major appliance industry, most dealers sell their merchandise on a consignment basis. In other words, they don't have to pay the manufacturer for the merchandise until it is sold off the showroom floor.

In the book publishing industry, it is quite common for small, poorly financed bookstores to wait as long as six to nine months before getting around to paying a publisher's bills. In some cases, it is only the bookseller's need for other books from that publisher that prompts him to pay. Thus, the large publishers that regularly produce best sellers have a much better chance of being paid promptly than a smaller publisher offering a limited selection of new titles. The ability to force a customer to pay by threatening to stop shipments to him is referred to as "clout" in the publishing game. This credit scenario helps to explain why author contracts provide for payment of royalties up to a year after a book has been sold in a bookstore. In effect, it is the author who is helping to finance the bookstore.

Why do publishers tolerate this situation? Simple. They can use all the outlets they can get. So they help finance the bookstores by maintaining fairly liberal credit standards. Profits on the extra sales are expected to help cover the burden of such lax financing policies.

Capital Markets When confidence in the economy is strong, publicly held stocks may trade at high price-to-earnings multiples on the major exchanges. Given such conditions, it may be easy for businesses to raise money through the sale of new stock to the public in order to raise equity financing. If, in fact, the value of all the outstanding stock is substantially higher than the book value of the company, then selling additional stock to raise money may be an excellent idea.

Let's say that the book value of a company is $2 million. If the company has 1 million outstanding shares of stock, each of which trades at $10, the company is valued in the market at $10 million, or five times its book value. The board of directors may then decide to issue 250,000 new shares of stock at $10 a share. This offering would bring an additional $2.5 million into the company treasury, thus raising the book value to $4.5 million. The market value of all of the stock outstanding would be $12.5 million, or less than three times the company's book value. Although the stockholder's equity has been diluted through the issuance of new stock, the financial condition of the company has been dramatically improved.

However, when public confidence in the economy is low, the stock market fares poorly. Companies are unable to find buyers for their stock at any reasonable price. After all, no company wants to sell new stock that would have to be sold at *less* than the book value of the company.

Given such circumstances, debt financing is the only recourse the companies have. Unfortunately, this means greater demand for loan funds than are available from the lenders, and so interest rates skyrocket. In such a credit crunch, companies tend to "stretch

FORTY MONEY SOURCES

Lender or Investor	Type of Financing Available	
	Debt	Equity
Closed-End Investment Companies		X
Colleges, Universities, and Other Endowed Institutions		X
Commercial Banks	X	
Commercial Finance Companies	X	
Consumer Finance Companies	X	
Corporate Venture Capital Departments or Subsidiaries	X	X
Credit Unions	X	
Customers	X	X
Economic Development Administration	X	
Employees	X	X
Equipment Manufacturers	X	
Factoring Companies	X	
Family Investment Companies	X	X
Financial Consultants, Finders, and Other Intermediaries	X	X
Founders	X	X
Industrial Banks	X	
Insurance Companies	X	X
Investment Advisers		X
Investment Bankers	X	X
Investment Clubs		X
Leasing Companies	X	
Mutual Funds		X
Mutual Savings Banks	X	
Parent Companies	X	X
Pension Funds		X
Private Individual Investors		X
Private Investment Partnerships		X
Privately Owned Venture Capital Corporations		X
Relatives and Friends	X	X
Sales Finance Companies	X	
Savings and Loan Associations	X	
Securities Dealers		X
Self Underwriting		X
Small Business Administration	X	
Small Business Investment Companies	X	X
State and Local Industrial Development Commissions	X	
Tax-Exempt Foundations and Charitable Trusts		X
Trade Suppliers	X	
Trust Companies and Bank Trust Departments		X
Veterans Administration	X	

Source: *Up Your OWN Organization! A Handbook on How to Start and Finance a New Business* by Donald M. Dible

their suppliers," and instead of paying within 30 days as is normally the case, they wait 60 to 90 days. In crisis periods such as this, companies are forced to investigate every possible means of securing financing.

When money is tight, and competition for available funds becomes intense, it's the company with a plan—the company that's going places—that will succeed in getting the financing it needs. A basic knowledge of money sources and a little financial imagination can do wonders. To help you further, we have included the chart on the preceding page. It is a comprehensive list of financing sources that should prove quite valuable in planning for the financial needs of your business.

RECOMMENDED READING

Belew, Richard C. *How to Win Profits and Influence Bankers: The Art of Practical Projecting.* New York: Van Nostrand Reinhold Company, 1973.

Dougall, Herbert E. *Capital Markets and Institutions.* 2nd ed. Foundations of Finance Series. Englewood Cliffs, N.J.: Prentice-Hall, Inc., 1970.

Goldsmith, Raymond W. *Financial Institutions.* New York: Random House, 1968.

Hoffman, Cary. "The Venture Capital Investment Process: A Particular Aspect of Regional Economic Development." Unpublished Ph.D. dissertation, The University of Texas at Austin, 1972.

Magen, S. D. *The Cost of Funds to Commercial Banks: An Econometric Analysis.* New York: Dunellen, 1971.

Shapiro, Eli; Solomon, Ezra; and White, William L. *Money and Banking.* 5th ed. New York: Holt, Rinehart and Winston, Inc., 1968.

Solomon, Ezra, ed. *The Management of Corporate Capital.* New York: The Free Press, 1959.

Index